THE
TIGERS
AND
THEIR
DEN

THE OFFICIAL STORY OF THE DETROIT TIGERS

BY JOHN MCCOLLISTER
FOREWORD BY AL KALINE
INTRODUCTION BY MICHAEL ILITCH

ADDAX
PUBLISHING
GROUP

Bob Snodgrass
Publisher

John Lofflin and Judy Widener
Editors

Nelson Elliott
Managing Editor

Darcie Kidson
Publicity

Randy Breeden
Art Direction/ Design

Dust jacket design by Laura Bolter

Cover photo by Mark A. Hicks, Action Image

Poem on page 240 by Nelson Elliott

Select photos courtesy Detroit Tigers and as noted

Select Opening Day photos courtesy Tim Bischoff and Gary Carson

Production Assistance
Michelle Zwickle-Washington, An Beard, Sharon Snodgrass

Published by
Addax Publishing Group
8643 Hauser Drive, Suite 235
Lenexa, KS 66215

ISBN: 1-886110-81-6

Printed and bound in the United States of America.

1 3 5 7 9 10 8 6 4 2

Library of Congress Cataloging-in-Publication Data

McCollister, John.
    The Tigers and their den / by John McCollister.
        p. cm.
    ISBN 1-886110-81-6 (hard)
    1. Detroit Tigers (Baseball team)—History. I. Title.
GV875.D6M375 1999
    796.357'64'0977434—dc21   99-27437
                                                                CIP

Dedication:

To daughter Beth, who learned mathematics
by calculating Tiger batting
averages and who will forever
remain one of the Tigers'
most loyal fans.

Acknowledgments

THE STORY OF THE DETROIT TIGERS and the magnificent ballpark they have called "home" for more than a century is not the work of just one person. Many gave of their time and expertise to turn this dream of a project into reality.

Deserving special praise are Tyler Barnes, Director of Media Relations for the Tigers and Melanie Waters, Public Relations Coordinator. David Matheson, Giovanni Loria and Christina Branham, also from the Office of Public Relations, were extremely helpful.

Todd Miller, Editor of *Tiger Stripes*, newsletter for the Mayo Smith Society, provided valuable editorial and research assistance for this project. Revelations by Charlie Cobb have gone a long way to set the record straight about his grandfather, "The Georgia Peach." Likewise, the eagle eye of editor John Lofflin demonstrated why he is a valued associate professor of journalism at Park College in Kansas City.

The author treasures the support and encouragement of announcers Ernie Harwell and Jim Price throughout the writing of this book.

Al Kaline, a Hall-of-Famer both on and off the field, became a role model even before the phrase was coined. Thank you for your willingness to write the foreword and to show class no matter where you go.

Sharon Arend, Company Historian for Little Caesars Enterprises, Inc., was instrumental in securing photographs. Photographer Mark Cunningham, too, provided photos. Your cooperation and assistance were extremely helpful.

Special thanks to Michael Ilitch, owner of the Tigers, and to John McHale, Jr., president and CEO of the club. Your encouragement and support are appreciated, indeed. Thank you, also, for your vision for the future and your willingness to make tough decisions.

Finally, the author joins the entire Detroit Tiger organization in giving a standing ovation to you loyal fans who have made baseball at Michigan and Trumbull a part of your fabric. May this book bring back for you those wonderful memories of Tigers baseball.

- J.M.

- Preface -

BASEBALL, MORE THAN ANY OTHER SPORT, is a blend of fact and myth. A challenge facing any baseball writer is to separate the two and report only the facts. For the purpose of illustration, permit me to be a bit personal. I was born June 1, 1935. That's a fact. On that day, George Herman Ruth decided to retire from baseball. That, too, is a fact. I would like to imagine that he said to himself, "Now that the McCollister kid is in this world, it's time I step aside." That's myth.

Separating fact from myth is not always so easy. Even if we baseball fans know something is not true, we are hesitant to let go of the myth. Abner Doubleday, for example, did not invent the game of baseball. Doubleday, a graduate of West Point who fought at Gettysburg, probably didn't know the difference between a cannon ball and a baseball.

Likewise, Babe Ruth never called the home run shot off Charlie Root in 1932. Pete Gray was not the first one-armed player in big league history. And although Jackie Robinson is identified in this book as the player who broke the color line, some astute historians would argue that Moses "Fleetwood" Walker, a catcher in 1884 for the Toledo Blue Stockings of the American Association, not Robinson, was the first African-American to play in the majors.

One of the pleasures of writing *The Tigers and Their Den* is the realization that the story of the Detroit Tigers is blessed with so many characters and so many wonderful happenings that no one has to reach into the grab bag of myths to lend color to the narration. The facts, in this instance, far outshine any contrived myths.

Here's wishing you a most enjoyable journey through the pages of the Tigers' spectacular history in a ballpark that radiated warmth and charm.

- John McCollister

Table of Contents

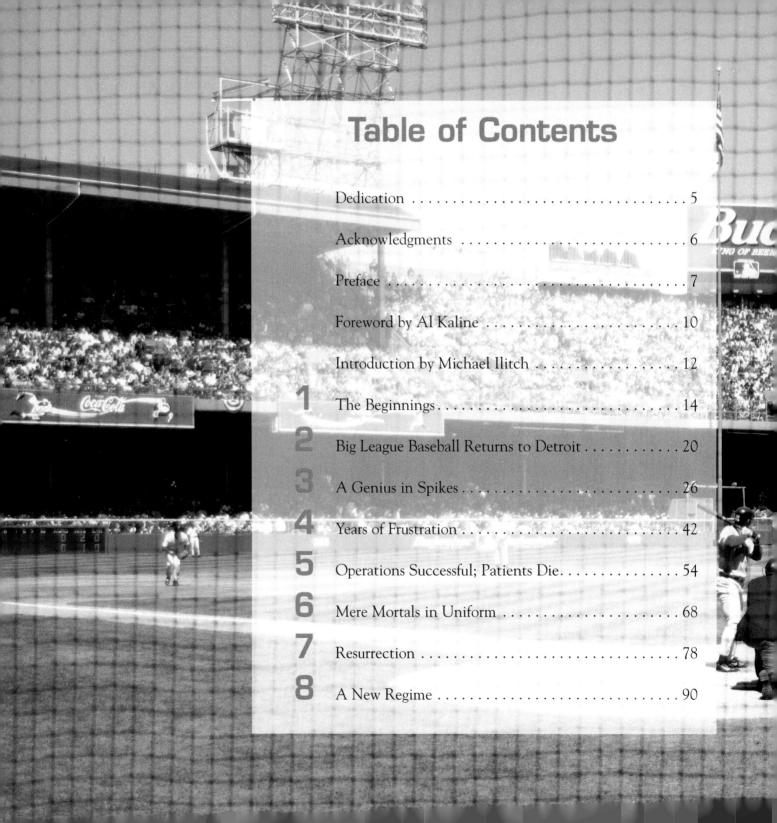

Al on Opening Day, 1999.

FOREWORD

by Al Kaline

I HAD JUST RECEIVED MY DIPLOMA from Baltimore's Southern High School in the spring of 1953 when I signed a major league contract with the Detroit Baseball Club. I thought I could never be happier. I was wrong. This was merely the beginning. I have been fortunate to share in many more exciting moments.

There was the first time I put on a Detroit Tiger uniform. I recall, vividly, my first hit on July 8, 1953, at Comiskey Park against the White Sox. There was the single in Game Five of the 1968 World Series that helped turn the corner in favor of the Tigers. My 3,000th hit on September 24, 1974, in Baltimore was wonderful; I only wish I could have done this in front of the Tiger fans. Then there was the induction to the Hall of Fame in 1980 and, on August 17 that same year, having my number 6 retired by the Tigers.

I was fortunate throughout my baseball career to have played for managers who allowed me to develop my skills. I am thankful for my teammates who were willing to welcome an 18-year-old kid fresh out of high school. And I am especially appreciative of the wonderful fans of Detroit who supported us all the way—through good times and bad.

Since I left the playing field as an active player and have moved to the broadcast booth, I can look back and put things in perspective. I have been blessed beyond all measure. I am proud to be known as a husband who has been fortunate to be married to a wonderful woman, as a father of two fantastic children and as a Detroit Tiger who gave his best in every game.

May *The Tigers and Their Den* bring back for you some wonderful memories of the most colorful team in the history of Major League Baseball and of the stadium at the corner of Michigan and Trumbull where the story of the Detroit Tigers unfolded day by day.

I am honored to have been a part of that story.

Al Kaline

Introduction

by Michael Ilitch

NOT LONG AGO, I asked veteran sportscaster Ernie Harwell a pointed question: "Why do I like you so much? Why do I, along with millions of fans, enjoy listening to you broadcast a baseball game?"

That question may have floored others with less experience and security. But Ernie and I had gotten to know each other well enough that I was not afraid to ask the question and he was not hesitant to answer it.

"I keep it simple," said the Hall-of-Fame broadcaster. "Baseball is a simple game. Fans want to hear about the guys who make it work. They're interested in what player got the winning hit or which pitcher struck out a batter with the bases loaded. They also want to know something about the players and what makes them what they are. I try to bring those pictures to the fans."

Ernie Harwell said exactly what I feel. I treasure the rich history of the Detroit Tigers and the people both on and off the field who have made baseball a part of our culture. I appreciate, too, the legion of fans who have come to see the Tigers at the ballpark or have followed them through the news media. Let's face it, nothing would have been possible were it not for the support of the men, women and children who have been so proud to call the Tigers "our team."

That's just one of the reasons I am happy that this history of the team has been written by a fan. Throughout these pages, John McCollister shows us the glory of the championship seasons and the agony of the times things did not work out as well as we had hoped.

The Tigers and Their Den allows you to relive those wonderful days when Ty Cobb ruled the basepaths, when Charlie Gehringer redefined the art of fielding second base, and when Hank Greenberg responded to catcalls about his religious faith by pounding baseballs out of the park. It also reveals the appeal of some of the modern day heroes—Al Kaline, Willie Horton, George Kell, Kirk Gibson, Alan Trammell and Lou Whitaker, plus some of the budding superstars currently wearing uniforms with the familiar Olde English "D."

I now invite you to become a part of the ongoing history of the Tigers as it unfolds at our new baseball diamond at Comerica Park. I promise to do whatever I can to make this an exciting time for you.

Chapter 1
The Beginnings

"Professional baseball is on the wane. Salaries must come down, or the interest of the public must be increased in some way. If one or the other does not happen, bankruptcy stares every team in the face."

- Albert Spalding
1881

1887 Detroit Wolverines
National League Champions
Top row - Bennett, Brouthers, Thompson, Ganzel, Twitchell, Baldwin
Third row - White
Second row - Briody, Dunlap, Watkins, Hanlon, Shindle, Getzein
First row - Rowe, Weidman, Richardson

Players demand more money.

Owners refuse to budge from their offers.

Sportswriters predict high salaries will kill the game.

Fans grow disgusted with the whole mess.

No, these are not headlines from a current newspaper. They were controversies that dominated baseball reporting more than 120 years ago.

The National Baseball League was not yet three years old when it had its first significant conflict between players and owners. At impasse were players' salaries.

Club owners attempted to curb escalating salaries among players (the average was $200 a month) by playing another kind of hardball. On September 29, 1879, they secretly agreed to a "reserve clause" through which five players (normally the five best players) would be named by a club owner as "reserved." No other club would be allowed to approach these designated players or to sign them without consent of their current owner. This meant that a top player had little if any say in the amount of money he was paid. He had two choices: accept his owner's offer or leave baseball.

Even if the player chose to retire from baseball, he was still property of the team that reserved him and could not sign with any other National League club.

News of this secret agreement was leaked to the press. One of the first reporters to challenge the issue was O. P. Caylor, sports editor of the *Cincinnati Enquirer*. Players for the Cincinnati Reds, baseball's first professional team, rebelled against this clause. "It looks like they want to make slaves of us all," said pitcher Will Wright, who had posted a 43-31 record that season.

Cincinnati had objected to earlier high-handed decisions by the National League. The final blow came at the end of the 1880 season when the league, in an attempt to give the game a better image, banned Sunday baseball and the sale of beer at games. In contrast to the practice that year initiated by President Rutherford B. Hayes and First Lady "Lemonade Lucy," who refused to serve alcohol in the White House, attending Sunday afternoon games while sipping a local brew was one of the few joys left for citizens of a blue-collar town such as Cincinnati. Consequently, the team voted to leave the National League and made plans to play elsewhere.

Cincinnati's decision to walk left a void in the league. Filling that slot was a team from Detroit called by two names: the "Wolverines" and the "Detroits."

Many people were instrumental in bringing Major League Baseball to Detroit. The most influential was Detroit Mayor William G. Thompson. Thompson, also president of the Detroit Baseball Club, used his persuasive powers and political muscle to generate interest by the citizens.

Some of his colleagues silently wondered if Detroit could compete with major markets. After all, Detroit had yet to identify itself. Since French explorers first settled there in 1648, and 15 years before Henry Ford completed his first automobile, the city had no major industry. Instead, it had slowly grown from a predominantly farming community to a center for exporting of produce to Canada and the East via the Detroit River, Lake St. Clair and Lake Erie.

Lack of industry didn't phase Mayor Thompson. He reminded anyone who would listen that America was also in a stage of transition. He was right. The nation was licking the wounds of the Civil War which had ended only 16 years earlier. Voters had just elected James A. Garfield president of these United States. He would serve only four months before being assassinated.

Baseball was also emerging. The earliest rules established by Alexander Cartwright were quite different from those of today. Pitchers, for example, could toss underhanded only. Instead of throwing from a mound, they were stationed in a chalk-marked box just 50 feet from home plate. If a pitcher was ineffective and had to be removed, he was "knocked out of the box"—a designation that still applies. A batter received an intentional pass after eight balls.

As a way of publicizing his major league city of 116,340 residents, Mayor Thompson preferred to call his team the "Detroits"; newspaper reporters adopted the name "Wolverines."

The team played its home games at Recreation Park near Brush and Brady—the far northeast corner of the city at that time. The field had just a few bleachers along the first and third-base lines. Spectators, many of whom rode to the games in horse-drawn buggies, placed themselves behind the outfielders, thereby determining the outfield "fence." Visiting teams sometimes complained that when Detroit batters came to the plate the fans moved in closer; when the opposing team was at bat, they moved several feet back.

Detroit prepared for an 84-game schedule with the Chicago Colts (with Adrian "Cap" Anson and Michael "King" Kelly of "Slide, Kelly, Slide" fame), the Providence (RI) Grays, the Buffalo Bisons, Troy (NY) Trojans, Boston Red Caps, Cleveland Blues and Worcester Ruby Legs.

On May 2, 1881, more than 1,200 fans paid between 15 and 65 cents each to see their team beaten by Buffalo, 6-4.

The National League's newest entry, managed by Frank Bancroft, had three star players: rookie first baseman Martin Powell, who led the club with a .338 average; outfielder Ned Hanlon, one of the league's best defensive players; and catcher Charlie Bennett, a three-year veteran of the league who hit .301 and led the team with seven homers. Bennett is said to be the first catcher who got into a crouch position behind batters; others merely placed themselves several feet behind the batter and caught a pitched ball on the first bounce.

The Wolverines carried only two pitchers. Both performed magnificently. George Derby (29-26) was the "ace," but George "Stump" Weidman (8-5) topped the National League with a 1.80 ERA.

Solid hitting and pitching earned the surprising Wolverines a

fourth-place finish in their freshman year in the National League.

The next year, 1882, produced the National League's first rival. Led by the departed Cincinnati squad, a new league—the American Association—was born. For all intents and purposes, however, this league was looked upon by the nation as a minor league.

Detroit slipped to sixth place in 1882, even though it posted a winning record of 42-41. Leading the Wolverines in hitting and in fan popularity was catcher Charlie Bennett. His .301 mark was the only one to crack the .300 barrier. Once again, Derby and Weidman handled the starting mound chores.

Also in 1882, Detroit crowned its first home run champion. Outfielder George Wood led the National League with seven circuit blows.

Individual statistics meant little to the fans; of greater importance was sponsoring a championship team. The team was just two years old, but Detroit fans already displayed little patience with mediocrity. They clamored for a "winner."

The team's most unusual victory of the '82 season occurred off the field. Following a 1-0 loss for Detroit, Owner Thompson discovered that second-year umpire Richard Higham had met with some gamblers in a Detroit pool hall prior to the game. He complained to the National League. Upon further investigation, the league expelled Higham from its roster of arbiters.

Fan discontent and fights with umpires took their toll on Owner-Mayor Thompson. Following the

1882 season, he chose to focus on civic matters and sold his club to businessman Charles H. Marsh.

The National League attempted to enhance its overall appearance in 1883 by regulating the color of team socks. The color of the uniforms and design of the logos were left to the individual owners. The league was concerned only with the stockings worn by each player. The Detroit "Wolverines" were assigned the color brown.

In '83, the New York Gothams and the Philadelphia Quakers replaced the struggling teams of Troy and Worcester. Even with two new entries, the Wolverines could not improve on the previous year's record. A disappointing 40-58 season behind new manager Jack Chapman resulted in a seventh-place finish.

Bennett (.305) and Wood (.302) were the sole consistent hitters. The only one to top the league in any category was Martin Powell, who had the dubious honor of leading all first basemen with 54 errors.

Beginning with the 1884 season, the scope of baseball changed radically when, for the first time, pitchers were permitted to throw overhand.

Had they been allowed to face only underhand tosses by opposing pitchers, the 1884 Wolverines would probably still have fielded a sorry team. With only 28 wins all season, they finished in last place on merit. In one game, James "Pud" Galvin led Buffalo to an 18-0, no-hit thumping of Detroit as the Wolverines were able to get only one batter to first on an error.

Catcher Bennett (.264) was the closest regular to hitting .300, and no pitcher enjoyed a winning record. It was a year management and fans would rather forget.

Two managers, Charlie Morton and Bill "Wattie" Watkins tried to rejuvenate the club in 1885, to no avail. All they produced was a sixth-place finish.

Now the fans really showed their anger. Many openly rebelled by boycotting games. Wolverine management suffered severe losses in gate receipts. To save the club from bankruptcy, Frederick K. Stearns, a wholesale druggist who captained the University of Michigan 1877 baseball team, invested a lot of cash into the operation. He became majority stockholder and president of the club.

Buffalo and Providence were not so blessed with local investors. Red ink forced both franchises out of the league following the '85 campaign. Replacing these teams were the Washington Statesmen and the Kansas City Cowboys. Players from departed Buffalo and Providence teams became free agents. Detroit took advantage, and purchased for a grand sum of $8,000, four established stars who had formed the Buffalo infield: first baseman Dennis "Dan" Brouthers (pronounced "Broo-thers"), second baseman Hardy Richardson, shortstop Jack Rowe and third baseman "Deacon" James White. The investment paid off handsomely.

Brouthers (.370) and Richardson (.351) led the club in hitting. They also tied for the league lead in homers with 11. Rowe (.303) was sensational at short, and White (.289), a master at third.

Southpaw Charles "Lady" Baldwin dominated hitters as demonstrated by his league-leading 42 wins against 13 losses.

This roster gained for Detroit not only respect, but also a second-place finish, just 2 1/2 games behind first-place Chicago.

Wattie Watkins and his Wolverines knew they had a contender. Financial woes forced Kansas City and St. Louis out of the National League in 1887. Replacing them were the Pittsburgh Alleghenys and Indianapolis Hoosiers.

From Opening Day of 1887, Detroit left no doubt they were the team to beat. Right fielder Samuel "Big Sam" Thompson had a banner year, leading the league in hitting with a blistering .372 and 166 RBI. For the record, baseball rules in 1887 allowed bases on balls to be counted as hits. In spite of the inflated averages, Brouthers (.338), Rowe (.318), Richardson (.328) and White (.303) made that $8,000 purchase price look like the greatest bargain in sports history.

By season's end, Detroit had won its first National League pennant, beating out second-place Philadelphia by 3 1/2 games.

A first-place finish alone was not good enough for Owner Stearns. In a letter dated September 23, 1887, Stearns challenged Chris Von Der Ahe, president of the St. Louis Browns—winners of the American Association pennant—to a series of 15 games that would be played in a variety of cities. Each player for the winning team would collect $100. Von Der Ahe accepted. Detroit won

its eighth and deciding contest by the 11th game, but the players continued with the schedule. By the end of the round robin, Detroit had won 11 games and the Browns only 4.

Detroit had many years of practice on how to be a good loser; none, however, on how to be a good winner. Momentum from the previous season failed to carry over to the next. Plagued with injuries and substandard performances, Wattie Watkins' team struggled to a fifth-place finish. With 38 games remaining in the season, Bob Leadley replaced Manager Watkins. Even the fact that Detroit became the first team ever to issue rain checks could salvage fan support.

Before the season ended, Frederick Stearns sold most of his interest in the club to Charles W. Smith. Both Smith and Stearns grew weary of baseball in a very short period of time. High salaries for star players made it impossible for them to foresee any genuine possibility of profits. They had to make bold, quick moves in order to survive. That included unloading some high-priced employees. Walking the plank were Brouthers, Richardson and Bennett, sold to Boston; White, Rowe and Hanlon were shipped off to Pittsburgh; Thompson went to Philadelphia. Quietly, the remainder of the team was sent off to Cleveland. When no players were purchased to replace them, Detroit fans soon realized that the eight-year history of the Wolverines in the National League was just that—history.

On Opening Day, 1889, Detroit was no longer a major league city.

Chapter 2

Big League Baseball Returns to Detroit

"Pop Dillon for President."

- Slogan chanted by Detroit fans following the opening day win, April 25, 1901

Bennett Park, where the Tigers played their first American League games.

BY 1889, BASEBALL HAD LARGELY DEVELOPED into the game we see today. Three strikes and you were out; four balls and you got a free pass to first base.

Rules changes notwithstanding, Detroit fans grew restless. They missed big league baseball. Some pastors, priests and rabbis even urged their flocks to pray for a team. Their prayers were answered, but not until 1901.

Owner George Arthur Vanderbeck, a native Californian, ensured that Detroit would have a professional team, even though it might not be in the "Show"—the term used to designate the major league. As a result, from 1889 to 1900, Detroit was host to several minor league teams, including one in the Western League.

If the city had any hope of returning to the National League, Pittsburgh Pirate owner William W. "Captain" Kerr, who served on the league's membership committee, smothered it. "Detroit has not the remotest chance of getting back into the league," he wrote in the October 14, 1893, edition of *The Sporting News*. "It was no stayer when it was a member of the league and sold out."

On January 9, 1894, Detroit fans were shocked to learn that one of their all-time favorites, catcher Charlie Bennett, was the victim of a tragic accident. While on a hunting trip with friends, Bennett slipped attempting to re-board a moving train. He lost his footing, and fell under the wheels. He lost his left foot; his right leg was cut off at the knee.

Charlie Bennett, the reliable and plucky catcher whose career was cut short due to a freak accident.

Following the 1895 season, Owner Vanderbeck hired George "Tweedy" Stallings as manager for the 1896 campaign. During that year, Stallings attempted to add a dash of flash to the team by replacing the mundane brown uniform socks with black and yellow striped stockings. He told author Frederick Lieb: "I didn't think of their resemblance to a tiger's stripes at the time, but the fans and some of our early writers noticed it and soon started calling the club the 'Tigers.'"

Another version of the origin of the team's name says that a year earlier, an unidentified headline writer wrote in the April 16, 1895,

edition of the *Detroit Free Press*, the following: "Tigers Showed Up Very Nicely." Throughout the year, a column of statistics appeared in the paper labeled as follows: "Notes of the Detroit Tigers."

A new team name was not the only change in Detroit baseball. Owner Vanderbeck invested $10,000 to construct a hastily built stadium on the corner of Michigan and Trumbull Avenues for Opening Day, 1896. It was the start of a new location for the Tigers—one that would serve as their home for more than 100 years.

Of particular delight to the 8,000 fans who squeezed into the 5,000-seat stadium on that brisk afternoon of April 28, 1896, was the ceremonial opening pitch. Hobbling to home plate to catch the toss was none other than Charlie Bennett. As soon as Bennett caught the pitch and the crowd finished its roar of approval, Mr. Vanderbeck announced that, beginning this day, the new home of the Tigers would be named "Bennett Park."

Tears fell at home plate, in the ballpark and throughout the city of Detroit.

Detroit won the first contest played at Bennett Park when it defeated the "Athletics," a local semi-pro team, 30-3. The game was never in doubt when Detroit sent six runners across the plate in the top of the first. The home team in that day enjoyed the option of starting the game in the field or at bat.

Despite watching such overpowering victories, Detroit fans were not satisfied with anything short of big league baseball.

Growing fan discontent with the current status of Detroit baseball coupled with problems in Arthur Vanderbeck's personal life, including a divorce and pending lawsuits, led Vanderbeck to sell the club on March 6, 1900, to James D. Burns and other investors.

Burns, a quick-tempered Detroit saloon owner and former Wayne County Sheriff, was more accustomed to settling arguments with swinging fists while working in his Irish pub, or with a billy club when wearing a badge, than with sophisticated negotiations and diplomacy required of big business. Later that year, Ban Johnson, president of the Western League, another flamboyant leader, led a group of club owners in forming the American League. Insiders felt the quick-triggered personalities of Burns and Johnson would never allow a meeting of the minds. The 42-year-old Johnson, former sports editor for the *Cincinnati Commercial-Gazette*, regarded Burns and his Detroit organization as threats to his strong rule. Few, therefore, gave Detroit much chance to gain admission to the new league.

In addition, with a population of fewer than 296,000 citizens, Detroit was the smallest city among prospective franchises.

Burns, however, proved equal to the challenge. In 1901, his Tigers were invited to join the Milwaukee Brewers, Chicago White Stockings, Boston Somersets, Philadelphia Athletics, Baltimore Orioles, Washington Nationals and Cleveland Blues in the formation of the American League.

Following a 12-year hiatus, Major League Baseball finally returned to Detroit.

On Thursday afternoon, April 25, 1901, 10,023 fans not only saw their first American League game, they also witnessed one of baseball's most amazing come-from-behind victories.

The Tigers fielded a rather solid line up that first game:

Frank "Pop" Dillon - first base

William "Kid" Gleason - second base

Norman "Kid" Elberfeld - shortstop

James "Doc" Casey - third base

William "Kid" Nance - left field

Jimmy Barrett - center field

James "Ducky" Holmes - right field

Frederick "Fritz" Buelow - catcher

Emil Frisk - pitcher

Aided by seven Detroit errors, pitcher Pete Downing and his Milwaukee Brewers led the upstart Tigers 13-4 after eight innings. Many of the hometown fans groaned as they left the park to get ahead of the crowd that would follow after the last out. Everyone knew the game was lost ... except the Detroit players.

Leadoff hitter in the bottom of the ninth was James Patrick "Doc" Casey. The tiny (5' 6", 150-pound) third baseman lined a ground-rule double into the crowd of faithful fans standing in left field. That began a barrage of hits—nine of them—mixed with a walk and a Milwaukee error. The Tigers were down by only one run. With two outs and two runners on the sacks, first baseman Dillon blasted a line drive toward the overflow crowd standing in left field. A partisan Detroit fan, said one reporter, reached out and batted the bouncing ball away from the Brewers' left fielder. Both runners scored easily on Dillon's fourth double of the afternoon. The Tigers won 14-13.

Cheering fans raced onto the field, lifted Dillon on their shoulders and gave him a hero's ride to the center-field clubhouse.

The Tigers, in their debut season in the American League, made a solid impression. Elberfeld (.310) led the club in hitting. Roscoe Miller, in his only full season with Detroit, led the Bengals with a 23-13 mark on the mound. Utility man Lewis "Sport" McAllister filled in as a catcher, infielder and outfielder whenever necessary and hit an impressive .301. The heretofore-untested Tigers compiled a 74-61 record and a third-place finish.

The team worked well together. Management did not. Field manager and minority owner George Stallings constantly bickered with majority owner Burns. They accused each other of less-than-ethical handling of gate receipts. One insider commented: "Stallings and Burns had a simple system of bookkeeping. Whichever one got to the cash box first got the money."

As a remedy for this embarrassing situation, League President Ban Johnson forced both Stallings and Burns to sell their interests in the club. Railroad tycoon Samuel F. Angus headed the new owners.

If any of the Tiger hopefuls were ready to celebrate a league championship in 1902 based on the bright promise offered by the previous year's squad, they soon would be disappointed. Led by new manager Frank Dwyer, the Tigers languished near the bottom of the league, ending the season 52-83 and in seventh place.

Jimmy Barrett (.303) was the only one to crack the .300 mark in hitting. No pitcher had a winning record, although Ed Siever (8-11) led the league with a 1.91 ERA.

Attendance dropped 28 percent that year. As a means of reaching more people, Owner Burns authorized the playing of Sunday games. Games on church days were forbidden if not by law, certainly by so-called "community standards." However, the rules were much more relaxed in farming areas. Burns, therefore, moved the Sunday games three miles west of Bennett Park to a place he dubbed "Burns Park," on Dix, between Livernois and Waterman.

One would think that fans watching a game on a Sunday afternoon would be quite subdued. Not so. Fights aplenty broke out during these contests. Future owner Walter O. Briggs attended most of these games. "You used to see more fights there on a Sunday afternoon than you see now in the big leagues in five years," he recalled. "The players fought each other and the fans; the fans fought the gate tenders; and the tenders fought the groundskeeper. Fights started before a ball was pitched, lasted throughout the game, and continued long afterwards."

League President Ban Johnson, no fan of Detroit, was ready to pull the carpet from under the franchise. Detroit management, however, vowed to clean up its act, and Johnson backed away from any threat to move the team.

Manager Ed Barrow led the Tigers to an improved 65-71 record in 1903. Even with the solid hitting of Barrett (.315) and "Wahoo Sam" Crawford (.325 and a league-leading 25 triples)—the six-foot left-handed hitter from Wahoo, Nebraska, purchased from Cincinnati before the start of the season—the team never posed a threat to take the pennant, ending the year in fifth place, 25 games behind Boston.

Until 1903, most baseball experts looked down their noses at the allegedly inferior American League. That opinion changed quickly after the National League Champion Pittsburgh Pirates agreed to play the Boston Pilgrims (the new team name) in the first World Series. To the surprise of everyone, especially the Pirates, Boston won the best-of-nine-games Series five games to three.

On January 22, 1904, Angus sold his interest in the Tigers to 28-year-old William Hoover Yawkey, heir to a lumber fortune and uncle of future Boston Red Sox owner Tom Yawkey. Yawkey knew little about the nuts and bolts of running a baseball franchise, so he brought on board another young man, Frank Navin, to oversee the day-to-day operations of the club. Yawkey promised, in time, to bring a winning team to Detroit.

That "time" was not 1904. Ed Barrow lasted just over half a year at the helm of the hapless Tigers before being replaced by Robert Lincoln "Bobby" Lowe, who also played second base for the club, becoming Detroit's first player-manager. Lowe was a weak hitter (.208) and, as it turned out, just as weak a manager. He was not offered a contract to manage the Tigers the next year and remained content to serve as a utility infielder for three more seasons.

Once more, no Tiger batted over .300. Only right-handed pitcher William "Wild Bill" Donovan, in his second year with the team, had a winning record (17-16).

No team legitimately wore the World Series crown in 1904. Still suffering from the humiliation of the previous season, New York Giants manager John McGraw refused to accept the challenge of the American League pennant-winning Boston team to play a second World Series. The Boston players, as a result, declared themselves as World Champions by default.

"Wahoo Sam" Crawford was a hitter with power.

Chapter 3
A Genius in Spikes

"I had to fight all my life
to survive.**"**

- Ty Cobb

Ty Cobb revolutionized the game with his savvy on the basepaths.

NO OTHER PLAYER IN TIGER HISTORY COULD GENERATE as much excitement per game as did Tyrus Raymond Cobb. Ty Cobb embodied a lust for survival that dominated Detroit during the first part of the 20th century.

The 6' 1", 175-pounder from Narrows, Georgia, used everything in his power to get a hit, steal a base or score a run. If he could do all this within the rules, that would be fine. If it meant stretching the rules or even breaking them without being caught, that would be fine as well.

Fans and sportswriters knew that this feisty player, dubbed "The Georgia Peach" in 1906 by Joe Jackson of the *Detroit Free Press*, would do whatever it took to bring home a victory for their beloved Tigers. They were seldom disappointed. Between 1905 and 1926, Detroit fans saw Cobb help the Tigers win games in every imaginable way—and some they could never have conceived.

Some say that Ty Cobb was the best ballplayer ever to roam an out-field. His home run production may fall short of one George Herman Ruth, but his overall record earned him the right to join Ruth, Honus Wagner, Christy Mathewson and Walter "Big Train" Johnson as the first five players elected to baseball's Hall of Fame in Cooperstown, New York, on February 2, 1936. In fact, Cobb received more votes—222 (out of a possible 226)—than any other player. Babe Ruth, for example, received 215 votes.

For 23 years, Ty Cobb batted over .300. He won 12 American League batting championships (twice by hitting over .400); nine of those were consecutive. At one point, he held an astounding 90 major league records, including the highest career batting average (.367) ever compiled by any major leaguer before or since.

A plaque unveiled on the Trumbull Avenue side of Tiger Stadium on July 17, 1963, summed up his career:

TYRUS RAYMOND COBB
1886 - 1961
Greatest Tiger of All
A Genius in Spikes

Ty Cobb revolutionized the game with his agility on the basepaths. It wasn't just his ability to steal a base, although he would soon smash all records in that department. It was his gutsy running during otherwise routine plays. Often, he scored from second on a ground out. He stole home a record 54 times. He had the opposition convinced he could steal any base any time he wanted. "The base runner has the right of way," insisted Cobb, "and that man who blocks it does it at his own peril."

Cobb's teammate, Herman "Germany" Schaefer, would add a touch of anxiety to the opposition when, after Cobb swiped a base, he would yell from the dugout: "Hold onto your pants or he'll steal them, too!"

Baseball historians seldom refer to Cobb as a long-ball hitter. Yet he did slam 118 homers in an era of the so-called "dead ball." He actually led both leagues with nine round-trippers in 1909.

Prior to a game in May 1925, Cobb told a reporter that he was tired of reading about Babe Ruth's home runs. "I'll show you something today," he promised. That afternoon, the Peach slammed three homers, plus a double and two singles. The next day he hit two home runs.

Ty Cobb remains fourth among all major leaguers in career doubles, second in career triples and fourth in career RBI. In addition, he remains second on the all-time hit list and third in total stolen bases (having led the league six years in that department).

Some skeptics claim that Cobb's batting average was high in an era most players had a higher average compared to modern day hitters. The facts dictate otherwise. Currently, major leaguers average .260. A batting champion hits from 80 to 90 points higher. In Cobb's era, players averaged less than .250. When winning his batting crowns, Cobb typically hit 100 to 140 points higher.

Sam Crawford recalled many years after he retired that players in those days sometimes played an entire game with just one ball. By game's end, it was lopsided and full of tobacco juice and licorice stains. "Pitchers used to have their own way," he said. "Spitballs and Emory balls and whatnot."

Ted Williams—arguably the greatest hitter of the modern era—credits Ty Cobb's success to his intelligence. "He was as intelligent a guy as I ever met in baseball," says the Splendid Splinter. "He studied each catcher's style—the different way each one called his game—and could readily adjust his hitting strategy to a change of catchers. Not only was Cobb intelligent, he was also talented and completely fearless—a deadly triple threat."

The legacy that dominates the image of Ty Cobb in the minds of most fans is his rather ungentlemanly conduct both on and off the diamond. One classic photograph shows him sliding into third base, feet high, ready to spike the fielder who dared get in his way. Other witnesses tell of his willingness to fight players and fans within seconds after he became irritated. Most of the time these agitations stemmed from something insignificant.

Cobb didn't deny this. "Baseball is a red-blooded game for red-blooded men," he once said. "It's no pink tea, and mollycoddles had better stay out. It's a survival of the fittest. Every veteran is not only fighting against the other side, but he is trying to hold his own against some youngster on his bench. Why not boldly admit this?"

Detroit Tiger brass had heard of the 19-year-old Cobb in 1905 when he was playing in the South Atlantic (Sally) League for Augusta—site of the Tigers' spring training camp that year. Frank Navin, by 1905 holder of a large share of stock in the club, along with pitcher Bill Donovan and infielder Schaefer, went to see the youngster in practice. What Navin saw was a diamond in the rough. The left-handed batter and right-handed thrower appeared awkward and clumsy. At the same time, he had remarkable speed and an exceptionally quick start.

Cobb was not invited to the Detroit club right away. Navin felt a year's seasoning would help smooth out the rough edges.

During the 1905 season, Ed Barrow, manager of the Indianapolis club, offered to buy Cobb from William Croke, owner of the Augusta club. Croke demanded $500. Barrow offered $300 for Cobb. "Not a chance," said Croke, and the deal was off. Years later, Barrow sadly confessed to a reporter, "I lost Ty Cobb for a lousy two hundred bucks."

Near the end of the 1905 major league season, Detroit needed some additional hitting prowess. Navin got Cobb for a reported salary of $750. Cobb, just a few days before, had been called home. His mother, Amanda, had accidentally killed his father, Herschel—a respected educator and state senator—with two shotgun blasts. Following the funeral, his mother was indicted for manslaughter; she would later be acquitted.

Some pseudo-psychologists theorize that this horrible scene was responsible for Cobb's sour attitude about life. Cobb, however, overcame even this tragedy when he played 41 games for Detroit in 1905, batting .240 with one home run.

Even if Cobb had hit his lifetime average, it would not have had a significant impact on the Tigers of 1905 who finished in third place with a record of 79-74, 15 1/2 games behind the Philadelphia Athletics.

Cobb's sophomore year proved to be a preview of his playing ability which would elevate him to lasting stardom. In 98 games during the 1906 campaign, the young right fielder hit .320 and stole 23 bases. Unfortunately, that did little to enhance the Tigers' standing in the league. When the season ended, Detroit was far down in the standings in sixth place, 21 games behind the league-leading White Sox.

Easing some of the tensions brought on by a losing season were the antics of "Germany" Schaefer. In contrast to the intense, focused Cobb, Schaefer delighted in using comedy routines to keep things in perspective. Once, for example, with Detroit leading late in a game and the umpires refusing to call the contest on account of darkness, Schaefer went out to his position at second base while holding a lantern. On another occasion, before the rule was changed, just after he hit a double, leaving him on second and another Tiger on third, Schaefer "stole" first base. Although the fans and other players laughed, he later explained that he tried to tempt the catcher to throw to first, giving the runner

"Germany" Schaefer added some comic relief to the tension-filled games.

on third a chance to score.

All of Schaefer's creativity on the diamond could not save the job of low-key manager Bill Armour, who compiled a mediocre 150-152 record during his two years at the helm. Replacing him was a most colorful figure—Hugh Ambrose Jennings.

Jennings, in contrast to his predecessor, refused to remain in the background. The blue-eyed, freckle-faced Irishman elected to place himself on the field as first base or third base coach. During a Tiger rally, Jennings often pulled up fistfuls of grass from the coach's box, raised his right leg and with a yell that could be heard as far away as the coal mines in his home town of Pittstown, Pennsylvania, bellowed: "Ee-yah! Ee-yah!" Fans loved to sit in the stands immediately behind the feisty manager and shout the unusual yell with him. It wasn't long before manager Hughie Jennings became known as "The Ee-yah Man."

No baseball expert would claim that a change in managers alone could make such a difference, but in 1907, Detroit, paced by its flashy right fielder from Georgia, made a marked turn-around. In fact, they led the league by scoring 694 runs. Even more impressive, they also ended the season in first place, 1 1/2 games ahead of second-place Philadelphia. Ty Cobb led the American League hit parade with a whopping .350 average and 116 RBI. He tied for second place in home runs with five; he also topped the junior circuit with 49 stolen bases, 212 hits, 286 total bases and a .473 slugging average.

All this came close to never happening. On March 16, during spring training, Cobb stood in the dugout and got into a shouting match with a groundskeeper. Words led to blows. Cobb's teammate, catcher Charlie "Boss" Schmidt, tried to stop the fight. Cobb turned his attention away from the groundskeeper and punched Schmidt in the jaw. Four teammates were needed to restore the peace.

Manager Jennings is often praised for his ability to handle the temperamental Cobb, whose vein-bulging outbursts had already become an American League staple. The new manager, who passed his bar examination while with the Tigers, also could have used a degree in psychology. However, even Jennings' patience had its limits. The manager with a "grin that echoed" was forced to consider the effect Cobb's antics would have on the rest of the team. He was not eager to have internal troubles plague his debut, so he offered to trade Cobb to Cleveland for outfielder Elmer Flick. Napoleon Lajoie, manager of the Indians, perhaps not wanting to add a problem child to his lineup, said, "Thanks, but no thanks."

Before the team broke camp to head north, Cobb quietly mentioned to a newspaper reporter that, if he wanted, he could whip Boss Schmidt and any of his other teammates in a fair fight. Schmidt took this as a personal challenge to his manhood and, within hours after the story broke, got into a knock-down-drag-out fight with Cobb. Cobb came out second best

with a broken nose and two swollen eyes. Consequently, he missed spring training's last two exhibition games.

The popular movie, *Field of Dreams*, contains a pointed scene in which great baseball players from the past somehow return to life to play ball on an Iowa farm. Missing from the ensemble is Ty Cobb. When asked why he wasn't there, one of the players responds, "We didn't like him when we were living; we still don't like him."

Ty Cobb, however, was never interested in winning a popularity contest. His chief goal—his only goal—was to win ball games.

In 1907, he helped Detroit do just that.

On August 2, the Tigers played against Washington and a young pitcher making his first appearance in the major leagues. His name was Walter Johnson. Cobb greeted the youngster with a bunt down the third-base line that he beat out for a single. Johnson pitched for nearly eight innings, gave up six hits, including an inside-the-park home run by center fielder "Wahoo Sam" Crawford. Detroit gave Johnson his first loss by a score of 3-2.

Less than three weeks later—on August 18—the Tigers played their first Sunday game at Michigan and Trumbull. Detroit defeated the New York Highlanders 13-6, but that still did not please many of the area's clergy, who protested the violation of a heretofore strict Sabbath Day observance. Owners of businesses within walking distance of the stadium, on the other hand, praised the decision. They saw another opportunity to make

"Wild Bill" Donovan became one of Detroit's first pitching aces.

cash registers ring.

Sam Crawford enjoyed a banner year in 1907. Second in the league to Cobb in hitting (.323), he led the circuit scoring 102 runs, was second in doubles (34) and triples (17).

Tiger pitching stats that year featured Bill Donovan whose 25-4 record led the league in winning percentage (.862). His teammate, Twilight Ed Killian, had an equal number of victories and 13 defeats.

An overflow crowd sat on the outfield grass at Columbia Park in Philadelphia on September 30 to watch a double-header between the Athletics and the Tigers, who maintained a half-game lead for the American League pennant. Philadelphia got off to a comfortable 7-1 advantage in the first inning against Detroit's ace Bill Donovan. The Athletics' normally dependable George "Rube" Waddell (19-13) could not contain Detroit. The Tigers pecked away until Cobb tied the game 8-8 with a two-run homer in the ninth.

Each club added a run in the 11th. In the 14th inning, Philadelphia's Harry Davis hit a long fly ball into the spectators sitting on the grass in left-center field. Crawford backed into the crowd. One of the fans, a police officer, stood up either to make room for Crawford or to interfere; the interpretation varies with team loyalty. The two collided. One umpire ruled a ground-rule double. Another more senior umpire reversed the decision, called interference, and declared the batter "out."

The air was filled with language that should have curled the hair of any Philadelphia Quaker. After the cursing and shouting ceased, play resumed. The next batter laced a single to center that would have scored the runner had he been allowed to remain on second. Alas, no one scored. At the conclusion of the 17th inning, the game was called on account of darkness and remained on the books as a tie. The second game was never rescheduled.

Since rained out or tied games were not replayed in those days, Detroit left Philadelphia still holding on to first place and headed for Washington. They swept the Senators in the remaining four games of the year.

During that series, Cobb collected a bonus of $500 when he got his 200th hit of the year. Cobb, a superstitious man, credited his success to a black bat he used that possessed, in his words, "magical powers." More important than individual records or the effect of good-luck charms was the fact that for the first time in their brief history, the Detroit Tigers were the American League Champions.

Their challenge now was to take on the National League Champs—the Chicago Cubs.

That was quite a challenge, indeed. The Chicago Cubs, with their legendary trio of Joe Tinker, Johnny Evers and Frank Chance, posted 116 wins the year before. That was two more wins than the celebrated New York Yankees in 1998, and in fewer games. But they were defeated in the '06 World Series by the so-called "Hitless Wonders" of the cross-town White Sox. That gave the Tigers a ray of hope. The Tigers needed every ounce of hope because, in 1907, the Cubs again ran away with the National League pennant. Finishing the season with an impressive 107-45 record, they outdistanced second-place Pittsburgh by 17 games.

Helping the cause for the Cubs were five outstanding pitchers: Jack "The Giant Killer" Pfiester (15-9 and a league-leading 1.15 ERA), Orval Overall (23-7, 1.68 ERA), "Big Ed" Reulbach (17-4, 1.69 ERA), Carl Lundgren (18-7, 1.17 ERA) and Mordecai "Three Finger" Brown (20-6, 1.39 ERA).

Game One of the 1907 Series was played in Chicago. Detroit led 3-2 in the bottom of the ninth. With two outs and two strikes on the batter, fans in the Motor City prepared to celebrate. However, catcher Boss Schmidt (the same player who decked Ty Cobb in spring training) missed a pitch. The ball skipped back to the screen, allowing Chicago to tie the score. The game lasted three more innings before being called on account of darkness.

A tie game was not unusual. What looked like more than a coincidence was the fact that, earlier in the day, Ban Johnson, president of the American League, announced that the players would share not only in profits from the

first four games, but also for tie games. Fans from both Chicago and Detroit smelled a rat. A postgame investigation revealed no conspiracy. Johnson, however, ruled that henceforth, players would be paid for the first four games only, no matter what the score happened to be.

In Game Two, Chicago's Pfiester scattered nine hits to defeat the Tigers 3-1. Detroit's George Mullin took the loss.

Game Three the next day was much the same. The Tigers lost 5-1, getting only six hits against Chicago pitcher Ed Reulbach. Johnny Evers paced the Cubs attack with three hits, including two doubles.

Enthusiasm for the World Series waned in Detroit as witnessed by the scarce attendance of only 11,300 for Game Four who saw the home team again lose to Chicago by a score of 6-1. Orval Overall limited Tiger bats to only five hits.

The skies were overcast, the temperature hovered in the low 40s and a howling wind sent chills through the body. The weather reflected the mood of the city of Detroit that seemed ho-hum as the Cubs and Tigers met for Game Five. Crossing the turnstiles that day were only 7,370 fans—the smallest turnout for any World Series game in history.

The faithful few were not

George Mullin wore two hats, one as a steady pitcher, the other as an outfielder.

rewarded. The game was painful to watch as the Cubs starting pitcher—"Three Finger" Brown took the mound. Mordecai Brown earned his nickname because he was missing one finger on his pitching hand, thus he was able to release the ball between two extended fingers, much like today's fork ball, and make the ball drop sharply just before it reached the plate. The pitch most certainly was effective this game. Brown tossed a seven-hitter and blanked the Tigers, 2-0. As if to add an exclamation point to the Series, the Cubs stole four bases during the game, giving them a total of 18.

Following the final out, Detroit players sat in the locker room stunned. Nobody spoke. They just sat there, staring into space. Some of their gloom was erased when majority owner Yawkey turned over the club's share of the winnings to the players. Each player took home an additional $1,945.96—which, for many of the players, far surpassed their entire year's salary.

An unexpected bonus notwithstanding, the Tigers were humiliated at every turn in the Series. Chicago pitchers posted a team ERA of a stingy 0.75. They limited batting champion Ty Cobb to four hits and a .200 average.

Detroit fans were furious. They blamed everyone: the pitching, the hitting and the management. One of the nation's more famous sportswriters, I. E. Sanborn of the *Chicago Tribune*, penned a dark prediction: "There is only one conclusion to be drawn from Detroit's attitude toward its champions, and

that is the well-known adage that a city of that size will not stand for a loser, and I look for the disappearance of Detroit from the major league map within a few years."

One of those who did have faith in the Tigers was young Frank Navin. Principal owner Bill Yawkey appeared to be satisfied with winning his first American League pennant, so Navin, the one-time bookkeeper for the Detroit ball club, bought a half-interest in the Tigers for $40,000. Yawkey even loaned Navin enough money to make the first payment. "You've got a good club now," said Yawkey. "You can pay me the rest as you go along."

Frank Navin was a different kind of owner. He did not look like a person associated with baseball. He was not athletic. A bald, pudgy man who, even before he reached 30, appeared to be woefully out of shape. He seldom showed enthusiasm for victories or sorrow following a loss. He hid all emotions behind a poker face that seldom changed expression. Unlike most other owners with roots in the sport, Navin did not smoke or chew tobacco. He was also a teetotaler with a fondness for sweets. He did, however, love gambling. More importantly, he loved to win at gambling. His primary passion was playing a game of high-stakes poker. His other love was horses. He even owned some prize race horses and was a regular visitor to the track.

Frank Navin's association with games of chance, however, never interfered with his obligation to baseball. No one ever questioned his honesty or, for that matter, his skills in business dealings. The poker face that helped him bluff the best players in poker also served him well in negotiations for his ball club.

The following winter, Navin faced several uphill challenges from a variety of camps. He made a mistake in hiring non-union workers to make repairs at Bennett Park and the strong union contingent from Detroit threatened to boycott future games. Navin offered an apology that was accepted.

Other labor difficulties came from within the organization. Ty Cobb, wearing the coveted crown as American League Batting Champion, demanded $5,000—the same salary paid to the National League Champion, Pittsburgh's Honus Wagner. Navin argued that Wagner was a 12-year veteran. That didn't faze the 21-year-old pride of Georgia.

When Detroit fans started to take sides and express themselves in letters to the editor of Detroit's newspapers, Navin made his opinion known through a caustic quip to the Associated Press: "The creation cannot be greater than the creator. Cobb is not bigger than baseball." That statement did nothing but irritate the Georgia Peach, who stayed at his home in Georgia while his team held spring training in Little Rock. Less than a week before the start of the season, Cobb agreed to sign for $4,500.

Besides Cobb, outfielder Sam Crawford, who had hit .295 the year before, missed much of spring training due to his wife's illness.

The two Tiger stars were not in the best of shape at the ringing of the opening bell for the 1908 season. They and the rest of the Tigers languished in sixth place during the first few weeks of play. Before the end of May, however, the Tigers caught fire and tied the New York Highlanders for the league lead. New York cooled off and for the remainder of the season, three teams—the Tigers, Chicago White Sox and Cleveland Naps (named in honor of their star player, Napoleon Lajoie)—battled for first place. The winner of the race would not be determined until the last game of the season between Detroit and Chicago at Comiskey Park. The winner of that game would capture the pennant. The best Cleveland could hope for was second.

Detroit got on the board quickly with a four-run outburst in the top of the first. That was more than enough for Wild Bill Donovan, who gave up only two hits in the game. The Tigers pounded out 13 hits to win with ease, 7-0.

Donovan (18-7) and "Wabash" George Mullin (17-13) led the Tiger mound staff that year. Aiding in the pitching department was a rookie named Edgar Oren Summers, who posted a 24-12 record with his famed knuckle ball. Because of the erratic flight of his pitches coming at opposing batters, his teammates dubbed him "Kickapoo Ed."

Ty Cobb, for the second year in a row, led all American League hitters with, for him, a rather modest .324 average. Sam Crawford hit .311.

Forgetting about the disappoint-

Enterprising property owners of land just beyond the outfield walls of Bennett Park erected high bleachers where fans could view the game for as little as one nickel. These so-called "Wildcat Bleachers" were often filled with tobacco-chewing, liquor-drinking rowdies who shouted insults to opposing players and even spit tobacco juice on some. Prior to the 1911 season, Mr. Navin purchased the property, and the "Wildcat Fans" had to see the game from inside the stadium.

Southpaw Ed Killian was another mainstay with the Tigers' pitching staff.

ment of the previous year, Tiger fans supported the team as never before. A record 436,199 attended home games. The 1908 Tigers were even more popular than Henry Ford's newest product—the Model T.

Part of the reason for the Tigers' success in 1908 was a last-minute addition to the team of Owen J. "Donie" Bush, a 5' 6", 140-pound shortstop purchased from Indianapolis. He played in only 20 games, thus he was ineligible for World Series play, yet the hustling rookie was a sparkplug who filled a hole left vacant with an injury to Charley O'Leary.

The Tigers were determined to get revenge for the humiliation suffered the previous year at the hands of the Chicago Cubs who had also repeated as National League champions in '08.

The opening game took place in Detroit under a steady pour of rain. Groundskeepers were constantly in motion in an attempt to keep the turf of Bennett Park close to playing conditions. The teams exchanged leads throughout the contest. Chicago pitchers Ed Reulbach, Orval Overall and Three-Finger Brown were not at the top of their games. Detroit held a 6-5 lead going into the top of the ninth. Twilight Ed Killian started the game for Detroit but was knocked out of the box in the third. Ed Summers was able to hold Chicago in check. He appeared to have the Bengals' first Series victory in the bag until the dreadful ninth inning, when five Chicago runners crossed the plate. The final score: Chicago 10, Detroit 6.

Through a strange arrangement, Games Two and Three were played in Chicago. Bill Donovan held the Cubs to only one hit in seven innings, until Joe Tinker's home run sparked a six-run rally. Detroit lost Game Two by the score of 6-1.

As if to say: "Enough is enough," with the score 3-1 in favor of the Cubs in Game Three, Ty Cobb rapped out four hits to lead the Tigers to their first World Series victory 8-3, as George Mullin limited Chicago to seven hits.

That was the end of Detroit's momentum. Back in Detroit for Game Four, Three-Finger Brown shut out Ed Summers and the Tigers, 3-0, on just four hits.

Game Five was nearly a photocopy of the one played the day before. This time, however, the Tigers could scratch out only three hits as the Cubs and pitcher Orval Overall ended the season by besting Bill Donovan, 2-0.

The Detroit clubhouse resembled a funeral. All that remained was the administering of last rites. The Tigers were humiliated two years in a row. But Manager Hughie Jennings knew what he had seen and had to admit to his players and to the press, "We were beaten by a great team. A great team."

Cubs fans, to this day, still celebrate their 1908 World Championship - their last championship of the twentieth century.

With no early Christmas bonus this year from Bill Yawkey, the Detroit players pocketed only $870 and change for participating in the Series.

The neck-and-neck race for the pennant in 1908 and the two World Series losses were experiences neither Manager Jennings nor owner Frank Navin wished to repeat. Over the winter, they took steps to rebuild their club.

The familiar infield of Coughlin, O'Leary, Schaefer and Rossman were no longer in their plans, although they would retain Charley O'Leary as a utility infielder. Ira Thomas, a back-up catcher, was traded to New York for George Moriarty, a scrappy third baseman who would win fan approval with his aggressive style of play. Donie Bush, the promising youngster purchased the year before, was penciled in as the regular shortstop.

Detroit started early in the 1909 season showing its intent to walk away with the pennant. From April through August, they occupied first place for all but one day. Philadelphia, at the same time, was keeping pace.

Jennings, anticipating a tough race, asked Navin for more help. Second baseman Jim Delahanty came over from Washington in a trade for Schaefer. First baseman Tom Jones traded his Browns uniform for Tiger threads in a deal that sent Claude Rossman to St. Louis.

The energy of new blood kicked in. Detroit regained its dominating style of play.

Ty Cobb made certain that no one could underestimate the Tigers' eagerness to win. On August 24, Cobb slid into third base with his cleats high and spiked the Athletics' popular third baseman Frank Baker in the right arm. Cobb was roundly criticized for his style of play, especially by fans and sportswriters outside of Detroit. Some went so far as to accuse him of sharpening his spikes with a file before games, then purposely sliding with feet high just to injure infielders. Most of the Detroit writers and fans sided with Cobb. They labeled his behavior "aggressive play."

Cobb never denied these rumors, although no player ever claimed he actually saw the Peach sharpen his spikes. Those who knew Ty Cobb understood where he was coming from. For Cobb, baseball was not just a physical game; it was also mental. If he could do anything to agitate an opponent and, thereby, get him

Detroit Tigers
1907 American League Champions
Top Row - Eubank, Rossman, Crawford, Donovan, Mullin, Willett, Payne, Killian
Middle Row - D. Jones, Downs, Cobb, Coughlin, Schaefer, B. Jones
Front Row - Siever, Archer, Jennings *(manager)*, Schmidt, O'Leary

angry, the opposing player might well lose his concentration, giving Cobb the advantage.

To Ty Cobb, anyone wearing an opposing uniform was his enemy. Before the game or after the game, Cobb could be friends with the player, perhaps even share dinner with him. But once the first pitch was tossed, he was the enemy. Cobb, therefore, used every psychological ploy just to gain an edge. He was not afraid to use name-calling, insults or fear to gain a psychological advantage. In Cobb's mind, winning was everything and he was willing to pay the price for his behavior.

It came as no surprise to Cobb, then, when he and his Tigers returned to Philadelphia for a four-game series in September, that an avalanche of hate mail awaited him in the visitors' locker room. For one of the few times in his life, the crusty right fielder feared he might have gone too far. Tiger management feared for his life. They insisted their premier right fielder be escorted to and from the park by police motorcycles. During the game, uniformed officers stood in the front row, separating Cobb from the fans in the right field stands. Another 15 undercover policemen stationed themselves throughout the stadium looking for anyone who might take a shot at the controversial Georgian.

Philadelphia won three out of the four games and Detroit escaped Shibe Park 2 1/2 games ahead of the A's. Detroit eventually captured the American League flag by 3 1/2 games.

Much of the success of the '09 campaign was due to the prowess of Tyrus Raymond Cobb. He again led both leagues in hitting with a lusty .377. He also topped the American League in runs scored (116), stolen bases (76), RBI (107), slugging average (.517), hits (216) and for the only time in his brilliant career, in home runs (9).

Cobb and teammate Wahoo Sam Crawford were not the best

Detroit Tigers
1908 American League Champions
Top Row - Tuthill *(trainer)*, Stanage, Killian, Downs, Thomas, Rossman, Summers, Willett, Crawford, Mullin
Middle Row - Schaefer, Donovan, Winter, Navin *(president)*, Jennings *(manager)*, Coughlin, O'Leary, Bush, Cobb
Front Row - McIntyre, Malloy, D. Jones, Suggs, Schmidt, Killefer

of friends, but they provided Detroit with consistent hitting. Crawford batted a healthy .314.

Donie Bush, in his first full year, batted a respectable .273, and he played shortstop like a seasoned veteran. He also scored a whopping 114 runs.

Another late addition to the Tiger staff that year was catcher Oscar Stanage, who caught 77 games, hit .262 and showed all the attributes necessary to become a first-string receiver.

George Mullin's 29-8 record led the Tiger mound staff and the American League in the number of wins and winning percentage (.784). His fellow right hander, Ed Summers, also had a good year with a 19-9 mark. Ed Willet had a career-high 21 wins and only 10 losses. Bill Donovan, however, had an off year (8-7).

For the third season in a row, the Tigers represented the junior circuit in the World Series. This time, they played the Pittsburgh Pirates who had won the National League crown with a most impressive 110-42 record.

From the outset, the 1909 Series was dubbed as a duel between the two most feared hitters of the era—Cobb and the Pirates' Honus Wagner, quite possibly the greatest shortstop of all time. Game One was held at the newly constructed Forbes Field in the Steel City. It was the perfect setting for Cobb to show Wagner and the Pittsburgh fans who was truly the best player in the majors.

In the first inning of the game, Cobb hit a single to center. While standing on first, he taunted

Wagner: "Hey, Krauthead," he shouted. "I'm coming down on the next pitch."

As soon as Pirate pitcher Babe Adams released the ball, Cobb took off for second. The barrel-chested Wagner, with blacksmith-like arms, covered the bag and awaited catcher George Gibson's throw. Cobb slid, spikes high. The burly, six-foot, 200-pound Wagner sidestepped the onrushing Tiger, then swung his gloved hand across Cobb's jaw with a vengeance. The blow cut Cobb's lip and loosened two of his teeth. The umpire bellowed: "Yer out!"

Both the individual match-up and the game were won by Pittsburgh, as Adams outdueled George Mullin, 4-1.

In Game Two, Cobb regained some of his pride by stealing home

**Detroit Tigers
1909 American League Champions**
Top Row - Summers, Schmidt, Stanage, Gainor, Willett, Crawford, Cobb, Mullin
Middle Row - Delahanty, T. Jones, Killian, D. Jones, Jennings *(manager)*, Moriarty, O'Leary, Bush
Front Row - Tuthill *(trainer)*, Lelivelt, Donovan, Works, McIntyre, Beckendorf, Speer

Catcher Charles "Boss" Schmidt was a tough backstop who once had to curtail the aggressiveness of Ty Cobb. As a result, the two were never close friends.

twice. Combined with Bill Donovan's five-hit pitching, the Tigers pounded Pittsburgh, 7-2.

Cobb's base-stealing exhibition may have inspired Honus Wagner, who amassed three singles, scored three runs and stole three bases, leading the Pirates to an 8-6 victory in Detroit the next day.

In Game Four, Mullin struck out ten Bucs as the Tigers blanked Pittsburgh, 5-0.

Back in Detroit for Game Five, Babe Adams and his Pirates came out on top, 8-4, overcoming a stellar performance by Sam Crawford, who went 3 for 4, including a double and a home run.

A quick train ride back to Pittsburgh the next afternoon for Game Six proved more exhausting for the Pirates, who were defeated by George Mullin and the Tigers, 5-4. In the ninth inning, the Tigers suffered three injuries: Tom Jones ran over Pirate base runner Owen Wilson while chasing a ball and was knocked unconscious; Boss Schmidt and George Moriarty were spiked while attempting to tag Pirate runners.

Back in Detroit for the seventh and final game, Pirate ace Charles "Babe" Adams rose to the challenge and shut out the Tigers, 8-0. For the first time in baseball history, the Pittsburgh Pirates were the Champions of Baseball.

Detroit had yet to experience that thrill.

The trumpeted personal contest between Ty Cobb and Honus Wagner was not close, at least on paper. Wagner batted a healthy .333 during the seven games. Cobb hit a mediocre .231. But one event best remembered by the fans on both sides was the confrontation at second base in Game One between Wagner and Cobb.

Only two home runs were hit during the entire seven-game Series, both by Pirate player-manager Fred Clarke. Such limited long-ball hitting would be out of line with today's standards. However, in, 1909, that figure fell well within the norm.

Some modern-day observers liken baseball at the turn of the century to the state of the game today in which players are often ranked by the number and distance of home runs. Instead, baseball in the early part of the 20th century was driven by a different set of values. Superstars of that era were the scrappy players who used every weapon in their arsenals to score runs. Bunt singles … stolen bases … hit-and-run plays … spitballs … an occasional long ball. Whatever was necessary, they used.

Intelligent, determined, arrogant, spiteful, with limitless energy—from the first day he laced a pair of spikes to the day he died, Ty Cobb was the personification of that brand of baseball.

Prior to the start of Game One of the 1909 World Series, Ty Cobb discusses the finer points of hitting with Pirates superstar Honus Wagner.

Chapter 4
Years of Frustration

"Manager Jennings' experimental moves were slow in bearing fruit."

- Reach's 1912 Guide

Ty Cobb shows the classic swing that led him to win 12 league batting championships.

THE TIGERS GAVE EVERY INDICATION THEY WERE BUILDING a dynasty in Detroit. Cobb, Crawford and the newcomer Bush furnished power at the plate. The team also featured superb pitching; Mullin, Summers, Willett, Killian and Donovan headed a staff that outshone any other in the league. Orchestrating all this talent from his familiar third-base coach's box in the newly painted Bennett Park was the Tigers' spunky manager, Hughie Jennings. Unfortunately, all the stadium improvements, potential talent and "Ee-yahs" in the world could not get the job done in 1910.

On occasion, the Tigers showed flashes of the brilliance that had won three consecutive pennants. An 11-game winning streak rekindled the enthusiasm of Detroit fans. However, Connie Mack's Philadelphia A's won 13 in a row to win the American League pennant. In a nutshell, that was the story of the 1910 season for the Bengals. No matter what the Tigers did, Philadelphia, with the likes of Eddie Collins and Frank "Home Run" Baker, did a wee bit better. When the season ended, the Athletics sat atop the American League standings by 14 1/2 games over second-place New York. Detroit, despite scoring a league-leading 679 runs, wound up a distant third, 18 games behind Mack and his crew.

Bill Donovan regained his form with a 17-7 record. Mullin maintained his steady performance with 27 complete games and 21 wins in 33 trips to the mound. Ed Willett racked-up 16 wins, and Summers had a so-so, 13-11, year.

Ty Cobb won the batting championship by a whisper in 1910 with a remarkable .385 average. Cobb snatched his title from future Hall-of-Famer Napoleon Lajoie, with the help of last-minute strategy. He was just a few points ahead of Lajoie when Detroit began a four-game series in Chicago to end the season. During the first two games, the Peach got four hits in seven at-bats. He opted to sit out the last two games, hoping his average would stand.

Cleveland's Lajoie made Cobb re-evaluate his decision. Because of their anger at Cobb, the Browns allowed Lajoie to go eight for eight, including seven bunt singles, in a double-header on the last day. His efforts resulted in a .384 average—one point behind Cobb.

Another challenge to Cobb's future batting crowns was a youngster who played in only 20 games for Cleveland that year and hit .387. His name was Joe Jackson—an outfielder from Pickens County, South Carolina, who was so poor he could not afford a pair of baseball shoes. For the remainder of his career he would be known as "Shoeless Joe."

Hard-hitting Sam Crawford dipped below .300 (.285) although he led the league in RBI (120). Delahanty, Moriarty and Jones suffered injuries that kept them out of key games.

The Tigers' most troubling problems ran much deeper than a few injuries and sub-par performances. A report in *Reach's 1911 Guide* summarized the situation in just one pointed sentence: "Factional troubles existed and frequent rows helped make the days more unpleasant for Hugh Jennings, manager of the fallen champions."

At the center of controversy was, as might be expected, Tyrus Raymond Cobb who reportedly complained when a waiter on a train failed to show him due respect. The story made the front pages of the newspaper, adding to the growing numbers in the anti-Cobb army around the nation.

Prior to 1910, Michigan imposed an informal ban on regularly scheduled Sunday baseball. However, union workers around Detroit clamored for an opportunity to see a major league game on their only day off. Reluctantly, Frank Navin joined Chicago, St. Louis and Cincinnati by allowing games to be played in Detroit on an "experimental basis."

Clergymen from many of the surrounding churches led a protest, citing the Ten Commandments that demanded keeping the Sabbath Day holy. The fact that those same Commandments also

The "ee-yah" man, manager Hughie Jennings, in action.
[Photo: *The Detroit News*]

Cobb displays his unique batting style. Note how far apart he holds his hands. "That gave me better control of the bat," insisted the Peach. [Photo: *The Detroit News*]

Was Ty Cobb the meanest, most acid-tongued player ever to sharpen a pair of spikes? "Yes," say most writers. Testimony by opposing players seems to support that claim. However, with our 20-20 hindsight and from observations shared by those who knew him best, a growing number of historians are re-examining their opinions. They are convinced that Cobb was the first player ever to use to his advantage both the physical and mental dimensions of baseball.

referred to Saturday notwithstanding, the more fundamentalist factions of the Christian community made their impact. Navin and the rest of the Tiger brass knew they were on probation. They insisted that the players be on their best behavior and do anything necessary to insure that Sunday games would be played with dignity.

During that first-year "experiment" with Sunday ball, one incident nearly caused Navin to regret his decision. Boston was in town and had tied the score in the ninth inning. With two outs, the Tigers' third-sacker, George Moriarty, was on third. Suddenly, without any instructions from the bench, Moriarty took off in an attempt to steal home. He slid hard into Red Sox catcher Bill Carrigan. The umpire yelled: "Safe!" The Tigers won the game to the delight of the fans.

With the Tiger faithful cheering in celebration and Moriarty lying on the ground savoring the moment, Carrigan walked away from home plate, but not before he let go with a squirt of tobacco juice that hit Moriarty right in the eye. Moriarty jumped to his feet and smacked Carrigan in the jaw. Both benches cleared. Following a pattern begun in the earliest days of Detroit baseball, a few Tiger fans climbed the railing to assist their team. The normally reserved owner Frank Navin stood atop the Tiger dugout, struck the pose of a tent-meeting evangelist, held his hands high in the air and urged the crowd to leave quietly. The fans heeded his call for composure.

Spectators and players left the field with no further incident.

On Monday morning, American League President Ban Johnson slapped Moriarty with a $100-dollar fine. Author Frederick Lieb recalls a conversation the next day between Navin and Moriarty.

"That was quite a mess you stirred up yesterday," said Navin, "and on a Sunday, too."

"I'm sorry Mr. Navin," apologized Moriarty, "but under the circumstances I could do nothing else."

Navin promised to pay the $100 fine and warned his third baseman, "Don't let it happen again."

"No, Mr. Navin, I won't," said a relieved Moriarty.

As Moriarty left the office, Navin went to the door and shouted at him, "I mean don't ever let any of those fellows spit in your eye again."

The 1911 Tigers treated the previous year as ancient history. They stormed out of the gate winning 21 of their first 23 games. Suddenly, the wheels fell off the Detroit machine. Internal bickering took its toll. Sam Crawford and Donie Bush no longer spoke with Ty Cobb, partly because of his obnoxious treatment of innocent people such as waiters and groundskeepers. Cobb, in turn, resented what he considered a lack of support on the part of his teammates. Crawford fueled the flames when he accused Tiger management of giving favored treatment to its batting champion. He told a Detroit newspaperman Cobb could miss batting practice or break other club rules without penalty. "The rest of us would catch hell for doing the same thing," he said.

Cobb gave credibility to Crawford's observation when he waited until spring training was nearly over before reporting for an exhibition game in New Orleans. To the dismay of his manager, Cobb showed up woefully out of shape. Added to his once slim, athletic body was now a pronounced "pot belly." Even the loose-fitting baseball uniform could not hide his pudgy appearance. *The Sporting News* editorialized: "It may be that Ty is undergoing a steady, though gradual transition and that he will eventually lose his great speed."

Appearances aside, Cobb began the 1911 season where he left off a year earlier with a battery of base hits and stolen bases. The focus of attention by newspapers, however, was not on the Georgia Peach, but on a youngster named Del "Sheriff" Gainer. The tall right-handed-hitting first baseman, in his initial full year with the club, was an inspiration, even to veterans. In his first 70 games, he averaged more than a hit per game and was batting a solid .302. Without warning, this all came crashing down. During a game in not-so-friendly Philadelphia, Gainer was hit on the wrist by a high, inside fast ball tossed by pitcher Jack Coombs. X-rays revealed the worst: a season-ending broken bone. Gone not only was Gainer's potent bat, but also the principal source of inspiration for the Detroit ball club.

The Tigers played less than overpowering ball during the last part of the season, ending the year in second place, a distant 13 1/2 games behind Philadelphia.

Cobb, however, was brilliant. Pushed by the upstart Joe Jackson of Cleveland, he clubbed the ball at a blistering pace. Some say this was Ty Cobb's finest hour. He led his club and the league in batting average—a phenomenal .420. He also led in slugging percentage (.621), total bases (367), hits (248), doubles (47), triples (24), RBI (144), runs scored (147) and stolen bases (83). In addition, he tied the Red Sox' Tris Speaker for second place in home runs (8). All this earned for him the coveted Chalmers Award—akin to today's Most Valuable Player Award—for the American League.

Not too bad for an out-of-shape ballplayer.

Cobb later admitted that one of the reasons for his success was the pressure put on him by Shoeless Joe Jackson, who had a nine-point lead in the batting race with only 12 games to go. "Joe and I were good friends," admitted Cobb, "but I refused to talk with him. He thought he had done something to get me angry. While he was trying to figure out what it was all about, I beat him out of the title. If he had been relaxed and hitting naturally, I would have never overcome that nine-point lead."

Other players earning praise that year were reliable Sam Crawford (.378 and 7 home runs) and first baseman Jim Delahanty (.339), who had replaced the

> "Tyrus, Dear Boy ... The presence of man and the jargon of artificiality and show do not crowd out the grand aspect of God's handiwork. ... It is truly great to have a mind that will respond to and open the door of the soul. ... Be good and dutiful, conquer your anger and wild passions that would degrade your dignity and belittle your manhood."
>
> - Letter from Sen. Herschel Cobb to his son, Tyrus Raymond Cobb, 1902

injured Del Gainer.

George Mullin (18-10) led the Tiger pitching staff, and Ralph Works, with his career-best 11-5 record, was a pleasant surprise. Ed Willett (13-14), Ed Summers (11-11) and Bill Donovan (10-9) had marginal seasons.

Detroiters' support of their team continued to increase. A loyal fan base had already developed. Now it was becoming fashionable for parents to take their children to the games, thus generating fans for the future. Frank Navin realized this and added seats, increasing the capacity of Bennett Park to 14,000 in 1911. During the following winter, Mr. Navin ripped out the old wooden stands and replaced them with a large, single-deck concrete stand seating 23,000 people. In addition, he moved home plate from what would become the right field area to the southwest corner of the field.

Even the name of the ballpark changed. Everyone—sportswriters, fans and the rest of Tiger management—agreed that the park should be christened in honor of the driving force behind its reconstruction: Frank Navin.

Although Bennett Park shared the same location, the opening of Navin Field was the beginning of Tiger Stadium, the home of the Tigers through the 1999 season.

Formal dedication of Navin Field was scheduled for Opening Day, April 18, 1912. A typhoon-like downpour postponed the celebration for two days. It was worth the wait. The Tigers, behind right-hander Mullin, defeated southpaw Sylveanus "Vean" Gregg and his visiting Cleveland Naps with a hard-earned 6-5 win. Detroit outfielders—rookie Oscar "Ossie" Vitt, Crawford and Cobb—got ten of the team's 12 hits. Cobb also stole two bases.

Ty Cobb again made front-page news in 1912, not so much with his activities in the bat-

Oscar "Ossie" Vitt played both infield and outfield for the Tigers from 1912-1918.

ter's box or on the bases, rather it was his off-the-field antics that gave his manager premature gray hair. Even before the first drum beat of a parade and the remainder of the Opening Day ceremonies at the new ballpark, Detroit played a three-game series in Chicago. The night following the first game, Cobb had a difficult time sleeping due to noise from a train yard just outside his hotel room. The clamor of arriving and departing steam engines kept him awake throughout the evening. He called the front desk and asked that his room be moved. The hotel clerk did nothing. Cobb then awoke his manager from a deep sleep. "I don't know what I can do this time of night," said Jennings. "I'll see what I can do tomorrow."

That was not good enough for Cobb. He dressed, packed his clothes, left the hotel and hopped a late-night train for Detroit. The Tigers were forced to play the remaining two games in Chicago without their hitting star. Some of the other Tiger players openly grumbled when Manager Jennings refused to discipline Cobb for leaving the club.

Cobb's display of emotion was but an overture to what would take place one month later in New York City. During a May 15 game against the Highlanders, one fan— a local politician named Lueker— heckled Cobb unmercifully, punctuating his remarks with sailor-like curses that insulted Cobb's southern heritage. Cobb took all he could. Suddenly, the Peach bolted from the on-deck circle, leaped the

George Moriarity showed that it was not nice to spit tobacco juice in someone's eye.

railing, ran into the stands and punched the unsuspecting Lueker into submission.

Umpires Westervelt and O'Loughlin thumbed Cobb out of the game. League President Ban Johnson, no fan of Cobb, suspended the Tiger outfielder indefinitely.

The next day was a typical Thursday open date for travel. On Friday the Tigers, without Cobb, defeated the A's in Philadelphia, 6-3. Prior to the game, the Tigers held an impromptu meeting. They all signed a petition to be sent to Ban Johnson in stating that Cobb may not be among their favorites as a person, but as a player, he was

George "Hooks" Dauss got his nickname because of his wicked curve ball.

for-a-day" was a seminarian, Albert Travers, who was later ordained a Jesuit priest. Travers was paid $25 for the game, while the rest of the players each received $10. The Athletics treated Travers with little reverence; they pummeled him with 25 hits and won a laugher 24-2.

President Ban Johnson was furious with what he considered a mockery of the game. He took the first train to Philadelphia to squelch this uprising. The next day served as a cooling-off period because Sunday baseball was still banned in Pennsylvania. Johnson unilaterally canceled Monday's game at Shibe Park. Instead, he met with the Tiger players and flexed his authoritative muscle. He threatened to run out of baseball any player who failed to take the field against Washington in the next scheduled game on May 21.

Some of the players dug their heels into the sand and were set to ignore the president's threat until Ty Cobb himself urged the players to give up the strike. The players endorsed Cobb's advice and agreed to play the game. As a final display of his authority, Ban Johnson hit each of the Tiger players with a $100 fine. Cobb was fined $50 and given a 10-day suspension.

Later that year Cobb was driving with his wife to the train station in Detroit when three hoods jumped on the running board of his car and attacked him. One of them, holding a knife, reached inside an open window, slashing away at Cobb. Ty stopped his car, got out, and while bleeding, fought off all three thugs. The attackers

the best. They sided with his aggressive action against Lueker. The most daring part of the petition was a promise that the team would refuse to take the field on Saturday unless Cobb's suspension was lifted immediately.

Manager Jennings telephoned Frank Navin in Detroit. Navin knew he would be fined $5,000 for every game the Tigers refused to take the field. "You have to get a team somehow … somewhere," Navin ordered.

Jennings and his coaches issued an urgent call for players. They amassed a group of semi-pro players from the area to don Tiger uniforms. The pitcher for the "Tigers-

were never caught, but talk on the street was that the assault was a payback for Cobb's slugging of the New York fan.

That turmoil was the apex of excitement for Detroit baseball fans in 1912; their Tigers struggled to a 69-84 record and a sixth-place finish.

Cobb once again hit a smoking .410 to lead the league, beating out Shoeless Joe by 15 points. Jackson was shell-shocked. "What a hell of a league this is?" moaned the back-woods native of South Carolina. "Ah hit .387, .408, and .395 the las' three years and Ah ain't won nothin' yet!"

Ty Cobb also led the American League in slugging average (.586) and was third in home runs (7) behind Frank "Home Run" Baker and Tris Speaker, who tied for the lead with 10. Sam Crawford hit a very convincing .325, and Donie Bush showed some maturity as a hitter with his .294 average.

Pitching left much to be desired. Manager Jennings had cut former ace Bill Donovan, and Charley O'Leary left to manage a team in Rhode Island. Attempting to take up the slack were Ed Willett (17-15) and newcomer Jean Dubuc who had a career-best year, posting a 17-10 record and a 2.77 ERA. The rest of the staff, including George Mullin (12-17), did not compile Hall of Fame sta-tistics.

The best thing that can be said of the 1913 season is that it was played. Finishing again in sixth place, the Tigers were gradually undermining the fan enthusiasm that had been building over the past several years. Highlights were few, indeed. Ty Cobb, for the sev-enth straight year, led the American League in hitting (.390), and Crawford was right up there among the leaders at .316. In the pitching department, Dubuc (14-14) and George Dauss (13-12) were the only hurlers without los-ing records. This was Dauss' first full year with the Tigers and the beginning of a solid 15-year career in which he would rack up 222 wins and 182 losses.

The Detroit Tigers were in a rut. A fourth-place finish, 19 1/2 games behind front-running Philadelphia in 1914 gave little reason for excitement in the Motor City. Sportswriters would not be criti-cized were they to pen in the name of Ty Cobb as batting champion before the toss of the first pitch on opening day. Had they done so, they would have guessed correctly for the eighth year in a row. Cobb dominated the league in batting average (.368) and slugging aver-age (.513). Meanwhile, his stolen-base total dropped off to a mere 35. Some insiders openly questioned if Cobb still had his legs.

Rookie George Burns hit the ball at a .291 clip and with five homers, showed sufficient power to establish himself as the starting first baseman. He was good enough to convince Tiger management to unload the popular Del Gainer to Boston. Gainer, unfortunately, never re-captured the form he had prior to being hit on the wrist in 1911.

The Tigers' best fresh face in

"Ty Cobb told of how he spent two years devising a single play. When he reached third base, he liked to bluff as if he were continuing to home. He saw that one particular player liked to throw to third base to try to catch him. Cobb sprung his trap in the ninth inning of a tie game. When he saw the fielder throw to third, Cobb simply kept on going and scored the winning run."

- Bill Osinski, Columnist, *The Atlanta Journal-Constitution*

1914 was Harry Coveleski (born Harry Kowalewski)—a Polish left-handed pitcher from the coal mining town of Shamokin, Pennsylvania. Six years earlier, Coveleski grabbed headlines when, as a rookie with the Philadelphia Phillies in the National League, he beat John McGraw's mighty Giants three times during the last week of the season, thus eliminating them from the pennant race. Coveleski was dubbed "The Giant Killer" from that moment on.

In his first year in the American League, Coveleski showed the same raw talent as he led the Detroit club with a 22-12 record. His teammate, George "Hooks" Dauss was 18-15; his four saves, enough to lead the American League in that department.

A disruptive factor for all of big league baseball in 1914 was the formation of the Federal League, a pseudo major league backed by wealthy investors who were unafraid to offer attractive salaries to any players who wanted to swap uniforms. While some teams lost several key players to the upstart league, only pitcher Ed Willet left the Tigers for a bigger paycheck promised by the St. Louis Terriers.

Both Cobb and Crawford were targets for the new league. Neither had signed a contract with Detroit and elected to bypass the 1914 spring training camp held in Gulfport, Mississippi. Cobb eventually signed for a whopping $20,000. Crawford, now 35 years old, realized he was nearing the end of his career. He was happy to sign a four-year contract with the Tigers. It was one of the first multi-year contracts in the history of baseball.

The Federal League lasted only two years and outside of losing Willett, caused little concern in Detroit. At the same time, the fans and management grew increasingly impatient with their team. They realized that the Tigers had serious internal problems. The paying customers felt they deserved much more.

Navin Field Grand Opening
(April 20, 1912)

DETROIT	AB	R	H	O	A	E
Vitt, LF	5	2	3	3	1	0
Louden, 3B	3	0	0	4	2	0
Cobb, CF	4	2	2	4	0	0
Crawford, RF	5	1	3	1	0	0
Delahanty, 2B	5	0	1	1	1	2
Gainer, 1B	3	0	0	12	1	1
Bush, SS	4	1	1	1	2	2
Stanage, C	5	0	1	7	1	0
Mullin, P	5	0	1	0	7	0
Totals	**39**	**6**	**12**	**33**	**16**	**5**

CLEVELAND	AB	R	H	O	A	E
Graney, LF	6	1	2	1	0	0
Olson, SS	6	1	1	2	1	1
Jackson, CF	4	1	1	1	0	0
Lajoie, 2B	5	1	2	2	5	0
Ryan, RF	4	1	1	2	1	0
Hohnhorst, 1B	6	0	2	15	2	0
Turner, 3B	5	0	2	1	2	0
Easterly, C	4	0	1	0	3	0
Gregg, P	5	0	0	0	5	0
Totals	**45**	**5**	**12**	**32**	**19**	**1**

*Two out when winning run scored

Inning	1	2	3	4	5	6	7	8	9	10	11	Final
Detroit	2	0	1	0	0	0	0	2	0	0	1	6
Cleveland	1	0	2	0	2	0	0	0	0	0	0	5

Two-base Hits - Crawford, Olson, Jackson, Lajoie, Ryan, Turner.
Sacrifice Hits - Louden (2), Ryan.
Stolen Bases - Cobb (2), Gainer (2), Graney, Jackson, Hohnhurst.
Double Plays - Gregg, Hohnhurst and Easterly.
Left on Bases - Detroit 7, Cleveland 13.
First Base on Balls - Off Mullin, 4; off Gregg, 3.
First Base on Errors - Cleveland 4.
Hit by Pitcher - By Mullin (Ryan); by Gregg (Gainer).
Struck Out - By Mullin 5; by Gregg 4.
Passed Balls - Easterly.
Time - 2:32.
Umpires - Perrine and Dineen.
Attendance - 24,384.

Chapter 5

Operations Successful; Patients Die

"Do you smell something? Something around here really stinks!"

- Ty Cobb, whenever his arch rival, Babe Ruth, walked by

Navin Field, American League Park, Detroit, Mich.

Navin Field, 1918.

As poet John Greenleaf Whittier once wrote: "For all sad words of tongue or pen, the saddest are these: 'It might have been.'" That pragmatic insight best described the 1915 Detroit Tigers.

Detroit looked forward to a genuine chance to win the American League pennant that year, especially since Connie Mack dismantled much of the power-laden Athletics. When many of his star players threatened to leave his team for the higher paychecks of the Federal League, Mack cleaned house. He would rather work with young, inexperienced players who were loyal to him and his team than dicker with those whose dedication was ruled by dollar signs.

The 1915 season, however, fell far short of Detroit's expectations. It became the type of year that compelled Hughie Jennings to change his spirited "Ee-yahs" into agonizing groans. To pilot a talented club to a 100-54 season only to learn that another team would represent your league in the World Series would be enough to tempt a less secure baseball manager to search for a new job in the "Help Wanted" column of the *Detroit Free Press*. When the curtain came down on the final game of the 1915 season, the Boston Red Sox had a 101-50 record.

"This was my biggest disappointment in Detroit," moaned Jennings. It sent Tiger fans into depression as well.

Throughout the season, Detroit and Boston handled opposing teams with relative ease. The Tiger outfield of Cobb, Crawford and Bobby Veach could have been a starting trio in the All-Star Game had there

From under the roof of the grandstand at Navin Field, 1919.

right-hander Dauss had 22 and 24 wins, respectively. Rookie Bernie Boland chimed in with a 13-6 mark.

The Tigers played well; Boston fared better, especially in head-to-head contests. The Red Sox appeared to play their best during their games with Detroit, winning 14 out of 22 encounters.

One series proved to be fatal for Detroit. In mid-September, two weeks prior to the end of the season, Detroit traveled to Fenway Park for what some newspapermen called "the little World Series."

Dauss won the first of the four-game series in relatively easy fashion, 6-2, before a packed house. The Bosox, however, swept the remaining three games, dashing the hopes of Tigers fans.

During the series, the target for abuse by Beantown fans and sportswriters was Ty Cobb. During the last two innings, rookie pitcher Carl Mays took the mound in relief for Boston. Perhaps in an effort to gain respect, Mays pitched Cobb high and inside, compelling the Peach to drop to the ground. The fans, who had been jeering Cobb all afternoon, let out an ear-shattering cheer. That was all Cobb needed. He rose to his feet and threw his bat at Mays. The whirling bat resembled a boomerang as it sailed over the pitcher's head. Before Cobb had a chance to continue the confrontation, uniformed police ran onto the field, surrounded the Detroit outfielder and convinced him to leave with their protection, lest the irate fans hurt him.

The Boston Globe contained this

been such a contest. Cobb had another phenomenal year. The scrappy center fielder led the majors in batting average (.369), hits (208), total bases (274), runs scored (144) and swiped a mind-blowing 96 bases.

"I've always regretted I didn't make it a hundred steals that year," Cobb recalled. "With just a little greater effort, I could have gotten those four extra bases."

Right fielder Sam Crawford led the circuit with 19 triples, tied teammate Veach with 112 RBI and hit a solid .299. Besides sharing RBI honors with Wahoo Sam, Veach slammed a league-leading 40 doubles while hitting the ball at a .313 clip.

Ralph Young, a 5' 5" rookie second sacker, hit only .243. At the same time, his constant chatter on the field instilled the kind of enthusiasm for the game that had been missing since the days of Del Gainer.

Pitching for the Tigers in 1915 produced some notables as well. Both southpaw Coveleski and

report the next day: "Boston is willing to concede Cobb to be a great ballplayer and give him full credit for what he does as a player, but there is a limit beyond which even he can't go."

Detroit fans chanted: "Wait 'till next year." They were merely setting themselves up for another disappointment. The Tigers 87-67 record was good enough in 1916 for only third place, four games behind pennant-winning Boston.

The Tigers gave their followers a glimmer of hope in late August when they held onto first place two full days.

The real shocker of the 1916 season was the realization that perhaps … just perhaps … the immortal Ty Cobb was more human than thought. For the first time since 1907, the Peach failed to win the batting crown. Normally, his .371 average would have been good enough to win hands down. Instead, it got him second best. Cleveland's Tris Speaker, traded from Boston at the start of the season, finished with an eye-popping .386. Cobb offered no excuses. He did not enjoy losing the batting title, but if anyone were to win it, he was happy that it was Speaker. Cobb would later admit that "Smoke," as he called him, was one of the few people in baseball he could call a friend.

Playing his first full season in the majors in 1916 was young Harry Heilmann. That year, "Harry the Horse" split his time in the outfield, at first base and second base. He hit .282 and showed enough long-ball potential to suggest he was a star of the future.

Heilmann (sometimes called "Slug") would play 15 years for the Tigers. Once the 6' 1", 195-pounder hung up his cleats, he became the first in a long line of former players to sit behind the microphone as a sportscaster, calling Tiger games on radio from 1934 – 1950 and on television from 1947 – 1952.

Enthusiasm for the Tigers waned in 1917. A so-so 78-75 season certainly did little to generate excitement. In addition, the nation's attention was focused on battles across the ocean. Germany's Kaiser Wilhelm II and his disciplined troops marched over Europe, threatening the free world. War was imminent.

The full impact of the war was not felt in the States. Americans, by and large, remained interested, but passive observers.

The Tigers also appeared to be little more than observers during spring training that year, while other teams worked themselves into shape. Most of Detroit's players reported to training camp in the little-known town of Waxahachie, Texas. Heavy rains thwarted many of their practice sessions. "We might as well have trained in Detroit," said Bobby Veach.

Ossie Vitt held out for more pay and remained home in California until he eventually signed just

Harry "Slug" Heilmann played right field for the Tigers from 1914-1929. The Hall of Famer later became a popular broadcaster for Tiger games.

prior to Opening Day. As happened before, Ty Cobb chose to conduct his own spring training at home. He did, however, join his team as the Tigers and John McGraw's New York Giants began a barnstorming trip prior to the start of the season.

During one of those games in Dallas, Texas, Cobb stole second base, but not before he gashed second baseman Charles "Buck" Herzog. Later that night, Cobb saw Herzog in the lobby of the Oriental Hotel. Historian and newspaperman Frederick Lieb recalled the conversation.

"If you didn't get enough this afternoon," said Cobb, "see me in my room. I'll be there all evening."

"I can't take that," muttered Herzog to one of his nearby teammates.

A few minutes later, Herzog and two of his friends paid a visit to Cobb in his room. Immediately Herzog started to throw punches. Cobb grabbed Herzog and wrestled him over the foot of the bed. With Herzog bent helplessly over the footboard, Cobb cocked his right fist and asked, "Have you had enough?"

"I guess so," said Herzog.

Cobb backed off, and the three intruders left the room.

That may have been the spark Cobb needed to help resume his familiar spot as the king of American League hitters. His .383 average in 1917 was 31 points better than defending champion Speaker, who was third behind George Sisler of the Browns. His 55 stolen bases led the league, as did his 225 hits, 336 total bases, 44

doubles, 23 triples and .571 slugging average. It tempted Tiger brass to encourage all of the Tigers to take spring training at home.

Bobby Veach (.319) topped the league with 103 RBI, but Father Time finally caught up with Sam Crawford, who played only 71 games in his final season, batting an anemic .173. Prior to his last game, he shook hands with every one of his teammates … except Ty Cobb.

Pitching was fair, not spectacular. Dauss (17-14) and Bernie Boland (16-11) were the most consistent. Harry Coveleski slipped to a disappointing 4-6 record.

When America declared war on Germany on April 6, 1917, baseball realized that the 1918 season would be different from any other that came before. President Woodrow Wilson predicted this would be a "war to end all wars." Caught up in this enthusiasm to ensure world peace for future generations, Americans willingly sent their fathers, sons and brothers overseas.

From Washington came an official "work or fight" order, which meant that every draft-eligible man had to serve in the military unless he had an "essential job for the war effort." Since baseball was not considered "essential," Detroit and the rest of Major League Baseball agreed to a shortened season that would conclude on Labor Day.

Exchanging baseball uniforms for the Army brown was a legion of Detroit players, including: Bill James, Howard Ehmke, Bernie Boland, George Cunningham,

John "Red" Oldham and Del Baker. In addition, George Burns was sold to the Athletics.

As soon as the shortened season of 1918 came to a close, Cobb enlisted in the Army's chemical warfare section and was quickly awarded the rank of captain. Manager Jennings, too old for the draft, volunteered the next year as a Knights of Columbus worker; he made it to France just prior to the signing of the peace treaty.

Meanwhile, Detroit and the rest of the league went through the motions of offering big league ball. With rosters depleted due to the war effort, Bill Donovan came out of retirement after he was let go as manager of the New York Yankees (the team name changed from the "Highlanders" five years earlier) to pitch several games for his old pal, Hughie Jennings. In fact, Jennings himself filled in at first base on occasion.

Several young and untried players entered and left the revolving doors of the Tiger clubhouse. Jennings was the sixth first baseman to fill that slot during the '18 season.

Only three players were what might be called "steady." Donie Bush hit a weak .234 but played shortstop as well as any other American Leaguer. Before enlisting in the Army, Ty Cobb won the league batting title with .382, and Bobby Veach's 78 RBI led the junior circuit in that department.

As fine as these numbers appeared, the hitting of a Red Sox pitcher who doubled as an outfielder was gaining most of the attention from sportswriters. The big left hander with the face of a cherub who would be known simply as "The Babe," tied for the league lead with 11 home runs. He helped Boston win the American League pennant and for the last time in more than 80 years, the World Series. These 11 home runs would be the first of many hit by "The Bambino."

The Tigers' 55-71 record produced a seventh-place finish in 1918.

Germany signed an armistice on November 11 that year. Americans could now concentrate on more pleasant things.

The war's quick ending surprised major league owners. In pre-season meetings, they had agreed to reduce the number of games for the 1919 season from 154 to 140 and to cut salaries. This last decision laid the groundwork for one of baseball's all-time scandals, the impact of which would not be felt until the following year.

Ossie Vitt was traded to Boston for catcher Eddie Ainsmith, outfielder Charles "Chick" Shorten and Edward "Slim" Love, a tall (6' 7") southpaw.

Dauss led the team with a 21-7 record. Hubert Benjamin "Dutch" Leonard, who was purchased from Boston for a whopping $7,500—a tidy sum in those days—proved to be an expensive investment; Leonard ended the 1919 season with 14 wins in 27 outings.

Ty Cobb, now an "old man" at nearly 33 years of age, won his twelfth and final batting championship with an average of .384. Second to him in the race for the batting crown was teammate,

Bobby Veach (.355).

Early in the 1919 campaign, Frank Navin became full owner of the Detroit Baseball Club when William Yawkey died. Within a year, he brought on board two silent partners—John Kelsey and Walter O. Briggs—as a way of getting the necessary money to expand Navin Field.

The Tiger faithful had supported their team through the past decade without the reward of a first-place finish. In the entire history of the club, they had yet to celebrate a World Series championship.

The 1920 season would not fill that void in franchise history.

The club got off to a miserable start, losing its first 13 games. An eventual seventh-place finish, 37 games behind league-leading Cleveland, showed the fans and press the Tigers were going nowhere fast.

Ty Cobb batted .334, tenth among American League hitters, far behind the Browns' George Sisler, who hit .407, and Cleveland's player-manager Tris Speaker (.388). Cobb was limited to playing in only 112 games during the 1920 season due, in part, to a June 7 collision with fellow outfielder Ira Flagstead. Torn ligaments in Cobb's left knee kept him off the field for several weeks. In addition, his lack of speed limited him to only 14 stolen bases.

Navin tried to get Jennings some much-needed pitching help that year. He hired Jack Coombs, former ace for the Athletics and Brooklyn Dodgers, as pitching coach. A parade of young pitchers signed contracts, only to be sent home after a few games.

The only young player to show any genuine talent was not a pitcher, but a third baseman named Ralph "Babe" Pinelli. Although he lasted with the Tigers for only one season, he developed into a regular player for Cincinnati. Several years later, he traded his baseball uniform for a chest protector and became one of the game's great umpires.

Talk around baseball throughout the 1920 season centered on two things. The first was the impact of a new dimension of the game— power. Babe Ruth was traded from Boston to the Yankees at the beginning of the season. In his first full campaign as an outfielder, he astonished the nation by slamming 54 home runs, while no other American League *team* hit more than 50 that year. Some of Ruth's homers were massive shots deep into the upper decks of Yankee Stadium and other parks. Reporters wrote that when the Yankees came to a particular city, people who had never before seen a ball game came just to watch this heralded slugger. Even the most casual fan had to admit that the emphasis of baseball was shifting from the scrappy style of play personified by Ty Cobb to a power game featuring tape-measure home runs.

The second concern was about what happened the previous year in the World Series. America was shocked and saddened by the revelation that the American League Champion White Sox, heavy favorites to win the Series, purposely lost to the Cincinnati Reds. Fans demanded the "Black Sox

Scandal," as it was called, be resolved as quickly as possible. The solution was found in the person of a judge from Chicago. In a bold move to demonstrate their sincerity to maintain a spotless image, club owners appointed a respected and eminent judge, Kenesaw Mountain Landis, as the game's first commissioner.

Landis, as it turned out, was more than a commissioner. He was a dictator. A stern dictator at that. With the spirit of a town marshal in the Old West hired to rid the area of outlaws, Landis issued unilateral decisions that included suspensions for life for some of the Sox players. One of them was "Shoeless Joe" Jackson, the man who challenged Ty Cobb for the batting crown just a few years earlier.

Landis imposed stern orders that major league personnel must never be seen betting on the game. According to Judge (some called him "Czar") Landis, gambling threatened the integrity of the game. At the same time, everyone in baseball knew that Tiger owner Frank Navin enjoyed games of chance. At the same time, Mr. Navin was always careful never to mix baseball with his passion for gambling.

As an old baseball saying goes, "Major League Baseball knows only two kinds of managers—those who have been fired and those who will be fired." When the Tigers tumbled to seventh place at the end of the 1920 season, Frank Navin and the rest of the Tiger front office determined that in the best interest of the club, the

beloved Hughie Jennings had to leave.

This was not a decision that Navin wished to make. Jennings was not only a good baseball man, he was also Navin's cherished friend. Pressure from grumbling fans, however, left Mr. Navin no choice.

Ironically, the one person with the most empathy for Jennings during his waning days with the club was the man who caused him the most grief—Ty Cobb. Together, they would sit up late into the night planning strategies for next day's game.

The haunting question in the Tiger camp, however, was who would replace the popular Hughie Jennings? Navin considered his options and at the suggestion of Jennings, offered the hot-tempered Ty Cobb an opportunity to run his team.

Player-managers were not uncommon in this era. After all, from his post in center field, Tris Speaker had directed his Cleveland Indians (the name changed from the "Naps" five years earlier) to a World Championship.

Ty Cobb would earn more money while wearing two hats, but he certainly did not need the extra cash. While he may have demonstrated instability in his social life, he was an astute investor. Unlike other players who squandered their money on booze and wild women, Cobb parlayed his funds into three different industries: the cotton market, with which he was familiar, a new corporation in Detroit known as "General Motors," and an upstart company in Georgia that created and bottled a new soft drink called "Coca-Cola."

Cobb considered many factors before accepting the post. The most influential factor was the fact that the Chicago White Sox spoke with Frank Navin in an attempt to get Cobb as their player-manager. Cobb, for all his faults, maintained a strong sense of loyalty toward his Tigers. To ensure his tenure in Detroit, Cobb accepted Navin's offer.

At the beginning of spring training in 1921, Cobb left no doubt in anyone's mind as to who was in charge. He felt strongly that when a player was on the field he should think only of the game, nothing else. Harry Salsinger, a sports editor for *The Detroit News* caught the spirit of Cobb's philosophy when he wrote: "With Cobb … we get baseball on the field and off. Baseball until midnight and baseball before breakfast."

One of Cobb's first decisions raised a few eyebrows. He elected to move himself to center field and put Harry Heilmann in right. The strategy worked. Heilmann hit a solid .394 to lead the American League. With Cobb's second-best .389, and left fielder Bobby Veach's .338, Detroit provided a powerful one-two-three punch at the plate.

Although these three talented players rivaled any outfield in the majors, they were seldom on speaking terms. Cobb thought Veach never lived up to his potential because he was too much of a "nice guy." Unlike Cobb, who considered anyone with a different uniform as his lifelong enemy, Veach liked to chat with opposing players, even go to dinner with them following a game.

Cobb initiated a plan that he hoped would change all that. He asked Heilmann, who followed Veach in the batting order, to harass his teammate. Heilmann did not want to endanger his friendship with Veach, but Cobb set his mind at ease by promising to explain the plan to Veach after the season.

Heilmann accepted the challenge. While Veach was at the plate, Heilmann accused him of being a "quitter" and a "yellow-bellied coward." The tactic worked wonders. Veach took his anger out on opposing pitchers and pounded the ball at a career-high clip.

Immediately following the last game of the season, with an unimpressive 71-82 record and sixth-place finish, Cobb took off for Georgia without taking time to explain to Veach that Heilmann's remarks were scripted. Heilmann attempted to explain all this to Veach himself, to no avail. Veach never again considered Heilmann his friend.

Cobb challenged his teammates, opposing players, even umpires. During the 1921 campaign, he nearly came to blows three times in one game with his bitterest foe—Babe Ruth. In another game against the Senators, Cobb was outraged when arbiter Billy Evans called him out after an attempted swipe of second. Cobb argued with Evans and challenged him to meet him under the stands after the game. Evans accepted. The two went at it in front of an audience of players, some fans and even

Cobb's own son. Both Cobb and Evans got in several blows before a strong-armed groundskeeper broke them apart.

The second umpire, George Hildebrand, reported the incident to Ban Johnson who took no action. Commissioner Landis, however, suspended Cobb indefinitely as a player but not at all as a manager. He would be reinstated before the 1922 season.

A scrappy posture showed little improvement in the Tigers' standing. Adding a fresh face or two for the 1922 season also would not help. The Tigers had some ingredients for a solid contender. Two catchers—Johnny Bassler (.307) and Larry Woodall (.363)—proved they could equal any backstop's numbers. Luzerne Atwood "Lu" Blue played first base and hit .308. Bobby Jones (.303) showed he belonged as a regular third baseman. Baseball experts agree, however, that the strength of a ball club has to be up the middle. That's where the Tigers were vulnerable. Young had a rough time at second. Shortstop Donie Bush lost his edge, was put on waivers and claimed by Washington. Major surgery was need in pitching.

A popular song in 1921 was "Toot, Toot, Tootsie, Good-bye." Tiger management echoed that theme to a number of its players, especially those in the infield and on the mound. Furthermore, some quality players had to be added to Detroit's roster to give the team extra spark.

Replacing Bush at short for the 1922 season was rookie Emory Elmo "Topper" Rigney, who sur-

prised even the most optimistic seer by batting an even .300. The second base slot was occupied by George Cutshaw, a seasoned veteran from the National League, who held his own both in the field and at the plate.

The most colorful addition to the 1922 squad was another rookie, Robert Roy "Fats" Fothergill. The 5' 10", 250-pound (when he was in shape) roly-poly first baseman looked more like a bit player in a Laurel and Hardy movie than a professional ball player. "Fat Bob," as he was called even to his face, surprised everyone with his agility and quickness. His .322 average was testimony that he chose the right vocation.

Ty Cobb's .401 average (the third time he surpassed the .400 mark) trailed only George Sisler's .420. Heilmann hit .356 and Veach .327. Once again, the outfield was the envy of any club owner.

Cobb's final average was a source of debate among American League officials. A New York writer, John Kieran, the designated official scorer, gave New York Yankee shortstop Everet "Deacon" Scott an error on an infield ground ball hit by Cobb. Detroit writer Frederick Lieb ruled it a hit and Lieb sent his scorebook to the Associated Press. Cobb was credited with a hit. Following the season, American League President Ban Johnson was informed of the disputed call. He ruled that the official scorer's version should stand, thus giving Cobb a .399 average. However, to this day, nobody has ever changed the original .401 average.

Herman Polycarp "Old Folks" Pillette, who made a brief appearance with Cincinnati five years earlier, was a welcome addition to the mound staff. His 19-12 record led the club. The remainder of the hurlers were fair, at best.

Considering the fact that pitching left much to be desired, the Detroit club did well in finishing third with a 79-75 record.

Could it be that Ty Cobb was turning the club around?

Pitching was still the key to winning pennants. Both Cobb and Navin knew that. In an attempt to bolster the staff, they both agreed to trade Howard Ehmke, a six-year veteran. Ehmke had talent, but Cobb, who was not known for his patience, thought he could do better. And he let Ehmke know that. In the 1922 season Ehmke pitched .500 ball (17-17), but it was his 4.22 ERA that concerned Cobb the most.

Ehmke and Floyd "Babe" Herman, a rookie first baseman, were sent to the Red Sox in exchange for second sacker Del Pratt and pitcher Warren "Rip" Collins.

The trade proved to be one of the worst in Tiger history. Old age had caught up to veteran Pratt, who had slowed considerably; he had to be replaced by Fred Haney, a fair infielder who later became a big league manager. Collins was hit with injuries. He won only three games and lost seven that year. Cobb, never a candidate for Mr. Congeniality, let Collins know how disappointed he was in his mediocre performance. Meanwhile, Ehmke led the last-place Red Sox with 21 wins, and later found power in his bat when, a few years later, he hit .393 and smacked 35 homers for the Brooklyn Dodgers.

Leading the Tiger lumber company in 1923 were outfielders Cobb (.340), Veach (.321) and Heilmann (with a league-leading .403). Others checked in with solid performances, including Rigney (.315), rookie Henry Emmett "Heinie" Manush (.334), and Fothergill (.315).

Dauss helped the pitching cause with 21 wins, but Pillette won the dubious honor of showing only 14 wins and a league-leading 19 defeats.

All in all, the Tigers fared quite well in 1923, finishing in second place, 16 games behind Babe Ruth and his Yankees, who had just completed their first year at the

Another member of baseball's Hall of Fame is outfielder Henry "Heinie" Manush who roamed left field for the Bengals from 1923-1927. [Photo: _The Detroit News_]

new ballpark, Yankee Stadium.

The Tigers were on their way up. Cobb believed that. Navin believed that. Everybody in Detroit believed that.

Bill Yawkey, the man from whom Navin purchased his half of the club, had died in 1919. Walter O. Briggs, Sr., and John Kelsey purchased his stock. Each owned 25 percent of the team.

The City of Detroit was growing rapidly. With the success of Henry Ford's auto industry, the population now surpassed one million people. In addition, fan support for their baseball team was on the rise, especially when they had winning clubs for which to cheer.

Unlike his field manager, owner Frank "Old Poker Face" Navin seldom outwardly expressed enthusiasm for success, or displeasure for things that went wrong. However, following the 1923 season's second-place finish, Navin could no longer contain his enthusiasm. "We have to make our park big enough to handle all the people during big games," he said.

Briggs and Kelsey supported him all the way.

Six thousand seats were added to the stadium by building a double-deck grandstand from third base to first base. A special section on the roof was added for the press. When the fans entered the turnstiles on Opening Day in 1924, they saw a delightful new ball park designed to hold up to 29,000 fans. On August 3, however, during a Sunday game with the mighty Yankees, more than 42,700 people squeezed into Navin Field, some of whom had to sit on the outfield grass.

Veach, whom Manager Cobb felt never gave his all, was sold to Boston prior to the start of the season. Heilmann (.346) and Cobb (.338) shared the outfield in 1924 with the youngster, Manush, who batted .284 and clubbed nine homers.

Second base was still a weak link in the Tiger defense. Pratt was tried again and failed. Several players attempted to fill the void, but nobody stood out. Late in September, however, a youngster from Fowlerville, Michigan, was invited to give it a try. He did and impressed Cobb. His name was Gehringer. Charlie Gehringer.

The most exciting games that year were between Detroit and the New York Yankees. Not only were they two of the top teams in the American League, but a strong animosity had built up between Cobb and America's newest hero, Babe Ruth. Cobb maintained that he, too, could hit home runs, but insisted he was more valuable to the club as a steady hitter for average. When he came to town, it was Ruth, not Cobb, who was surrounded by newspapermen. That irritated Cobb, who was accustomed to being the center of attention. If Cobb saw Ruth on the diamond, he did not speak with him. Instead, he'd yell to a teammate: "Do you smell something? Something around here really stinks!"

One particular game at Navin Field exemplified the bitterness between the two clubs. On June 13, more than 40,000 partisans witnessed their Tigers struggle in an attempt to overcome a 10-6

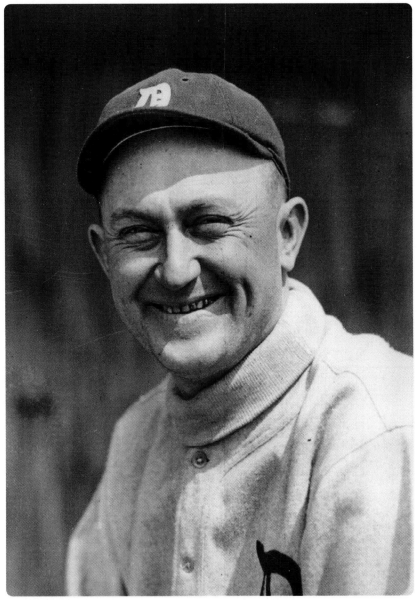

In his last days as a Tiger player and manager, Ty Cobb may well have been the first to use "mind games" in order to distract opposing players. When he joined the first five to be honored in the Hall of Fame, Cobb received more votes than any other inductee, including Babe Ruth.

[Photo: *The Detroit News*]

deficit when, in the late innings, Detroit pitcher Bert Cole hit the Yankees' Bob Meusel in the back with an errant toss. The normally reserved Meusel thought it was intentional. He flung his bat at Cole and charged the mound. Players leaped from both dugouts and ran toward the mound. Ruth and Cobb collided; neither fell to the ground. Joining the fracas were nearly 1,000 fans who poured out of the standing-room-only stands and swung at anyone wearing

Yankee pinstripes. Some of the more rowdy fans actually tore seats from the stands and tossed them onto the field. It took a half hour for the umpires to restore order and eventually forfeit the game to New York.

Detroit ended the season in third place, six games behind the surprising Washington Nats, and only four games behind the second-place Yankees.

The success of the club and the you'll-never-know-what-you-might-see anticipation before any game drew more than one million fans to Navin Field. It was the first time in history the Tigers had ever drawn so many people.

Navin and Cobb certainly earned their paychecks that year.

Were a Hollywood screenwriter to compose a fictional account of Ty Cobb, he would show the Georgia Peach rallying his team to play better than they knew how as they captured the World Championship for themselves and the City of Detroit. But baseball is not scripted. Unlike a children's fairy tale, it does not guarantee endings in which the "good guys" end up victorious. Every devout fan realizes the rewards of baseball are greater than those offered by any other pastime; they know, too, the heartbreaks are oft times unbearable.

Ty Cobb was a player who must be regarded as the finest of his era. The statistics speak for themselves. Many fans assumed, therefore, Cobb would be a great manager. He was not. Certainly, the record shows that he was a good manager who, like Billy Martin who would follow him many years later, could instill a shot of adrenaline into a floundering club and once in a while, encourage a player to reach beyond his abilities. But he was not a patient man with those who were not as baseball savvy. Some of his players claimed he was a poor teacher, unable to generate the sort of team spirit necessary to go all the way. Perhaps, instead, Cobb could not understand why a player would not hustle every minute he was on the field.

That became apparent during Cobb's final two years as Tiger manager. In 1925, Detroit slipped back to fourth place, 16 1/2 games behind pennant-winning Washington. Heilmann won the batting crown with a .393 average. Cobb hit .378. Absolom "Red" Wingo, who filled the shoes of the departed Bobby Veach, was right behind his manager with .370.

Cobb thought the fresh prospect, Charlie Gehringer, needed more seasoning, so he sent him to Toronto to learn the basics of the game. He may have been wise to use Gehringer, who could not have done worse than those who attempted to fill the keystone slot in Detroit.

Pitching was disappointing again, with only Dauss (16-11) and Leonard (11-4) showing anything noteworthy. Rip Collins, the pitcher obtained in the trade for Ehmke, posted a 6-11 mark.

The next year, 1926, was one in which nobody seemed to want the pennant. Detroit fell to sixth place in the final team standings, but only 12 games behind front-running New York. The Yankees, with their famous "Murderer's Row"—Ruth, Lou Gehrig, Meusel, Tony Lazzeri and Earle Combs—won just 91 games that year, finishing three games ahead of second-place Cleveland.

Heinie Manush (.378) became the newest Tiger to win a batting crown. Manush, who would later be inducted into the Hall of Fame, was notorious for getting his bat on the ball. Throughout his career, in 7,654 at-bats, he struck out only 345 times. For the 1926 season, his teammates, Heilmann and Fothergill, both hit .367. Cobb, limited to only 79 games due to injuries and some eye problems, hit .339.

The diamond in the rough that year was young Charlie Gehringer—dubbed "The Mechanical Man"—who hit .277 and was to fielding second base what Fred Astaire was to dancing.

The Tigers attempted to bolster the pitching staff by signing untested talent. Sam Gibson, Ed Wells and Owen Carroll are but three of the hurlers brought on board to curb opposing batters. None was effective enough to answer the Tiger's prayers.

Chapter 6
Mere Mortals in Uniform

"This image, mighty and of exceeding brightness, stood before you, and its appearance was frightening. The head of this image was of fine gold, its breast and arms of silver, its belly and thighs of bronze, its legs of iron, its feet partly of iron and partly of clay.**"**

- Daniel 2:32-33

Slick fielding Charlie Gehringer, "The Mechanical Man," was guilty of larceny with a glove, as he robbed many hitters of "sure" singles up the middle.

RUMORS FLEW FASTER THAN A WACO BIPLANE out of City Airport on Detroit's East Side. Word on Woodward Avenue was that Tiger owner Frank Navin would not offer Ty Cobb another contract to manage his team. Since his club's lowly sixth-place finish in 1926, Navin had been conspicuously silent about Cobb's future with the Tigers. The press and fans alike knew that the front office was concerned, especially about Cobb's impatience with players. In late October 1926, Navin confirmed these rumors. "Ty Cobb will not be retained as manager of the Detroit Tigers," he announced. He then added the reason for his decision: "The Detroit club of 1926 was badly demoralized and it did not get the results I thought it capable of attaining."

This was the same year Henry Ford introduced a 40-hours/five-day workweek at his automotive plant. That may have seemed appealing to Ty Cobb who by now was exhausted from the frustration of leading an uninspired team. Instead, he accepted an offer to play right field for Connie Mack's Philadelphia Athletics.

A few days later, Navin appointed George Moriarty Cobb's successor. Moriarty, a former Tiger third baseman, was umpiring in the American League when he received the call.

Within weeks, Cleveland's player-manager, Tris Speaker, was discharged. Cleveland had finished second in the league standings in 1926, just three games behind the Yankees, so poor performance should not have been the reason for his firing.

Baseball insiders were baffled. Something didn't seem right.

Ty Tyson was the nation's first announcer to broadcast baseball games on a regular basis.

Their questions were addressed before year's end. Baseball Commissioner Landis revealed that he had called Cobb and Speaker to his Chicago office along with Joe Wood, former Red Sox and Cleveland pitcher, and former Tiger pitcher Dutch Leonard. All but Leonard agreed to attend.

The meeting focused on a September 25, 1919, game between Detroit and Cleveland. Leonard, angry with Cobb for releasing him in 1925, produced some hand-written letters from Cobb and Wood indicating that players on both sides wagered on games. Leonard offered these letters to league president Ban Johnson for a fee of $15,000.

Johnson considered the letters so damaging that he gave both Cobb and Speaker the chance to resign, thus saving their families from embarrassment. According to Johnson, both Cobb and Speaker agreed, then changed their minds. They were determined to fight the charge.

Johnson was furious. He took his case to the public and announced, "As long as I am president of the American League, neither one of them will manage or play on our teams." Then, as if to offer a partial olive branch, Johnson added, "I don't believe Ty Cobb ever played a dishonest game in his life. It is from Landis that Cobb should demand an explanation. I love Ty Cobb. I never knew a finer player. I don't think he has been a good manager and I have had to strap him as a father straps an unruly boy. Ty Cobb is not a crooked ballplayer. We let him go because he had written a peculiar letter about a betting deal that he couldn't explain and because I felt that he had violated a position of trust."

In a surprising gesture of support, club owners rallied around Cobb. They chastised their league's president for his comments and suspended him with pay. Tiger owner Frank Navin assumed the duties of president on an interim basis.

On January 27, 1927, Commissioner Landis donned his former judge's robe and announced his verdict. Stressing Leonard's refusal to face the accused, Landis declared the matter closed. In his opinion, no evidence existed that either Cobb or Speaker had fixed a game.

Ty Cobb played two years while wearing the uniform of the Athletics. If age was catching up with him, his hitting eye didn't show it. In 1927, while the press was giving headlines to Babe Ruth's pursuit of his record-breaking 60 home runs, Cobb batted .357. His salary that year, including his bonus and percentage of the gate, was $70,000. In 1928, his last year in baseball, Cobb compiled a lofty .323 average.

Before he rendered his final decision in the Cobb-Speaker case, Judge Landis had another matter to consider. Charles "Swede" Risberg and Arnold "Chick" Gandil, two of the players suspended by Landis following the "Black Sox" scandal, alleged that, nine years earlier, Detroit and Chicago fixed the outcome of games that eventually allowed Chicago to edge out Boston for the league championship.

During a spirited hearing, Risberg and Gandil were the only two supporting this claim. For the defense, former players for the 1917 Tigers, including Cobb, Oscar Stanage, George "Hooks" Dauss, Willie Mitchell, Bill James, Bernie Boland, Howard Ehmke, Ben Dyer and Donie Bush, took the stand. Bush, now manager of the Pittsburgh Pirates, expressed the sentiments of his entire group when he looked at Risberg and shouted, "You're still a pig!"

Landis suspended any more testimony and declared the charge inappropriate due to the time between the alleged infraction and the accusation. He did, however, issue a stern warning that would affect players in the future. He announced that anyone who was guilty of betting on a game with a duty to perform in a particular way in that game would be banned from baseball for life.

After the dust settled from these infamous hearings, baseball fans welcomed the start of the 1927 season. Unfortunately, new manager Moriarty was unable to get his Tigers out of second gear, finishing in fourth place with an 82-71 mark, offering the Yankees no genuine threat in their quest for the World Championship.

On April 19, 1927, Detroit added another pioneer to its roster of celebrities. Ty Tyson, an announcer for WWJ Radio, sat behind a microphone and broadcast a game between the Tigers and the Cleveland Indians. More than five years earlier, Harold Arlin of Pittsburgh broadcast a Pirates game on an experimental basis, but Tyson, who would be the Tigers' radio voice for 17 years, was the first to air a full season of baseball. The broadcasts had some restrictions. Only home games were aired from 1927 to 1943. Sunday games were not broadcast from 1930 to 1932, and neither Saturday nor Sunday games were broadcast in 1933.

A high point for Tiger fans in 1927 was the homecoming for their idol, Ty Cobb. Although it would be strange to see him wearing the uniform of another team, Detroiters waited for an opportunity to cheer, once again, for their Georgia Peach during a May 10 match up between the Tigers and the visiting Athletics. Yet the festive occasion was nearly scuttled before it had a chance to materialize.

Five days earlier, in a game between the A's and Red Sox,

In 1931, the Tigers wore numbers on their backs for the first time. This aid for the fan came two years after the New York Yankees initiated the custom. The Yankees gave numbers to players in line with their batting order in the lineup, hence Babe Ruth wore number 3, Lou Gehrig number 4, and so on.

Rick Ferrell suffered the pangs of frustration and the joys of winning World Championships during his tenure as general manager from 1929-1947.

Cobb had hit what appeared to be a home run down the left-field line.

According to witnesses, the ball left the park barely in fair territory but curved around the foul pole and landed in seats just to the left of the pole. Plate umpire Emmett "Red" Ormsby called it a foul ball. Cobb was incensed. He and teammate Al Simmons argued with Ormsby. According to the umpire, Cobb and Simmons shoved him. That called for an immediate ejection from the game.

Fans reacted by throwing bottles and other debris. Ban Johnson slapped indefinite suspensions on both players.

Detroit fans protested with gusto. Thousands signed petitions asking the league to remove the suspension. Their pleas were heeded. Cobb and Simmons were reinstated in time for the May 10 game.

More than 35,000 people crammed inside Navin Field to greet their former local hero. Hundreds had to stand on the right-field grass behind a temporary rope barrier. The crowd cheered every move by Cobb. For the first time anyone could remember, they saw Cobb respond with humility. Between innings he even shook hands with fans who were standing behind the ropes, thanking them for their loyalty and support.

Cobb enhanced his image when he led off the top of the first by lining a screaming double into the right-field crowd driving in two runs.

Following the Athletics' 6-3 victory, Sam Green, a reporter for *The Detroit News*, crystallized the feelings of the witnesses: "For daring and strategy on the bases, for the knack of taking advantage of every slip—mental and mechanical—by his opponents, for skill with the bat, Cobb is still Cobb."

During the last day of the season, Slug Heilmann trailed the A's Al Simmons by two points. Simmons went two for five that day, giving him an average of .392. Heilmann went four for five in the first game of a scheduled doubleheader against visiting Cleveland to put him a few points ahead of Simmons. Instead of sitting out the final game guaranteeing a batting crown, "Harry the Horse" opted to play, delighting the hometown fans with a three-for-four output that gave him a six-point margin of victory with a .398 average.

Another remarkable demonstration of hitting came from the bat of Fat Bob Fothergill, who hit .359. The only thing expanding more rapidly than his batting average was the genial first baseman's waistline, as he ballooned to over

250 pounds. Seeing this overweight, yet light-footed ballplayer was, in the view of many Tiger faithful, worth the price of admission alone.

Fothergill played two more years with the Tigers before ending his 12-year American League career with Chicago and Boston. He died in Detroit when he was only 40.

Navin knew that the real drawing power for fans was a winning ball team. In an attempt to bolster a sagging pitching staff for the 1928 season, the Tigers' owner traded popular Heinie Manush and Lu Blue to the St. Louis Browns for pitcher Elam Vangilder, outfielder Harry Rice and shortstop Clarence Galloway. The trade proved unfavorable with Detroit fans, however, when Vangilder ended 1928 with a so-so 11-10 record. Rice hit .302, but Manush, as if to let the Tigers know they had made a mistake, tied his career-high average at .378.

Moriarty and his Tigers slipped to sixth place in 1928 with a 68-86 record. Heilmann's average dropped to .328; Fothergill hit .317; right-hander Owen Carroll had his best year posting a 16-10 mark.

Unnoticed by the newspapers was a blurb sent from Beaumont, Texas, that the New York Giants had purchased the young Detroit prospect, Carl Hubbell, for $40,000.

Because he failed to rally his team to any great heights, Manager Moriarty was not offered a contract to manage the 1929 season. Having his fill of pressures known only to big league managers, he returned to a less stressful job—

calling balls and strikes behind the plate.

The three years spent under Moriarty's leadership left some highlights that fans would remember for years. Automobile workers repeated these stories while tossing down a Stroh's Beer at their local watering holes. Parents and grandparents passed them along to their offspring. Few, if any, such memories were awarded Tiger fans for the next five years.

Selected to manage the Tigers was Stanley "Bucky" Harris, who had earned some solid credentials piloting the Washington Senators. He not only had baseball savvy, he also had a winsome personality that resulted in a legion of friends.

Shortly before he died of tuberculosis in 1928, former manager Hughie Jennings had recommended Harris to fill the managerial slot. The two came from the same coal mining area of Eastern Pennsylvania. Harris, in fact, was invited to try out for the Tigers before he signed with Washington.

The Tigers in 1929 were just another version of the "good hit, no field" teams of before. Slug Heilmann hit .344 and Charlie Gehringer .339. Rookie first baseman Dale "Moose" Alexander pleased management with 25 home runs and a .343 average. Fats Fothergill led the club at .350.

Less than overpowering pitching and errant fielding, however, allowed opposing teams to score more runs. As a result, the Tigers completed the season with another sixth-place finish.

Frank Navin sent shock waves

Harry Heilmann, one of Detroit's all-time great players and announcers was nicknamed "Slug" because of his poor speed and lack of defense.

Heilmann batted behind Ty Cobb and won four batting titles, each in an odd-numbered year, from 1921-1927. Heilmann compiled an impressive .342 career average and had 2,660 hits, including 542 doubles and 151 triples.

through the city when he announced shortly after the season that he was selling popular Harry Heilmann to the Cincinnati Reds. Much of the reason for the abrupt departure was that Heilmann and Harris never hit it off. Arguments became public. Harris tried to discipline his slugger by keeping him out of starting lineups.

Gehringer batted over .300 in 13 of his 16 full seasons, just one of the reasons why he was elected to the Hall of Fame in 1949.

The fans knew what was happening. They blamed Harris for the problems and the decision to send Heilmann to Cincinnati. For the next four years, Manager Harris would use all his skills of diplomacy in an attempt to win back fan support.

Those fans clamored even louder for a team that reflected the positive image of their community. Compared with other cities, Detroit became a haven for progressive families. Chicago, for example, had recently been the venue of the St. Valentine's Day Massacre as prohibition gangs fought for turf. A dozen clones of Eliot Ness could not have given a feeling of security. Cleveland was notorious for its waterfront crimes. Detroit, on the other hand, was safe, yet alive and vibrant. Its factories turned out more than 5,300,000 vehicles annually. A decade of prosperity resulted in the construction of the Penobscot Building, the General Motors Building, the Fisher Building, the Detroit Zoo, the Ambassador Bridge and the Detroit-Windsor Tunnel. The city had its problems, certainly. But they were solved through ballots, not bullets, as demonstrated when Mayor Charles Bowles was recalled and Frank Murphy was elected without one display of violence.

The curtain abruptly came down on this delightful drama on Tuesday, October 29, 1929, with the crash of the stock market. The vision of an upbeat future for Detroit suddenly gave way to a foretaste of tragedy.

A fifth-place finish in the 1930 standings did little to turn the public's attention away from the gloom of everyday life. Along with Harry Heilmann, another fan favorite was eliminated from the Tigers' roster. Because Harris could not convince Fothergill to lose weight, he and Navin sent the portly first sacker to the White Sox on waivers. Others sent packing were Owen Carroll, Harry Rice and part-time infielder George Wuestling - all to the Yankees - in exchange for pitcher Waite Hoyt and shortstop Mark Koenig.

Making their first, albeit brief, appearances for the Tigers in 1930 were two youngsters who would become fixtures in the lineup. One was right-hand pitcher Tommy Bridges. The other was a tall, powerfully built Jewish boy from the Bronx named Henry Benjamin "Hank" Greenberg.

Beyond the walls of Navin Field, the Depression transformed the city of Detroit. Automotive production dropped nearly 50 percent in 1930. Gangs now controlled the illegal liquor trade spawned by Prohibition. In less than one year, more than 75,000 workers lost their jobs. Michigan's unemployment rate hit 40 percent.

Frank Navin attempted to give the hometown a diversion from the sadness of the day. But if he thought that moving up from sixth place in 1929 to fifth place in 1930 was a trend of better things to come, he was sadly mistaken. His '31 Tigers showed signs of crum-

bling from within. Detroit lingered in the league basement more than a month and was fortunate to end the season in seventh place, a full 47 games behind the revitalized Athletics.

John "Rocky" Stone, a third-year outfielder, led the club with a .327 average and 10 homers. Charlie Gehringer hit .311 but missed a third of the season due to injuries. To praise the accomplishments of anyone else would take the skills of a fantasy writer.

Detroit actually had a winning record (76-75) in 1932, resulting in a fifth-place finish. Substantial improvement came from the mound. Earl Whitehill, now in his 10th season with the Tigers, led his team in victories with a 16-12 record.

The most memorable pitching performance in 1932 came from Thomas Jefferson Davis "Tommy" Bridges on August 5 in Washington. Bridges, who on any given day could be either extremely sharp or look like a poor excuse for a sandlot player, enjoyed one of his best outings. The right-hander from Tennessee mowed down the Nationals as if he were Davy Crockett with a rifle. For eight innings he did not allow one batter to reach first base. With his club ahead, 13-0, the outcome of the game was never in doubt. The only question remaining was whether or not young Tommy Bridges would become the sixth major leaguer to pitch a perfect game.

The partisan Griffith Stadium crowd warmly greeted Bridges as he stepped on the mound to begin the ninth. He quickly disposed of the first two Nats he faced. The crowd cheered every out. They rose to their feet, realizing they could be eyewitnesses to history.

Scheduled to bat was pitcher Bob Burke. Washington's manager, the immortal Walter Johnson, elected instead to insert a pinch-hitter named Dave Harris, a .337 hitter that year. The reserve outfielder swung at Bridges' first pitch and laced it into left field for a single.

The crowd moaned. Some of the Washington fans even booed Johnson for ruining a perfect game.

After the next batter was retired on a weak ground ball, the 25-year-old Bridges showed a maturity that surpassed his age by not criticizing Washington's manager. He agreed with Johnson that the game should be played as if you intend to win until the last out.

Twice more within the next two years, Bridges would come close to pitching a no-hitter. In each game only one batter got a hit. Neither of those games, however, drew as much frustration for him as did that fateful contest on August 5, 1932.

By 1933, the Depression sank America to its economic basement. Just before spring training, President Franklin Delano Roosevelt ordered all banks closed for audits. Helping to overcome their frustrations and uncertainties, the citizens of Detroit voted on April 3 to repeal Prohibition.

Prior to the '33 season, Bucky Harris and Frank Navin agreed to ship the club's best pitcher, Earl Whitehill, to Washington in exchange for Fred "Firpo"

Marberry, one of the game's first relief specialists. Like some of the trades at that time, Detroit came out second best. Marberry had a fairly good 16-11 year, while Whitehill enjoyed his best year with the World Champion Nationals winning 22 and losing only 8.

Two Tigers made their impressions on the press and the fans, both growing tired of so-so records. The first was a 6' 5", 210-pound high school student from Eldorado, Arkansas, named Lynwood Thomas Rowe. The nickname "Schoolboy" was appropriate and stuck. The right hander showed promise with his 7-4 record. This certainly was not bad for a club that would end the season with 75 wins and 79 losses, and another fifth-place finish.

The other superstar in the making was 22-year-old Hank Greenberg, who joined the club in June after more than three years of seasoning in the minors. In spite of missing a third of the season, the slugging first baseman led the Tigers with 12 round-trippers in 1933 and hit .301. He and Charlie Gehringer (.325) were the only Detroiters to hit over .300.

In spite of his terrific numbers, this son of Romanian immigrants had trouble being accepted by all of his teammates, let alone opposing players. Hank Greenberg was a Jew. In the early 1930s, Jews were much more visible and acceptable in New York City than in Detroit. Anti-Semitism ran rampant around the nation. Slurs and taunts against Greenberg came from crowds not only on the road but in Detroit as well. The fact that the slugging right hander stood 6' 4" tall and weighed 210 pounds encouraged most of the spectators to limit expressions of their bigotry to name-calling from behind the protective screens of the stadium. "Nonetheless," admitted Greenberg years later, "that made my life a living hell."

Greenberg, however, never lashed back at players and fans, nor did he moan to the press about unfair treatment. He remained a calm, cool, and collected gentleman both on and off the field. In doing so, he gradually won the hearts of even the most callused critic with his work ethic—he took extra batting practice after the rest of his teammates left the ball park—and timely hitting. He also gained a lot of respect for his decision not to play ball on Yom Kippur—the Day of Atonement on the Jewish calendar.

Bucky Harris realized he was unable to move the Tigers off dead center. Two weeks prior to the season's end, he submitted his resignation to Frank Navin. Even though Navin would have issued him a contract for the next year, Harris apologized to him and to the fans of Detroit for not doing better. "If a manager cannot deliver in five years, he should resign," said Harris.

The manager's mea culpa aside, Detroit fans and the normally supportive press grew increasingly impatient. Malcolm Bingay, editor of the *Detroit Free Press* wrote a stinging editorial following the final game of the season. It was directed at Frank Navin and anyone else responsible for rebuilding

the Tiger organization. The headline contained only six words, but made its point:

"WE WANT TIGERS,
NOT TAME KITTENS"

An emphatic reply to the paper's supplication would come sooner than anyone could imagine.

Hubert "Hub" Walker and his brother Gerald "Gee" Walker shared outfield duties for the Tigers in the mid '30s.

Chapter 7
Resurrection

**"This is the happiest day
in my life."**

- Mickey Cochrane
October 7, 1935

**Charlie Gehringer, Schoolboy Rowe and Goose Goslin pictured at an
Old-Timers Game in 1958. [Photo: *The Detroit News*]**

FRANK NAVIN WAS GROWING INCREASINGLY CONCERNED. His once prosperous baseball club was turning into a liability. Attendance since the market crash had dropped off steadily. Nearly 900,000 fans passed through the turnstiles four years earlier; in 1933 fewer than 321,000 journeyed to Michigan and Trumbull on game days.

In addition to dwindling attendance, other pains caused by the crash of October 1929 became increasingly acute. Navin, like the rest of the club owners, had to find ways to get extra cash to save the club from going bankrupt.

Outside of fielding a team that would have a genuine chance of capturing the American League pennant and the first World Series Championship in the club's history, the Tigers needed three ingredients to bring fans back to Navin Field. The first was a successful manager. The second was a solid catcher who could be a field general. The third was a "name" player who could attract fans.

Following the ho-hum 1933 season and the resignation of Bucky Harris, Navin realized his team had no Ty Cobb-like player who would draw fans just to see him play.

Frank Navin got a brilliant idea. He knew the most popular player in all of baseball was Babe Ruth. The "Sultan of Swat," like no other ballplayer in history, was responsible for making America forget about the Black Sox scandal of 1920. He made the home run the most important offensive weapon in baseball. He alone was credited with bringing enough fans to Yankee Stadium to pay for its construction; hence it was

Yankee legend Babe Ruth visited the Tiger dugout prior to the opening game of the 1934 World Series. One year earlier, he could have been the Tiger manager had it not been for a schedule conflict. Appearing with "The Bambino" were starting pitcher Dizzy Dean and manager Frankie Frisch from the St. Louis Cardinals and manager Mickey Cochrane and starting pitcher Schoolboy Rowe from the Tigers.

often called "The House that Ruth Built."

Would Ruth ever consider leaving New York? The answer was a resounding "Yes!" First, Ruth was nearing 30 years of age; he was slowing down and his home run totals and distances were dropping off. Second, he was at odds with his manager, Joe McCarthy, who had given the Babe a rough time about his training or lack of it. Finally, Ruth had an unquenchable thirst to manage a major league team.

Navin received permission from Col. Jacob Ruppert, Yankee owner, to speak with Ruth about managing the Tigers. Navin telephoned Ruth, asking him to come to Detroit to discuss the possibility of becoming player-manager for the Tigers. However, Ruth was just about to leave for Hawaii to play some exhibition games arranged months earlier. Navin wanted to get the matter settled and insisted that Ruth come to Detroit right

away. Ruth declined. After Ruth fulfilled his obligation in Hawaii, he wrote Navin demanding a lucrative salary plus a percentage of the gate. Navin, still smarting from Ruth's refusal to come to Detroit earlier and bowled over by the high dollar demand, dropped the offer.

He turned, instead, to Connie Mack, owner and manager of the Athletics. Like Navin, Mack had been hit hard by the Wall Street collapse of '29. Mack needed instant cash. He even borrowed $25,000 the previous winter to fund his club for spring training. One way to get the necessary funds would be to sell a marketable player. Navin realized this and asked Mack if he would part with Gordon Stanley "Mickey" Cochrane, his outstanding catcher. Mack agreed, but for a stiff price— $100,000.

Navin met with Walter Briggs who now owned half of the team, purchasing 25 percent from the estate of the late John Kelsey. Briggs gave his imprimatur. "If he's a success here," said Briggs, "he may be a bargain at that price. I'll furnish the money. You get Cochrane."

Had Mickey Cochrane gotten his way, he would have never been a big league catcher. This native of Bridgewater, Massachusetts, was an outstanding football player at Boston University. He loved the sport, but knew there was no opportunity to earn a living in football, so he elected to play baseball. He reported to a minor league team in Dover, Delaware, as an outfielder. The team manager, Jiggs

Donohue, asked Cochrane to put on a catcher's glove.

"But I'd rather play outfield," said the young collegian.

"Outfielders I got. You catch," said Donohue, "or it's off the payroll."

That afternoon, Mickey Cochrane became a catcher.

And what a catcher. He lacked experience and polish, but made up for these deficiencies with aggressive determination. By the time he got to the major leagues in 1925, he was able to lead the Athletics to a second-place finish and hit .331. Three years later, he was voted the league's Most Valuable Player.

In 1934, America began a national house-cleaning. Prohibition was over. Clyde Barrow, Bonnie Parker, John Dillinger and Charles Arthur "Pretty Boy" Floyd were gunned down by lawmen. As if to give Detroit a kick-start from a higher power, former baseball player turned evangelist, Billy Sunday, opened his second revival in the Motor City.

Before the start of the 1934 season, Frank Navin made another fortunate trade when he obtained outfielder Leon "Goose" (so-called because of the size of his nose) Goslin from the Nationals in exchange for John "Rocky" Stone.

Ty Tyson had been broadcasting Tiger games on WWJ radio since 1927. Earlier in the '34 season, he shared broadcasting duties with popular ex-Tiger Harry Heilmann. George W. Trendle, president of station WXYZ Radio and creator of nationally-aired classics such as

The Lone Ranger starring Brace Beemer and *The Green Hornet,* paid the Tigers $25,000 for the rights to broadcast games on five outstate stations he called the "Michigan Broadcast Network." He appointed Heilmann to serve as his play-by-play man.

Tyson and Heilmann were complete opposites as broadcasters. Tyson was reserved, announcing only the plays, thus leaving long periods of "dead air" between pitches. Heilmann, on the other hand, had no reservations about sharing stories and anecdotes during the contests. Tyson would continue broadcasting Tiger games for eight more years; Heilmann kept Detroiters fascinated with his yarns and descriptions of the games through the 1950 season.

The '34 campaign had Tiger fans buzzing again about their team. Conversation around the office water coolers focused on the "Tiger G-men"—Gehringer, Greenberg and Goslin. One wonders if these fans could have known that when they went to Navin Field and watched these three players along with Manager Cochrane, they would be seeing four future Hall-of-Famers.

Mickey Cochrane was an outstanding manager.

Gehringer, now deemed the best second baseman in all of baseball, hit a remarkable .356, just seven points behind league-leading Lou Gehrig of the Yankees. Greenberg's powerful swing produced 26 home runs, 63 doubles, 7 triples and 139 RBI along with a .339 average. Goslin smacked 13 homers and hit .305.

Another valuable ingredient to Detroit's success was switch-hitting Billy Rogell, now in his fifth year and wearing a Tiger uniform. He hit .296 that year and with only three homers to his credit, knocked in 100 runs.

The flashy short-stop, who would later become a Detroit city councilman, was a spark-plug for the Tigers. This was never more obvious than during a mid-season clash with New York. Vernon "Lefty"

When outfielder Leon "Goose" Goslin joined the Tigers in 1934, he added punch to the lineup and helped the club win two straight league championships and its first-ever-World Series flag.

Gomez, ace hurler for the Yankees, held a seemingly insurmountable 9-1 lead over Detroit. The Tigers closed the gap to 11-8 in the bottom of the ninth when they scored four runs. The last came when Rogell sent a line-drive single to left scoring Goose Goslin from sec-

ond. Fans in the stands recalled Rogell standing on first, jumping up and down, shouting, "Run, Goose! Run, Goose!"

The glue holding the team together was Mickey Cochrane. Not only did he prove to be a noteworthy manager, he also hit .320 and won his second MVP Award.

Pitching finally came around in 1934. Schoolboy Rowe had 16 straight victories en route to a 24-8 season. Tommy Bridges (22-11) was consistently in control. The mound staff also got solid outings from Firpo Marberry (15-5) and rookie Eldon Auker (15-7).

Of primary importance to Detroit fans, press and management was that Mickey Cochrane was able to pull off a miracle. The Tigers won 101 games that year and for the first time in 25 years, ended the season in first place, a full seven games ahead of the mighty Yankees.

Fans asked if Mickey Cochrane had visited Lourdes on his way from Philadelphia to Detroit.

To make 1934 the best year in its history, the Tigers would need just one more miracle—to win the World Series against the St. Louis Cardinals' "Gashouse Gang" managed by player-manager Frankie "The Fordham Flash" Frisch. The Cardinals overflowed with characters of the game: Joe "Ducky" Medwick, James "Rip" Collins, John Leonard "Pepper" Martin and Leo "Lippy" Durocher. The pitching staff featured the famous brothers Jay Hannah "Dizzy" Dean and Paul Dee "Daffy" Dean.

Prior to the start of the 1934

World Series, Commissioner Landis suffered one of the few setbacks in his professional life. Landis barred popular Tiger broadcaster Ty Tyson from the microphone during the Series. In the Czar's opinion, Tyson would be "too partial." An avalanche of protest letters poured into the Commissioner's office. After considerable thought, Judge Landis changed his mind and permitted Tyson to describe the games over WWJ Radio.

During Game One on October 3, perhaps the Tigers were overwhelmed by the realization they were playing in the World Series. Whatever the reason, the normally solid infield committed five errors. Ducky Medwick collected four hits off three Detroit hurlers, including a home run. Dizzy Dean scattered eight Tiger hits, one of which was a homer by Hank Greenberg. In front of groaning hometown fans, the Tigers lost by the score of 8-3.

The Tigers shook off their stage fright in Game Two and played errorless ball. Schoolboy Rowe pitched well, but was on the short end of a 2-1 score going into the bottom of the ninth. With two on and two out, Gerald "Gee" Walker, a reserve outfielder for Detroit, hit a lazy foul pop-up between home and first that should have ended the game. This time it was St. Louis' turn to clutch. First-baseman "Rip" Collins and catcher Bill DeLancey both stopped running and let it drop between them. Walker promptly hit the next pitch over second base for a single to plate the tieing run.

Both teams failed to score until the home half of the twelfth. Following walks to Gehringer and Greenberg, Goose Goslin singled to left, scoring Gehringer with the winning run to give Schoolboy Rowe and the Tigers a dramatic, 3-2, come-from-behind win in Game Two.

The Series shifted to Sportsman's Park in St. Louis for Game Three. Detroit got nine hits but could only get one runner across the plate. They left 13 men on base as the Cardinals' Daffy Dean outdueled Tommy Bridges and two clutch extra-base hits by Pepper Martin combined to defeat the Bengals 4-1.

Hank Greenberg and shortstop Billy Rogell flexed their muscles in Game Four combining for seven RBI as the Tigers pounded St. Louis 10-4. Eldon Auker looked like anything but a rookie as he pitched all nine innings.

Game Four may be best remembered by fans as the setting for one

Tiger shortstop Billy Rogell playfully offers a steel helmet to the Cardinals' Dizzy Dean the day after Dean was knocked unconscious by Rogell's throw to first during the '34 World Series.
[Photo: *St. Louis Post*]

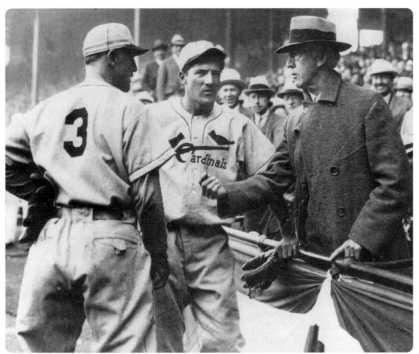

A testimony to the intensity of Detroit fans came when, on the last day of the '34 Series, Cardinals' outfielder Joe "Ducky" Medwick was called from the outfield and ordered to leave the game for his own protection by Baseball Commissioner Kenesaw "Mountain" Landis. Player-manager Frank Frisch (number 3) attempts to persuade the commissioner to change his mind, but Landis sticks by his decision.

of baseball's classic myths. With the Tigers leading by a score of 5-4, the Cardinals' Dizzy Dean was inserted as a pinch-runner during the home half of the seventh inning. On a potential double-play ball, Dean headed for second. Billy Rogell stepped on the bag for one out and threw to first. The ball hit Dean between the eyes and knocked him unconscious. He was taken to the hospital for observation and released within a few hours. A sub-headline in the *St. Louis Post-Dispatch* the next day allegedly read: "X-rays of Dean's Head Show Nothing." It's a great story; unfortunately, it's not true. The actual wording of the October 7, 1934, edition of the paper read: "X-Ray Photograph of Head Shows No Lasting Injury." As did Babe Ruth when stories circulated about his apocryphal "called shot" against pitcher Charlie Root, Dean never denied the myth.

With only one day's rest,

Tommy Bridges took the mound for Detroit in Game Five. He went all nine innings as he outpitched the legendary Dizzy Dean, who had obviously recovered from his injury the day before, and won 3-1. Gehringer's sixth-inning home run gave the Tigers the lead they would never forfeit.

Ahead in the Series three games to two, Tiger faithful envisioned a ticker-tape parade in Downtown Detroit. If this were going to happen, it would not be after Game Six. Dizzy's brother, Paul, and Detroit's Schoolboy Rowe battled back and forth. With the score tied at three in the seventh inning, Paul Dean got his only hit in the Series—a single that sent home the Cardinals' fourth run. That was the last of the scoring for the afternoon. Perhaps tomorrow would be a better day for Detroit.

October 9, 1934, could have been a red-letter day in the history of the Tigers, especially for the 40,902 rabid Detroit fans in attendance. Alas, this was not the case. A seven-run uprising in the third inning by St. Louis, continued timely hitting against six Tiger pitchers and a six-hit shutout performance by Dizzy Dean sealed the Tigers' fate. The 11-0 shellacking left no doubt about who deserved to be called "World Champions" that year.

The most memorable event during Game Seven came in the sixth inning. In the visitors' half, Ducky Medwick belted a long drive that hit high off the right-field wall. For most players, this would have been a double, but the speedy Medwick raced around second and slid hard into third baseman Marv Owen. Owen took exception to the aggressive slide and took a swing at Medwick. Medwick swung back. Neither would be mistaken for professional boxers and neither landed a blow before being separated by Umpire Bill Klem.

In the middle of the sixth inning, Medwick resumed his position in left field. Detroit fans sitting in the bleachers, frustrated at the realization that the Tigers would not win the Series, saw Medwick coming and were ready. They unleashed a chorus of boos. That didn't bother Medwick. More than a few fans let loose a shower of apples, oranges, rolled-up paper and anything else they could toss at Medwick, who held his hands over his head to protect himself.

Commissioner Landis, sitting in a front-row box seat, called Medwick in from the outfield and demanded a quick conference with him, Owen, managers Frisch and Cochrane, and the four umpires. Judge Landis, in characteristic style, made a quick, unilateral decision. He ordered Frisch to take Medwick out of the game for his own safety. When challenged by the St. Louis manager as to why he should do such a thing, Landis looked him squarely in the eye and said, "Because I said so."

Case closed.

Following the game, Tiger manager Mickey Cochrane went into the St. Louis clubhouse and congratulated his rival, Frankie Frisch. "I'm happy for the National League that you don't have more than two Deans pitching," he said.

The Detroit Tigers were saddened by the Series loss. Two things, however, made the coming winter much happier. The first was the fact that each player pocketed an extra $3,354.67— equal to or greater than the annual salary for many players. The second was the realization that the Tigers had a contending team that would serve notice on the American League that they were for real.

Could Detroit repeat as American League Champions? Was 1934 just a fluke? One thing was certain. The second-place New York Yankees did not appear to be as much of a threat to the 1935 Tigers. On February 26, Yankee President Jake Ruppert announced the unconditional release of Babe Ruth. He announced that the Bambino would be signed by the National League's Boston Braves as a player and vice president. Ruth, now slowed by age and a rather raucous social life dominated by women, booze, food and late-night partying, still managed to hit 22 homers the year before.

Spring training for the Tigers was held in Lakeland, Florida, the team's current winter home.

One of the Tiger aces was right hander Tommy Bridges.

The Cardinals start a rally in the last game of the '34 Series at Navin Field.

Schoolboy Rowe, though not as effective as the year before, managed to win 19 of 32 decisions. Alvin "General" Crowder, picked up from Washington the year before, impressed the club with his 16-10 mark.

Hitting with power, however, dominated the newspaper reports of Tiger victories. Hank Greenberg posted statistics that would earn for him that year the coveted Most Valuable Player Award. Not only did he bat a healthy .328, he also tied Philadelphia's Jimmy Foxx for the major league lead in home runs (36) and led the league in RBI (170) and total bases (389).

Others contributing to the offense were Charlie Gehringer (.330), Mickey Cochrane (.319), Pete Fox (.321) and Gee Walker (.301).

Solid hitting and pitching combined for Detroit to win its second pennant in as many years. Although the Ruth-less Yankees finishing in second place by three games and showed a zestful spirit, the final outcome was never in doubt all of September.

The Chicago Cubs had just won the National League pennant. Big guns for Manager Charlie Grimm and his team included Stan Hack, Phil Cavarretta, Chuck Klein and Gabby Hartnett. Heading the mound crew were Lon Warneke (who later became a National League umpire), Charlie Root and "Big Bill" Lee.

One question dominated the thoughts of the Tiger faithful: Were the Tigers building them up for just another letdown? Mickey Cochrane was determined that this

Instead of the upbeat tempo of a club that one would expect from the defending league champions, some of the players were displeased at what was developing.

Manager Cochrane angered Goose Goslin by benching him during some of the exhibition games for what Cochrane judged was Goslin's lack of enthusiasm for the game. Another disgruntled player, Isidore "Izzy" Goldstein, who had pitched briefly for the Tigers three years earlier, walked out of camp in a huff, never to return.

Some of those internal problems may have distracted the Tigers enough to affect their performance at the beginning of the campaign. Detroit did not resemble a pennant winner. Instead, during the first few weeks, they fought just to stay out of the cellar. By mid-season, however, the Tigers were growling again. Tommy Bridges, the staff ace, ended the year with a 21-10 record. Eldon Auker was 18-7 and

would be a year without any reason to look back and say: It might have been. . . .

During the first inning of Game One in Detroit, which was played on October 2, it looked as though Cochrane had allowed his optimism to override reality. Two Chicago hits and an error by pitcher Schoolboy Rowe, produced two Cub runs. That's all Lon Warneke needed as he tamed the Tigers on just four hits and shut them out, 3-0.

Twenty-four hours later, Detroit bats woke up. The Tigers came out swinging and in the first inning, pounded Charlie Root with four runs, including a long blast into the left-field seats by Hammerin' Hank Greenberg. Detroit's curve-balling right hander, Tommy Bridges, coasted to an 8-3 victory in Game Two.

The win, however, came at a tremendous cost. In the seventh inning, Greenberg attempted to score from second on a single. When the 6' 4" muscular first baseman collided at the plate with 200-pound Gabby Hartnett, those in attendance said you could hear the sound of the impact in the deepest center-field bleacher seat. Greenberg rose from the dust, holding his left wrist in pain.

Detroit Tigers
1934 American League Champions
Top Row - Marberry, Carroll *(trainer)*, G. Walker, Rowe, Hamlin, Hogsett, Bridges, Sorrell, Schuble
Middle Row - Owen, Doljack, Hayworth, Rogell, White, Auker, Gehringer, Fox
Front Row - Fischer, Greenberg, batboy, Clifton, Baker *(coach)*, Cochrane *(manager)*, Perkins *(coach)*, Goslin

Although he remained in the game, the pain did not go away. The next morning, X-rays revealed two broken bones. The verdict: Greenberg would be out of action for the remainder of the Series.

Cochrane and Navin met to discuss strategy. Navin suggested that Cochrane move Owen to first and position Herman "Flea" Clifton, a reserve infielder, at third. Cochrane was not receptive to the idea. Navin pulled rank and ordered Cochrane to make the move. "If we lose the Series," promised Navin, "it will be on my head."

Game Three at Wrigley Field in Chicago was marred by a running dispute throughout the game. Umpiring at second base was George Moriarty, former infielder

> "Us ballplayers do things backward. First we play, then we retire and go to work."
>
> - Charlie Gehringer

1935 World Series Program.

for the Tigers. Prior to the game, he chastised Cub manager Charlie Grimm about his team's verbal assaults during the first two games on some of the Detroit players, particularly the anti-Semitic slurs aimed at the injured Hank Greenberg. The Cubs were offended at this scolding and took every opportunity to question Moriarty's calls, particularly one on which Cavarretta was called out trying to steal second on a bang-bang play. The Cubs' anger was punctuated with shouts and curses. Moriarty had had enough. Before the game's end, he ejected Grimm and two players.

The harassment of Moriarty by Chicago players continued throughout the Series. More shouts and curses came from both camps. Following the Series, Commissioner Landis levied $200 fines on four of the more vocal Cubs, and on Umpire Moriarty for his part in contributing to the agitation.

Shouts and curses don't win ballgames, however. The Tigers, behind solid pitching by Auker and Rowe, won Game Three in 11 innings by a score of 6-5 when Joyner "Jo-Jo" White (a .240 hitter that year) singled home Owen with the tie-breaking run.

The next day, behind the five-hit pitching of General Crowder, the Bengals won a squeaker with the help of an unearned run in the sixth inning. The final score of Game Four was Detroit 2, Chicago 1.

Even with a 3-1 lead in the Series, the Tigers dared not get hopes too high in light of their demise the year before. Game Five gave every reason to support Detroit's apprehension. Future Hall-of-Famer Chuck Klein homered for Chicago, and Lon Warneke pitched six scoreless innings; Schoolboy Rowe and his Tigers lost 3-1.

Back in the friendlier confines of Detroit, more than 48,400 fans filled Navin Field on that memorable October 7 to cheer their Tigers in Game Six. They were to be amply rewarded for their support. Billy Herman's fifth-inning home run had put the Cubs ahead by one run, but Detroit came back to tie it in the bottom of the sixth.

Tiger pitcher Tommy Bridges surrendered 12 hits, but was able to bear down in the clutch. In the top of the ninth, for example, the Cubs' Stan Hack led off with a long triple, but Bridges calmly retired the next three hitters without allowing Hack an opportunity to budge off third.

That set the stage for the bottom of the ninth. With one out, Mickey Cochrane hit a ground-ball single past second base. He advanced to second on Gehringer's slow roller to first. Up to the plate stepped Goose Goslin, the man who began the year angry because of his treatment in spring training.

If there was any resentment in Goslin's bones, you couldn't tell it this day. He promptly lined the first pitch to right field, sending Manager Cochrane across the plate without any throw from the outfield. Cochrane jumped up and down on the plate several times so there would be no mistake that the winning run scored.

The stands erupted. For the first time in their history, the Detroit Tigers were World Series Champions.

Fans poured onto the field. Some lifted their newest hero, Goose Goslin, onto their shoulders and carried him into the Tiger dugout.

The normally stoic Frank Navin, in an unusual display of emotion, openly showed his excitement. "It's wonderful!" he shouted. "I've waited thirty years for this day."

Screeching fans, most of them hoarse from hollering at the game, refused to leave the stadium. They chanted for Mickey Cochrane to come back onto the field. Forty-five minutes later, they got their wish. Standing behind a microphone hooked up to a make-shift public address system, their beloved player-manager admitted while choking back tears: "This is

**Detroit Tigers
1935 World Champions**
Top Row - Schuble, Reiber, Carroll *(trainer)*, Hogsett, G. Walker, *(unknown)*, Bridges, Sorrell
Middle Row - Goslin, Rogell, Owen, Hayworth, Crowder, Auker, Rowe, Clifton
Front Row - Fox, Gehringer, Baker *(coach)*, Cochrane *(manager)*, Perkins *(coach)*, White, Greenberg, Roggins *(batboy)*

the greatest day of my life."

The fans knew exactly how he felt.

From Navin Field the spectators left the corner and paraded down Michigan Avenue to Woodward Avenue. By this time, many of the other citizens of Detroit had joined them. They formed snake dances through Cadillac Square and Grand Circus Park. Tavern owners forgot about the midnight deadline for selling alcohol. Some of the more popular hotel bars at the Book-Cadillac, Fort Shelby, Detroit Leland, and Statler, remained open until dawn.

Detroit was about to have its biggest collective hangover, but nobody seemed to care.

Chapter 8
A New Regime

"He [Mickey Cochrane] never got over being let go as manager by Mr. Briggs. And this wasn't getting hit on the head by Bump Hadley. Mike's hurt was in the heart, not the head."

- Hank Greenberg

Schoolboy Rowe meets with new Tigers' owner, Walter O. Briggs.

BY 1935, DETROIT, LIKE THE REST OF THE NATION, was becoming more sports conscious. Conversations, even at black-tie dinners, often focused on statistics, sensational plays and star players. The *Detroit Free Press* expanded its sports section by 50 percent in 1935. That came as no surprise to Detroit sports fans. The Motor City that year earned for itself a new title: "City of Champions." Not only were the Tigers the proud winners of the World Series, the Detroit Lions captured the National Football League championship and the Red Wings skated to the Stanley Cup. In boxing circles, insiders were abuzz about Joe Louis, a young heavyweight contender from Detroit known as the "Brown Bomber."

The Tiger family celebrated its good fortune for just over one month. They basked in the knowledge that they were World Champions. They celebrated with slugger Hank Greenberg who was named the American League's Most Valuable Player for the '35 season. Greenberg and his teammates had even more reason to celebrate as each of them took home more than $6,500 in bonus money for winning the World Series Championship Flag. The Tiger organization received a check for $150,000. Instead of pocketing the money, Frank Navin elected to pour all of it back into his stadium. He had ambitious plans for expansion.

Suddenly, and without warning, all of Frank Navin's dreams for the future vanished. On November 13, while riding at the Detroit Riding and Hunt Club, Navin was felled by a heart attack. He was rushed to the Detroit Osteopathic Hospital in Highland Park, where doctors worked

Right-handed slugger Hank Greenberg was Detroit's consistent long-ball threat.

"During my first year in the big leagues, the remarks from the stands and the opposing bench about my Jewish faith made life for me a living hell. But I was determined not to let that interfere with my concentration on the game. I owed my people that much."

- Hank Greenberg

frantically to save him. Their efforts were in vain. Within the hour, Frank Navin was pronounced dead.

Telegrams of condolence poured in from all parts of the nation, from political leaders, club owners, players and fans ... primarily from fans. They appreciated most what Frank Navin brought to their Tigers. They realized, perhaps more than any other group, that his primary purpose in life was to give the people of Detroit the best both he and baseball could offer.

Auto body magnate Walter O. Briggs purchased Navin's half of the team from his widow, Grace Navin, for $1 million. Almost immediately, Briggs started to restructure the organization. One of his first moves was to appoint his son, Walter O. Briggs, Jr., better known as "Spike," as treasurer and assistant secretary. He expanded Manager Mickey Cochrane's duties by naming him a vice president.

Cochrane, in an effort to add even more strength to his hard-hitting club, recommended that the Tigers purchase his old friend, Al Simmons, a long-ball-hitting center fielder from the White Sox. Briggs agreed and paid $75,000 for

the 34-year-old veteran.

Simmons hit .327 for the '36 Tigers and clubbed 13 home runs. But that was not enough to make up for what happened just two weeks into the season. Clean-up hitter Hank Greenberg, the first consistent long-ball threat in Detroit history, collided with Jake Powell of the Nationals at first base. Greenberg tagged the runner but sent a gasp through the Tiger dugout when he grabbed his left wrist—the same one that kept him out of much of the World Series. X-rays showed another fracture.

Greenberg hoped to return to the lineup by June. No way. The great slugger from the Bronx had to sit out the entire season.

Schoolboy Rowe won 19 games that year, but was not nearly as effective as the year before. He often complained to Cochrane that his arm felt weak. Cochrane accused Rowe of "dogging it." General Crowder suffered from a mysterious stomach ache and had to retire from baseball in July. Eldon Auker lost his effectiveness, as demonstrated by his 13-16 record. The only pitcher living up to his billing was Tommy Bridges, with a league-leading 23 wins and 175 strikeouts.

Hitting was still Detroit's strong suit. Along with the solid performance of Simmons, Gehringer (.354) led the league in doubles (60). Walker hit .353, Goslin .315, and Fox .305.

Manager Cochrane, a former masterful developer of talent, had abruptly become impatient with his men. In lieu of motivating players with a You-can-do-it approach, he scolded them and made them feel inferior.

Most disturbed by his manager's change in attitude was long-time friend Al Simmons. Immediately after the season's end, Simmons asked to be traded. The Tiger front office complied and sold him to Washington for a mere $15,000.

Pressures mounted on Cochrane. Some nagging injuries on the field, coupled with the building animosity among his players were just too much to handle. Just 45 games into the season, he suffered a nervous breakdown. Cochrane was ordered to take an extended vacation to pull himself together. Del Baker, Bengals' former catcher and now a coach, managed the team for 34 games.

Cochrane's therapy appeared to have been effective. He returned for the final 67 games to lead his club to a second-place finish, 19 1/2 games behind a revitalized New York Yankees team featuring a heralded rookie, Joe DiMaggio, and an aging veteran named Gehrig.

The 1937 Tigers followed much the same script, only with more tragic consequences. Cochrane showed growing impatience with Rowe, who moaned about his ailing arm. Cochrane slapped Rowe with a 10-day suspension for being "out of shape."

On May 25, the day Rowe returned to the mound following his suspension, the Tigers were in New York playing a critical game against the World Champion Yankees. Cochrane had given the Tigers the lead with a third-inning home run off Irving "Bump"

Hadley. When Cochrane stepped to the plate in the fifth, Hadley let loose with a high, inside pitch. Cochrane tried to duck but it was too late. With a sickening *thud!* the ball hit Cochrane's left temple. The Tiger catcher lay motionless on the ground as the Yankee crowd grew deathly silent.

Four players carried him off the field on a stretcher, and Cochrane was rushed to St. Elizabeth's Hospital. For three days, the powerful catcher hovered between life and death from what X-rays showed to be a triple fracture of the skull. On the fourth day, Cochrane suddenly showed signs of improvement. The prayers of New York pitcher Hadley, and the rest of the baseball world, were answered.

Del Baker assumed the temporary role as manager again until July 25 when, following a six-week stay at Henry Ford Hospital, Mickey Cochrane returned to the helm. Tiger fans, however, had seen the last of Mickey Cochrane as a player. Doctors warned him that another beaning could be fatal.

Through the gloom and depression of the season, the players continued to scrap for victories. Charlie Gehringer, now considered the game's best fielding second baseman, led American League hitters with a .371 average. Hank Greenberg tore the cover off the ball with 40 home runs, hit .337 and knocked in a whopping 183 runs—just one short of Lou Gehrig's league record. Gee Walker had 18 homers and a healthy .335 average; Pete Fox hit .331.

The only time Detroit's Heavyweight Champion Joe Louis fought in Briggs Stadium was September 20, 1939. In a championship bout with challenger Bob Pastor, the hometown hero drew over 33,000 who sat in a cold drizzle on chairs placed on the outfield grass. The soaking rain made the ground vulnerable to sinking chair legs and fans who tracked along the field.

Louis KO'ed Pastor in the 11th round. That was none too soon for the patient Detroiters who, now soaked, sloshed back to cars and busses through mud and uprooted grass.

Following the fight, Tiger owner Walter O. Briggs banned all prizefights from his stadium because of the damage done to the grounds.

The hottest player, for one month, anyway, was recently-acquired Rudy York, who smacked 18 home runs in August on his way to a 35-homer season. It was a major-league record for homers in one month until broken by Sammy Sosa in 1998.

Pitching faltered. Rowe managed only one win the entire season. Bridges posted a 15-12 record. About the only solid performance was by Albert "Roxie" Lawson (18-7), now in his fourth year with the club.

The Tigers' second-place finish was acceptable, especially in light of the dynasty now being created by the Bronx Bombers in New York.

Fan support for the Tigers continued to grow. That was incentive enough for Walter Briggs to fulfill the dreams of the late Frank Navin. Earlier Briggs had already increased the seating capacity of Navin Field to 36,000 when he added double decks in right field. Before Opening Day in 1938, Briggs spent an estimated $1 million on additional construction that allowed 56,000 paying customers to view a game.

The completed park was renamed "Briggs Stadium" in honor of its new owner, who had invested so much of his own money into building a ballpark second in size only to Yankee Stadium for the people of Detroit. That addition was the last significant change to the stadium's seating layout in its 87-year history.

Cochrane alienated many fans when he attempted to strengthen his mound staff with the acquisi-tion of Vern Kennedy from the White Sox. The price tag was high. The Tigers had to give up the popular Gee Walker, Marv Owen and homegrown catcher Mike Tresh. Along with Kennedy, Detroit received a utility infielder named Tony Piet and outfielder Fred "Dixie" Walker.

When it became obvious that Cochrane had lost the confidence of his players and the fans, and that the Tigers would not win the pennant, Owner Briggs called Cochrane into his office on August 6. Immediately following the meeting, Briggs offered a prepared statement.

"Mickey Cochrane and I had a conference today at which it was agreed that he would no longer continue his connection with the Detroit Baseball Club.... It seems apparent to both of us that, for the good of the club and in justice to the supporting fans, a change should be made."

The firing broke the heart of Mickey Cochrane. He died alone in 1962, in Lake Forest, Illinois. Hank Greenberg would later say, "He never got over being let go as manager by Mr. Briggs."

The 1938 season for Detroit will not be remembered for the club's fourth-place finish, rather for the chase for the all-time major league record for home runs by Hammerin' Hank.

The stoop-shouldered slugger had pounded out an astonishing 58 home runs during the '38 campaign with five games left to play. Fans packed the ballparks with the hope of seeing him surpass Babe Ruth's record of 60. As Greenberg recalled, in one of those five remaining games he was walked four times. Cleveland's "Bullet Bob" Feller fanned 18 Tigers in another (a record for one game at the time), including Greenberg twice. In the final contest of the season, the game was called after six innings on account of darkness. "I guess it just wasn't meant to be," Greenberg said later.

Shortly after the firing of Mickey Cochrane, Walter Briggs named Jack Zeller as general manager. Zeller, formerly head of the Tigers' minor league operations, would spend the next seven years molding clubs that would be contenders for the American League pennant.

Del Baker, for the third time, assumed the job as Tiger manager, following in the footsteps of Mickey Cochrane. For the 1939 season, however, the title "interim" was not used.

That year proved to be a good training ground for any new manager. Baker inherited a club in transition. Rudy York, while hitting a respectable .307 and slamming 20 home runs, was nosed out of his starting role by fourth-year backstop George "Birdie" Tebbetts. Hank Greenberg hit .312 and belted 33 homers. Charlie Gehringer, although out for a month due to injuries, hit .325 and showed a flash of power with 16 four-baggers.

Added to the roster shortly after the start of the campaign was a much-traveled pitcher, Louis "Bobo" Newsom, who racked-up a 17-10 record for Detroit. Newsom's strength to the ball club was not

only his performance, but also his ability to teach. One of his students was a rookie right hander, Fred Hutchinson, who would develop into a Tiger mainstay.

Undoubtedly, the best newcomer to arrive at the Tiger camp was an 18-year-old southpaw from Wilbur Wright Prep School in Detroit named Harold Newhouser. "Prince Hal," as he would later be called, pitched only five innings that year, but that was just the beginning of a career as one of baseball's outstanding pitchers.

The biggest blunder in 1939 came on July 24 when the Tigers waived reserve outfielder Dixie Walker. After he was picked up by Brooklyn, Walker developed into a solid hitter, helping the Dodgers capture some pennants. He was a fan favorite, dubbed "The People's Cherce," until Jackie Robinson broke the color barrier of major league baseball in 1947 and Walker demanded to be traded.

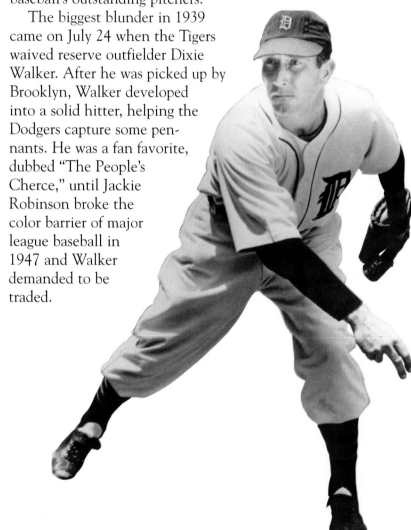

Adding to the pitching strength was Fred Hutchinson.

Overall, Detroit had a winning record (81-73) for a fifth-place finish.

Meanwhile, back in New York City, on August 26, 1939, legendary sportscaster Red Barber described the action during a televised broadcast of a game between the Dodgers and the Reds on experimental station W2XBS. This new medium would later play a major part of shaping the business of America's pastime.

The New York Yankees won their fourth consecutive World Championship in 1939. Everyone who knew anything about baseball could see no reason why the Yankees would not repeat. Certainly, no one expected a challenge from the second-division Tigers. Baseballs, however, often take strange bounces. The 1940 season proved just that.

The '40 campaign looked as though it would get off to a rocky start when Judge Landis accused several baseball executives, including Detroit general manager Jack Zeller, of negotiating with players who were still under contract. Detroit narrowly escaped losing sophomore pitcher Paul "Dizzy" Trout and the hard-hitting Rudy York in the fracas. A few trades were nullified and stiff fines imposed on the guilty. The Tigers were ordered to fork over more than $47,000.

Manager Baker had his own problems. What would he do with Rudy York who had some good years remaining? Birdie Tebbetts was his new starting catcher, but he hated to lose York's big bat. Baker found his answer. Move Rudy York to first base and Hank Greenberg to left field.

Greenberg at first objected. As an extra measure of persuasion, Jack Zeller raised his $40,000 salary to $50,000 if the Bronx slugger would play the outfield as an "experiment." That was enough to persuade Hammerin' Hank.

The experiment worked wonders. The agile Greenberg experienced some difficulties playing the outfield, as noted by his league-leading 15 errors. His home run swing, however, was not affected. He banged 41 home runs (tops in the American League), 50 doubles and had 384 total bases that year. In addition, he hit a blistering .340 and led the circuit with 150 RBI. The statistics impressed the astute Baseball Writers Association of America; they awarded Hank Greenberg his second MVP Award, making him the first player in major league history to win that honor at two different positions.

Rudy York adapted a bit more easily to fielding his new position and contributed to the hitting assault with a .316 average, 33 homers and 134 RBI.

"Rowdy" Richard Bartell, acquired in a trade with the Cubs for Billy Rogell, was a hard-crusted, John McGraw-type of shortstop who lit a fire under the team. At second base, Gehringer, though fighting the effects of lumbago, gave his usual solid defensive performance and hit .313.

Supporting these standouts was second-year center fielder Barney McCosky with his .340 average, his league-leading 200 hits and 19 three-baggers. Birdie Tebbetts

Owner Walter Briggs and son survey a model of the soon-to-be remodeled stadium in 1938.

showed he deserved the designation as number-one catcher by finishing the year just four points under .300 and showing a keen sense for directing the team in the field.

Shining lights from the mound included Bobo Newsom with his 21-5 record and Schoolboy Rowe, who staged a comeback with a 10-3 mark. John "Al" Benton kept the opposition in check with a league best 17 saves.

Throughout the season, Cleveland, New York and to the surprise of everyone, Detroit, battled for the first-place spot. The exciting pennant race drew a record-breaking 1,112,693 fans to

Briggs Stadium that year. Going into the final three games of the season, Tiger players were pinching themselves. Could this be a dream that they actually had a two-game lead with three games remaining with Cleveland? All the Tigers had to do was win just one game and the pennant would be theirs.

Cleveland, in second place, was determined to win all three contests. Before a sold-out hometown crowd, Cleveland manager Ossie Vitt started Bob Feller. The phenomenal Feller led the league in victories, games, innings pitched, strikeouts, and nearly every other category. Detroit countered with a

Construction to Briggs Stadium in 1938 made it possible for thousands more to see the game. View from Michigan Avenue.

relatively unknown rookie, Floyd Giebell, with his unheralded 1-1 record. The unorthodox strategy worked. With the help of Rudy York's two-run blast, the Tigers beat Feller and his Indians, 2-0.

For the sixth time in their history, the Detroit Tigers were American League Champions.

The National League Pennant-winning Cincinnati Reds, white-washed by the Yankees in the previous World Series, were determined to avenge themselves. Although they lacked the muscle of Detroit, the Reds had some fine country hitters such as Mike McCormick and Frank McCormick, who were not related. Cincinnati's strength, however, was on the mound with

William "Bucky" Walters, who led his league with 22 wins and Paul "Oom Paul" Derringer, a 20-game winner.

Detroit, by its own admission, started the series with an extremely confident, some might say cocky, attitude. "If we can beat the mighty Yankees," said some, "we should have no trouble with Cincinnati."

Game One at Crosley Field seemed to justify the Tigers' surety. The Tigers crossed the plate five times during the second inning, knocking Derringer from the box after only one and one-third innings. Newsom breezed to a 7-2 win.

In Game Two, Bucky Walters

An inside view of the additional seating constructed in 1938.

The Detroit Lions returned to playing at Briggs Stadium in 1941. Star player for the team was Byron "Whizzer" White—a tailback—who later became a justice for the United States Supreme Court.

One week following a 4-6-1 season for the Lions, the attack on Pearl Harbor dragged America into war. As with Major League Baseball, the National Football League continued play throughout the war years. Unfortunately, someone forgot to tell the Lions who played the entire '42 season without a win.

The 1943 to 1948 seasons—the last three of which the Lions finished in last place—proved to be no better. Attendance for games at Briggs Stadium sometimes dropped off to just over 6,000 a game.

tamed Schoolboy Rowe and the Tigers on just three hits en route to a 5-3 win before an enthusiastic hometown crowd.

Back in Detroit for Game Three, the Tigers shook off the previous loss as a bad memory. With Tommy Bridges in fine form and seventh-inning home runs by Rudy York and third-baseman Michael "Pinky" Higgins, the Bengals grabbed the Series lead with a score of 7-4.

Cincinnati came back in Game Four the next day, with Paul Derringer regaining his winning form and pitching all nine innings toward a 5-2 Reds win. Victim of a Cincinnati hitting barrage was starting pitcher Dizzy Trout who

was nailed for three runs in just two innings.

Bobo Newsom limited the Reds to just three hits, and Hank Greenberg's three-run blast gave him all the runs he needed as Detroit blanked Cincinnati 8-0 in Game Five. With a 3-2 Series lead, Detroit fans geared up for another snake dance down Woodward Avenue.

Schoolboy Rowe lasted only a third of an inning in Game Six the next day in Cincinnati as the Reds scored twice. Bucky Walters, on the other hand, overpowered the Tigers, 4-0. The Reds' pitcher helped his own cause with a solo home run.

In Game Seven played on

Following their 7-4 victory over the Cincinnati Reds in the 1940 World Series, Tiger players rush from the dugout to congratulate winning pitcher Tommy Bridges. [Photo: *The Detroit News*]

October 8 at Crosley Field, Bobo Newsom, winner of games One and Five, took the mound with only one full day of rest, hoping to capture Detroit's second World Championship. Paul Derringer, also pitching in his third game of the Series, started for Cincinnati.

Things looked good for the Tigers in the third inning when they scored a run without getting a ball out of the infield. Reserve catcher Billy Sullivan hit a weak grounder to first, but beat the toss to the pitcher covering the bag. Newsom sacrificed Sullivan to second. Following a strikeout, McCosky drew a walk. Gehringer hit a hard shot to third and a wild throw into the dirt at first sailed

past Frank McCormick. Sullivan easily scored from second.

Newsom held the Reds scoreless until Frank McCormick opened the seventh with a double. The next batter, Jim Ripple, hit a shot over the head of outfielder Bruce Campbell, playing his first season with Detroit. McCormick hesitated between second and third, not knowing Campbell would catch the ball. As soon as he saw the ball hit the ground, McCormick headed around third for home. Campbell quickly retrieved the ball and threw it to shortstop Richard Bartell. With his back toward the infield, Bartell had plenty of time to throw to the plate in an attempt to cut-down

Detroit Tigers
1940 American League Champions
Top Row - Hutchinson, Sullivan, Tebbetts, Greenberg, Benton, Gorsica, Seats, Smith, Campbell
Middle Row - Newsom, York, Averill, Croucher, Trout, Newhouser, Rowe, Meyer, McKain, Stainback
Front Row - Gehringer, Bartell, Kress, Hiller *(coach)*, Baker *(manager)*, Shea *(coach)*, Bridges, McCosky, Higgins, Fox

the slow running McCormick. But, with the sellout crowd roaring, Bartell could not hear the yelling of his teammates to throw home and just held the ball as McCormick scored the tying run. A sacrifice bunt moved Ripple to third, followed by a sacrifice fly scoring Cincinnati's second and final run of the game and the Series.

That was all the Reds needed. Derringer shut down the Tigers the rest of the way and Cincinnati became baseball's newest champions by a score of 2-1.

According to newspaper reporters covering the games, no team had ever taken the loss of World Series so hard.

When he emerged from the post-game shower, Bobo Newsom spoke for everyone when he moaned to Sam Greene of *The Detroit News*, "I feel like I need a good rest."

Chapter 9
The War Years

"We won for Steve O'Neill. There was no man on the club who didn't want to win for Steve—a man who never second-guessed a ball player and always understood."

- Hank Greenberg
  October 11, 1945

Owner Walter O. Briggs was determined to bring the World Championship back to Detroit.

FOLLOWING THE STOCK MARKET CRASH 12 YEARS EARLIER, one Wall Street broker explained his altered status this way: "Yesterday I was in the penthouse. Today I'm in the outhouse." The 1941 Detroit Tigers could identify with the broker's plight. Even though they lost the World Series the previous fall, they could, at least, fly an American League Championship flag over Briggs Stadium.

In 1941, that flag could have been flown at half-staff in memory of "a team that once was." A 75-79 record earned them a season-ending fourth-place tie with Cleveland. Meanwhile, the New York Yankees, led by Joe DiMaggio and his 56-game hitting streak, dominated everyone in the American League and eventually the Brooklyn Dodgers in the World Series.

Part of the reason for the club's abrupt demise was the fact that big Hank Greenberg answered the call of duty to serve in the armed forces. In doing so, he became the second player to join the military during World War II; the first was the Phillies' Hugh "Losing Pitcher" Mulcahy.

Radio news flashes over the past few months reported the *blitz* of German troops across Yugoslavia, Greece and the U.S.S.R. Even the innocent women and children of England had to hide in bomb shelters during raids initiated by Adolph Hitler and his "master race." In the Far East, the Empire of Japan enslaved Indochina, flexed its muscles and entered into a pact with Germany and Italy to form an alliance.

Americans were, by and large, sympathetic to England's plight but wanted to remain out of the war. Nonetheless, the nation realized that

The Tigers, in 1941, signed baseball's first "bonus baby" - outfielder Dick Wakefield.

we should be prepared in the event of an attack, as unlikely as that possibility appeared on May 7, 1941, when the 30-year-old Greenberg raised his right hand and swore to defend our country against foreign aggression.

Hammerin' Hank served only seven months in the military before Detroit's most eligible bachelor was discharged due to a new law that demanded all men over 28 years old be released from military duty. Just two days later, the "Day of Infamy," December 7, 1941, ushered America into World War II, and Greenberg donned his uniform once again.

On Opening Day 1941, fans sensed the Tigers were not the same squad as the year before. Players went through the motions of playing ball. Things that inspired them the previous year were now distractions. Sharp-tongued Dick Bartell, for example, in an attempt to motivate his team, got under the skin of most of the players. During the previous season when they were winning, his caustic comments were taken as attempts to prod his teammates

into becoming better performers. While they were losing in '41, those same remarks were considered nagging. General Manager Jack Zeller decided after just five games that year to release this source of unwanted irritation.

On July 8, Briggs Stadium was the setting for one of the most exciting All-Star Games in history. Managed by Del Baker, the American League squad overflowed with future Hall-of-Famers. A capacity crowd of 54,674 saw the Pittsburgh Pirates' Arky Vaughan smack two home runs to give his team a 5-3 lead going into the last of the ninth. With Yankee stars Joe DiMaggio and Joe Gordon on base and two outs, Boston's Ted Williams stood at the plate facing Claude Passeau of the Cubs. On the first pitch, Williams swung and sent the ball high into the upper deck in right field for a game-winning homer. Film taken of that moment still show us Williams' smooth, classic swing and his leaping around the bases as though he had just won the World Series.

The All-Star Game was just about the only reasons for Detroit fans to cheer in 1941. The Tigers' woes continued when Charlie Gehringer, plagued with lumbago, saw his average drop to .220. Bobo Newsom's 12 wins and league-leading 20 losses did not justify his annual $30,000 salary. While Al Benton posted a respectable 15-6 mark, Schoolboy Rowe's sore arm re-appeared. Everybody knew his days with Detroit were numbered.

Two waves of the future appeared in Tiger uniforms in 1941. The first Virgil "Fire" Trucks, who

established himself in the minors as a strikeout artist. The second was Dick Wakefield, often described as baseball's first "bonus baby."

Wakefield, a student at the University of Michigan, a 6' 4", 210-pound left-handed hitter, had all the tools necessary to make it as a big-league star. Although he was rough around the edges in terms of fielding, he could run, throw and hit with power. Several clubs presented tempting contracts, but the young native of Chicago did not jump at the first offer. The money became more attractive. Finally, Walter Briggs took a gamble and presented an irresistible contract that included a signing bonus of $52,000 and a new customized automobile. Wakefield accepted the Tigers' offer and was sent to Winston-Salem to develop his skills in the outfield.

Front-page headlines in Detroit newspapers during the 1942 campaign contained little mention of the Tigers. Instead, they told stories of United States GIs in European countries and on Pacific islands. Many of those troops consisted of former baseball stars, including Bob Feller, Ted Williams and Hank Greenberg.

The city of Detroit became directly involved with the war effort. Factories that once produced Ford, Chevrolet, Packard, Plymouth, Chrysler and Studebaker automobiles were now turning out parts for aircraft with strange-sounding names such as "Mustang," "Wildcat," "Hellcat," and "Lightning," along with a versatile vehicle known simply as a "Jeep."

On any given night, the people of Detroit could be ordered to turn off all lights in their homes, during

While war was seething in Europe in 1941, Americans vowed to keep focused on more pleasant things - such as the All-Star Game played in Detroit. Fourth from the right in the front row is Owner Walter O. Briggs. Standing to his left is his son, Walter "Spike" Briggs, Jr.

THE WHITE HOUSE
Washington

January 15, 1942

My dear Judge:

Thank you for yours of January fourteenth. As you will, of course, realize the final decision about the baseball season must rest with you and the Baseball club owners—so what I am going to say is solely a personal and not an official point of view.

I honestly feel that it would be best for the country to keep baseball going. There will be fewer people unemployed and everybody will work longer hours and harder than ever before.

And that means that they ought to have a chance for recreation and for taking their minds off their work even more than before.

Baseball provides a recreation which does not last over two hours or two hours and a half, and which can be got for very little cost. And, incidentally, I hope that night games can be extended because it gives an opportunity to the day shift to see a game occasionally.

As to the players themselves, I know you agree with me that individual players who are of active military or naval age should go, without question, into the services. Even if the actual quality to the teams is lowered by the greater use of older players, this will not dampen the popularity of the sport. Of course, if an individual has some particular aptitude in a trade or profession, he ought to serve the Government. That, however, is a matter that I know you can handle with complete justice.

Here is another way of looking at it—if 300 teams use 5,000 or 6,000 players, these players are a definite recreational asset to at least 20,000,000 of their fellow citizens—and that in my judgment is thoroughly worthwhile.

With every best wish,

Very sincerely yours
Franklin D. Roosevelt

Hon. Kenesaw M. Landis
333 North Michigan Avenue
Chicago, Illinois

which time volunteer "air-raid wardens" walked the streets to ensure that their neighbors abided by the law.

Briggs Stadium was not yet equipped with lights, so the ruling by Judge Landis that only day games would be played had no direct significance to the Motor City. The big debate, however, was whether or not Major League Baseball should be played at all. Plenty of Americans found it difficult to justify going to the ballpark for an afternoon of fun while our nation's young, brave men were laying down their lives for the sake of freedom.

President Franklin D. Roosevelt eased their anxiety when he penned a letter to Commissioner Landis on July 15, 1942, in which he expressed his desire that Major League Baseball should continue as, he put it, "for the best of the country." Almost as an afterthought in the same letter, Roosevelt encouraged that night games remain in order to give people who worked day shifts more opportunity to see a game.

Manager Del Baker and his Tigers entered the 1942 season with even more reason for dismay. Bobo Newsom refused to take a $20,000 cut in pay or to sign a contract. Before the end of spring training, he was sold to Washington. Schoolboy Rowe also bid farewell to Detroit when he was sold to Brooklyn after pitching in only two games in April.

Virgil Trucks (14-8) was the only consistent pitcher on the club, and no Tiger batter hit .300. A fifth-place finish, 30 games behind the first-place Yankees, was about as much as the team deserved.

Due to his inability to light a fire under his team, Del Baker was let go as Tiger manager and replaced by coach Steve O'Neill.

O'Neill, like Hughie Jennings, was another Tiger manager to come from the coal mining area of Eastern Pennsylvania. He was also a former major league catcher who had managed the Cleveland Indians for a little more than two years.

In 1943, O'Neill was handed a team sapped of strength by the military draft. Detroit certainly had its share of big leaguers in the service: Hank Greenberg, Barney McCosky, Pat Mullin, Birdie Tebbetts, Charlie Gehringer, Fred Hutchinson and Al Benton.

In the spirit of national pride, pitcher Hal Newhouser was set to hold his induction ceremony on the mound at Briggs Stadium, but a heart murmur kept the star southpaw on the 4-F list. Unable to fight in a military uniform, Prince Hal contributed to the war effort by working at nights in a defense plant.

In 1943, even the ball suffered from the war effort. War production needs were priorities in terms of available rubber. A gum called "balata" was substituted for the rubber normally used around the cork of a baseball. This "balata ball" reportedly was not as lively as the ones used before. The new ball, however, didn't seem to hurt Rudy York, who led the league with 34 home runs, 118 RBI and a .527 slugging average. In the pitching department, Dizzy Trout tied the Yankees' Spurgeon "Spud" Chandler with 20 wins.

Most celebrated of all Tigers in '43 was young Dick Wakefield. His .316 average was second only to veteran shortstop Luke Appling of the White Sox. In addition, the good-looking Wakefield became a hit among a new breed of fans—young ladies. The youngster became a matinee idol that rivaled the popularity of crooner Frank Sinatra. Added interest in the club or, in this case, a player, resulted in only one thing— larger attendance figures. Detroit's

Commissioned to direct the club to a World Series victory was manager Steve O'Neill.

Another fresh face with potential in '41 was Virgil "Fire" Trucks.

bonus baby added to the bottom line of the club's books.

Much of that boost created by female fans was thwarted following the '43 season when Tiger management ceased sponsoring "Ladies Day"—a chance for women to see Thursday afternoon games for 50 cents. The front office cited many complaints that came from men in the stands about the loud "screeching" emanating from the designated section of the stands set off for the ladies.

Another fifth-place finish, however, gave Tiger fans little cause for any kind of jubilation.

When the Tigers began the 1944 season by losing 12 of their first 13 games at home, and the light-hitting St. Louis Browns started with nine straight victories, Detroit fans let out a collective groan.

Their dismay deepened when even more Tigers left to serve Uncle Sam prior to the 1944 season. Trading baseball bats for military rifles were Dick Wakefield, Virgil Trucks and 37-year-old Tommy Bridges. Through the sort of bureaucratic mix-up that only the military could invent, Wakefield, who had started training as a Navy pilot, was given a 90-day leave until a decision could be made about whether the Navy needed more pilots. When Wakefield reported to the Tigers on July 13, his club was lingering around the American League basement. The young bonus baby gave the spark necessary for the Tigers to make an about-face. Batting .355 in 78 games, Wakefield helped the Tigers claw their way up the standings only to miss winning the pennant to the St. Louis Browns by one game. As it turned out, this would be the Browns' first and only American League Championship.

Detroit's success was due, mainly, to the arms of two pitchers. Dizzy Trout (27-14) was nothing short of phenomenal. He led the league with a 2.12 ERA, 352 innings pitched, seven shutouts and 33 complete games. Prince Hal Newhouser led the league with 29 wins against only 9 defeats and 187 strikeouts.

One of the reasons behind Newhouser's remarkable improvement was private coaching by veteran catcher Paul Richards, brought on board the year before as a replacement for Birdie

Prince Hal. [Photo: *Baseball Hall of Fame and Museum*]

Tebbetts. Richards worked not only on Newhouser's pitching skills, but also on his attitude. The hot-tempered southpaw often became his own worst enemy when he chastised himself for mistakes or losses. Richards' counseling helped the young pitcher to put things into perspective. The Baseball Writers Association of America agreed when they elected Newhouser as the American League's Most Valuable Player for 1944.

As Newhouser's star was rising, the career of Baseball Commissioner Judge Landis, who had led America's pastime through the sacrifices of the war, ended. On November 25, in Chicago, the crusty man who held fast to his convictions about the 1919 "Black Sox" scandal and that "no person of color" should be allowed to play Major League Baseball, died of a heart attack. He never sought praise for what he did in life; he refused to have it even in death. At his request, there was no funeral.

Experts claimed that had the Tigers been able to use the talents of Hank Greenberg, they would have played in the '44 World Series. But patriotism in Detroit, especially when it involved the military, ran high. On January 31, 1945, when Hamtramck-born Private Eddie Slovik became the

Hal Newhouser and Dizzy Trout - two pitchers that were the envy of every big league club.

only U.S. GI to be executed by firing squad for desertion, the people of Detroit showed little resentment.

The call to arms had depleted the major leagues. That paved the way for players such as Pete Gray, a one-armed outfielder for the Browns, to wear a big league uniform when he hit .218 in 77 games during the '45 season.

Gray and others moved aside as the regular players gradually returned from military service. Army Captain Greenberg was not released until General Dwight D. Eisenhower accepted the surrender of Germany on May 8—V-E Day. By the time Greenberg was given his honorable discharge, the 1945 baseball season was half completed.

More than 47,000 fans packed Briggs Field on July 1 to welcome Hammerin' Hank and his familiar number 5 back to the team. Greenberg did not let them down. In his first major league game in four years, one month and 24 days, he slammed a home run in the eighth inning off pitcher Charlie Gassaway to help beat Connie Mack's Athletics, 9-5. For the remainder of the season,

Greenberg showed that his batting eye had not disappeared. He socked 13 homers and knocked in 60 runs in just 78 games. None of the home runs he hit during his illustrious career, however, could top his last of the

regular season. It was one that Tiger fans in Detroit and throughout the Midwest who heard Harry Heilmann call it on WXYZ Radio would recall for the remainder of their lives.

Detroit and the rest of America were already in a celebrating mood. Six weeks earlier, Col. Paul Tibbets and his crew of the *Enola Gay* dropped the first A-bomb on Hiroshima on August 6. Eight days later, bells rang at the Old Mariner's Church on East Jefferson in Downtown Detroit. People that had assembled in Cadillac Square hugged and kissed complete strangers. They were celebrating the news of Japan's surrender and the end of World War II.

Celebrating victories in Briggs Stadium were also common events in 1945. The Tigers continued their winning ways and battled the Washington for first place most of the year. Washington (87-67) had completed its season by vacating its home park to make way for the start of the football season. Detroit (87-65) had two games to go in St. Louis, against last year's American League Champion Browns. If Detroit won just one of the games, the pennant would be theirs. A two-game loss called for a playoff.

The first game was rained out on Saturday. That meant a double-header had to be scheduled for the next day. On Sunday, September 30, a heavy downpour put the start of the games in doubt. The rain let up enough for the umpires to allow game one to begin one hour late. Patchwork by the grounds crew made the diamond semi-playable.

Detroit was leading 2-1 in the

On July 1, 1945, following four years in a military uniform, Hank Greenberg returned to the Tiger lineup. That afternoon, he slammed a home run. Nearly three months later, he would hit what many historians claim to be the most dramatic home run in Tiger history.

sixth when O'Neill called in Hal Newhouser from the bullpen to relieve Virgil Trucks. St. Louis scored two runs in the seventh to put the Browns ahead 3-2. The score held up until the top of the ninth. With the rain coming down a bit harder, Harvey "Hub" Walker, a .130 hitter in his only year playing for Detroit, led off with a pinch single for Newhouser. The Browns' first-baseman George McQuinn fielded shortstop James "Skeeter" Webb's sacrifice bunt but threw late to second. Both runners were safe. A sacrifice bunt followed by an intentional walk loaded the bases.

To the batter's box strode Mr. Greenberg. Digging in at the plate, holding high his 40-ounce bat, the slugger swung at the first pitch and sent it high toward left field. The ball seemed to part the rain and twilight as it sailed deep into the bleachers. His fellow players claimed they never saw Greenberg so happy as when he crossed the plate following that grand-slam home run.

Al Benton retired the Browns in the bottom half of the ninth, and, by a score of 6-3, the Detroit Tigers were American League Champs for the seventh time in their glowing history.

Game two of the double-header was only one inning old when it was called because of rain and darkness.

There was no darkness, however, in the hearts of the Detroit faithful. Hal Newhouser, winning pitcher in the crucial game, notched his 25th win of the season. It was impressive enough to

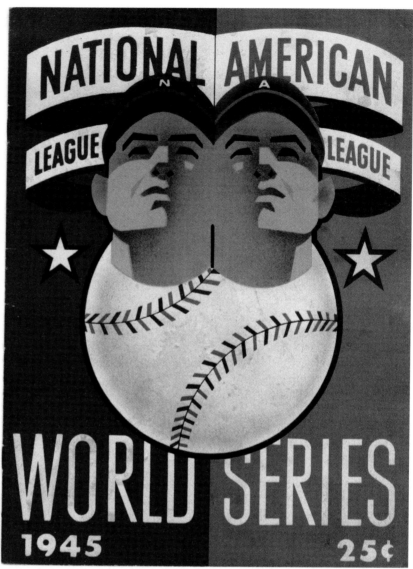

World Series program - 1945.

earn for him his second consecutive Most Valuable Player award. In all of baseball history, no other pitcher has won that honor in consecutive seasons.

The Chicago Cubs had just won the pennant in the National League. Charlie Grimm, the same manager who faced the Tigers in the World Series ten years earlier, led his solid-hitting club with batting champion Phil Cavarretta (.355), Andy Pafko, Harry "Peanuts" Lowrey and Bill "Swish" Nicholson. Hank Wyse (22-10) and Claude Passeau (17-9) led a

Detroit Tigers
1945 World Series Champions
Top Row - Hoover, Hostetler, Welch, Forsyth *(trainer)*
Third Row - Webb, Borom, Pierce, H. Walker, Houtteman, Swift, York, Cullenbine
Second Row - Wilson, Mueller, Outlaw, Benton, McHale, Overmire, Orrell
First Row - Cramer, Maier, Trout, Hills *(coach)*, O'Neill *(manager)*, Newhouser, Richards, Mayo
(note: Hank Greenberg was not present when the photo was taken during spring training)

fine Chicago pitching staff.

Viewing Game One of the World Series in Detroit from the Commissioner's Box was Albert B. "Happy" Chandler, the former governor of Kentucky, chosen by the owners to fill the shoes of the late Judge Landis. If the new commissioner was an American League fan, he and the 54,637 Detroit fans in attendance were disappointed. Pitching ace Hal Newhouser was racked for seven runs in just three innings, as Chicago's Hank Borowy humbled them by the score of 9-0.

Detroit came back strong in Game Two behind the strong arm of Virgil Trucks, who had been discharged from the Navy less than one week earlier. Trucks, pitching in his first game, scattered just seven hits and beat the Cubs, 4-1. Hank Greenberg's three-run homer in the fifth gave Trucks all the offense he needed.

Game Three, also held in

Detroit, raised the anxiety level of Tiger fans as Claude Passeau threw a brilliant one-hitter at the Tigers. Rudy York got the Bengal's only hit—a third-inning single. Frank "Stubby" Overmire was the losing pitcher for Detroit in this 3-0 loss.

When the Series shifted to Chicago for Game Four, Cubs fans had hoped that this would be their year. After Cubs pitcher Ray Prim retired the first ten Tiger batters to face him, those hopes looked more like realities. But the lingering curse on Chicago in the Fall Classic was about to make itself known once again. Four runs crossed the plate in Detroit's fourth inning. Dizzy Trout showed why he won 18 games that year as he five-hit the Cubs and won, 4-1.

Hal Newhouser shook off his Game One blues and struck out nine Cubs in Game Five. Hank Greenberg's three doubles keyed the Tiger attack. The final score was Detroit 8, Chicago 4.

Newspaper reporter Charles Einstein called Game Six of the 1945 World Series "the worst game of baseball ever played in this country." Einstein's hyperbole notwithstanding, the 3-hour, 28-minute contest went 12 innings.

Detroit had fallen behind, 7-3, when Hank Greenberg's eighth-inning home run paced the Tigers to a 7-7 tie. The score remained knotted until the bottom of the 12th. With a runner on first, Chicago's Stan Hack hit a lazy single to left field. When he saw the runner heading for third, Greenberg charged the ball with the idea of nailing the runner at third. The ball, however, hit some-thing in the outfield grass, hopped over Greenberg's head and rolled to the outfield wall. The runner scored easily, and the Cubs were 8-7 victors.

Chicago manager Charlie Grimm took a big gamble on October 7 before the Wrigley Field faithful. He named Hank Borowy to start Game Seven with only one day's rest. The gamble failed. Detroit greeted Borowy with three hits. Before he could register his first out, Borowy was lifted from the game. Detroit exploded for five runs in the first inning, which fea-tured a sacrifice bunt by slugger Hank Greenberg. Hal Newhouser scattered 10 hits and sent just as many Cubs batters down swinging. The Tigers coasted to a 9-3 win.

Four nights later, the World Champion Detroit Tigers were honored at a dinner hosted by Owner Briggs at the Book-Cadillac. Receiving special recog-nition were senior citizens—39-year-old Doc Cramer, who got 11 hits, and 34-year-old Greenberg, who belted two homers and knocked in seven runs during the Series. After the champagne corks were popped and the tributes given, Hank Greenberg stood behind the microphone and spoke for everyone: "We won for Steve O'Neill. There was no man on the club who didn't want to win for Steve—a man who never second-guessed a ball player and always understood."

A Roman Catholic priest, who had offered the invocation that evening, whispered: "Amen."

Chapter 10

A 23-Year Drought

"Baseball is a profession, not
a trade. The reserve clause
is the backbone of baseball.
Remove it and the game
will be ruined."

- H. G. Salsinger,
Detroit sportswriter

The '47 Tigers produced a "lumber company" of powerful bats. From
L-R, Lake, Kell, Cullenbine, Wertz, Evers, Mayo, Mullin, Tebbetts,
Trucks.

AN OLD EXPRESSION SAYS: "If it ain't broke, don't fix it." The 1946 Detroit Tigers should have done everything in their power to heed that sage advice. Instead, by design or accident, the defending World Series Champions picked apart a winning combination and set itself on a path of destruction.

Jack Zeller, Detroit's popular general manager, had, over the past few years, expressed his desire to retire due to his wife's failing health. Each year Owner Briggs was successful in convincing him to stay. No longer. Before the World Championship flag was raised over Briggs Stadium on Opening Day of 1946, Zeller resigned to take care of more important duties.

Prior to his departure, Zeller had radically changed the Tigers' minor league policy. In lieu of outright ownership of the clubs, the Tigers would maintain only a "working agreement" with selected teams.

Filling Zeller's shoes was George Trautman of Columbus, Ohio. Trautman was quick to initiate changes. He trimmed the Tiger roster by trading the popular Rudy York to Boston for shortstop Eddie Lake who led the league the previous year by assisting in 459 double plays. With the return of all the players who had served in the war—Greenberg, Wakefield, McCosky, Tebbetts, Hutchinson, Evers, Bloodworth, et. al.— the Tigers were now at full strength. Other fill-ins who had been added to the '45 squad were moved out to make way for these proven regulars. At the 1946 spring training camp in Lakeland, Florida, only 13 players on Detroit's roster just a year ago were wearing the Tiger uniform.

From Swifton, Arkansas, personable George Kell was a fixture at third base. Later he would gain added fame and fan loyalty from his position as a broadcaster. He was elected to the Hall of Fame in 1983.

Earlier that same year, teenage girls in Detroit wore black bobby socks. They mourned the news of the marriage of the city's most eligible bachelor—Hank Greenberg—to Ms. Carol Gimbel.

A record-breaking Opening Day crowd of 52,118 greeted the World Champion Tigers. Even that impressive figure was surpassed by nearly 100 on April 28—Detroit's first Sunday home game that year. What a contrast to the attendance at the 8,500-seat capacity of old Bennett Park.

Trautman continued purging the team. After only 26 games in 1946, outfielder Barney McCosky was sent to the Athletics in exchange for a 23-year-old third baseman from Swifton, Arkansas, named George Clyde Kell. Not many expected much of this personable youngster. The Dodgers had given up on him, and Philadelphia questioned his potential. In addition word around the scouting circles said that young George suffered from weak knees— an affliction he had since early childhood. But the scrappy Kell surprised even the most optimistic

seers by hitting .327 and fielding the hot corner with the skill of a seasoned veteran.

Other radical changes in baseball happened not so much in the major leagues, but in the minors. Less than a week after the final out of the 1945 World Series, Branch Rickey, vice president of the Brooklyn Dodgers, signed a superb black athlete from UCLA, Jack Roosevelt Robinson, to a minor league contract. Robinson was assigned to Montreal, the Dodgers' top farm team in the International League. Robinson's addition to the roster may have become significant news if more experts had been able to predict that baseball's color barrier would soon be broken.

Judge Kenesaw Mountain Landis, for all his noble accomplishments in breathing life back into baseball following the Black Sox scandal of 1919, had enforced a "whites only" policy for the major leagues. Few expected his replacement, the southern gentleman Albert "Happy" Chandler, to allow any change. Not only did Chandler *permit* change, he *encouraged it*. Wheels were set in motion, and before year's end, fans knew baseball would never be the same.

Until this time, African-Americans were relegated to playing baseball in what was known as the Negro Leagues. Legendary players emerged from these teams. James Thomas "Cool Papa" Bell, Josh Gibson, Leroy "Satchel" Paige and Detroit's own Norman "Turkey" Stearnes, were among the stars of the Negro Leagues.

Stearnes was a flashy outfielder for the "Detroit Stars" who played their games at Mack Park, located on the east side at Mack and Fairview. A .400 hitter during the late '20s, Stearnes earned his nickname from his habit of flapping his arms while running the bases. Of even more appeal were his towering home runs, some of which, according to newspaper accounts, sailed more than 520 feet. And this was in the era of the so-called "dead ball."

Stearnes and his Detroit Stars were so popular, they often outdrew the cross-town Tigers. Lawrence Carter, a writer for *The Detroit News*, reported that even some white folks attended the games just to watch Stearnes. "When Stearnes swung and missed," he wrote, "it would set up a great Pentecostal wind in Mack Park."

Following the 1927 season, some of the Tigers agreed to play the Stars on a barnstorming tour. The Tigers lost 11 of the 13 games. Ty Cobb refused to be a part of that show, however, and for good cause. Cobb, 16 years earlier, had agreed to join his team for an exhibition series in Cuba. Cobb regretted his decision. During the brief series he was overshadowed by the likes of John Henry "Pop" Lloyd, "Home Run" Grant Johnson and the Detroit Stars' catcher, Bruce Petway, who nailed the Peach each time he attempted to steal a base.

Most baseball clubs were not quick to join the Brooklyn Dodgers in seeking talented black ballplayers for their rosters. Lest we judge them too severely, we should remember that they were products of their time, continuing a long tradition in the history of baseball.

Two young ballplayers, for example, were good enough to be given a chance to prove themselves as potential Detroit Tigers. One was Wendell Smith, a student at Southeastern High School in Detroit in the early '30s. He could do anything demanded of a ballplayer. A Detroit scout, however, exposed the young man to the real world by telling him: "I wish I could sign you, kid, but I can't." Smith knew exactly what he meant, but there was not a thing he could do about it.

The other player showing promise in 1934 was an outfielder with a wicked throwing arm. Since he was not able to crack the major league barrier against blacks, Joe Louis Barrow concentrated on his second love— boxing.

In 1946, Hank Greenberg, who muscled 44 home runs to outstrip all major league sluggers, also led all hitters with 127 RBI.

Fred Mandel sold the Detroit Lions in 1948 to Edwin J. Anderson and Lyle Fife. They named Alvin "Bo" McMillan as head coach and signed Bob Mann and Mel Groomes—the team's first two black players. At quarterback, they hired the charismatic Bobby Layne who led his team with the sort of positive motivation that would be the envy of Norman Vincent Peale, and when the situation called for it, a royal reaming when a fellow player missed a key block.

Coach Raymond "Buddy" Parker replaced McMillan after the 1950 season. Fortunate draft picks and keen football savvy enabled Parker to fill the roster with solid players, including Jack Christiansen, Thurman McGraw, Cloyce Box, "Hunchy" Hoernschemeyer, Doak Walker and Leon Hart. One year later, rookies Yale Lary and Jimmy David bolstered the team's defense.

The chemistry worked. The Lions won four division titles from 1951 to 1957. They became NFL Champions in 1952, 1953 and 1957.

Increased attendance reflected the revitalized enthusiasm in this city known more for its support of baseball and hockey. More than 50,000 fans packed Briggs Stadium for each Sunday afternoon contest.

The glue to the team was still quarterback Bobby Layne. His remarkable ability to lead the team back for last-minute victories made Layne the first quarterback in NFL history to demonstrate the importance of a two-minute drill at the game's end.

Ray Boone had the difficult task of trying to fill the shoes of the popular George Kell.

Outfielder Roy Cullenbine, in the twilight of his career, had been brought back to the Tigers—the team with which he began his major league playing days eight years earlier. He showed that he still had some hits left in his bat as he led the Tigers with a .335 average. Not far behind was George Kell, with an impressive .327.

Hal Newhouser, with his league-leading 26 wins and 1.94 ERA, would have captured his third successful MVP Award were it not for the onslaught of Ted "The Thumper" Williams of the pennant-winning Red Sox. Williams led all American League hitters with 343 total bases, 142 runs scored, 156 walks and a .667 slugging average. Add this to a .342 batting average (second in the league) and 38 home runs (second to Greenberg), and the fact that his team ended in first place, the Baseball Writers Association of America voted him the coveted award. Detroit fans, however, felt cheated, although Newhouser never registered one word of complaint.

Although Detroit finished in second place that year, the battle for the pennant was no contest. Boston won it by 12 full games.

Along with the groundwork laid for blacks to join major league teams, baseball witnessed another preview of coming attractions in 1946. The owners use of the "reserve clause" which bound a player inextricably to a particular team had gone unchallenged. Up until that time, club management decided not only who would play, but where and when any person would play and how much money he would make. Players were bought, sold and traded at the whim of the front office. A Boston attorney, Robert Murphy, organized what he called "The American Baseball Guild." The concept was to create a union of ballplayers and give them a voice in their futures. Of primary concern to the players was the "reserve clause" by which a player was bound to a team even if he was eliminated from the roster.

We would think that the union-dominated industrial city of Detroit would have applauded this move. To the contrary, both the fans and the press sensed there was a difference between baseball and the work-a-day world. Veteran Detroit sportswriter H. G. Salsinger expressed this feeling when he wrote: "Baseball is a profession, not a trade. The reserve clause is the backbone of baseball. Remove it and the game will be ruined."

A radical change hit baseball and the Detroit Tigers in 1947. Jackie Robinson graduated to the major leagues April 15 when he stepped onto the diamond at Ebbets Field, taking his position at first base.

For Tiger fans, it wasn't the adding of a player that generated headlines; it was the leaving of one. In January 1947, superstar Hank Greenberg heard on the radio that he had been sold to the Pittsburgh Pirates of the National League. One of the reasons for his sudden release was his $75,000 salary.

Greenberg was truly disappointed with the announcement for two reasons. First, he hated to leave the Tigers; this was the only major league team he knew and he loved the people of Detroit as much as they had grown to love him. Second, he hoped Mr. Briggs would have told him face-to-face about the club's decision.

The slugger was determined to retire from baseball and not report to the Pirates until John Galbreath and the Bucs made him an offer he couldn't refuse. The proposed contract included a $25,000 raise, a private room on the road, the opportunity to travel by plane instead of train, and one of Mr. Galbreath's race horses. The Pirates agreed on each item, although Greenberg never saw the horse.

During his one-year stay in Pittsburgh, Hank Greenberg adopted an apt pupil. The National League Home Run King for 1946 was Ralph Kiner. Greenberg took the young slugger under his wing, passed along his work ethic and taught him the strike zone. His tutoring worked. Kiner went on to hit 51 round-trippers that year, beginning a successful journey on his road to the Hall of Fame.

After he left Pittsburgh, Greenberg served as a baseball executive for several clubs. He died of cancer in 1986 at age 75.

Rookie Vic Wertz was brought into the Tiger camp in 1947 with the hope of replacing the power lost with Hank Greenberg's departure. The left-handed-hitting Wertz, indeed, showed promise, but with only six homers for the season he was unable to fill the void. George Kell (.320) was the only Tiger to bat over .300.

League leads for the Tigers in 1947 were dubious honors, at best. Hal Newhouser (17-17) led the circuit in losses. Sitting atop the American League in errors at their respective positions were shortstop Eddie Lake (43) and third-baseman Kell (20). It's amazing, therefore, that Steve O'Neill was able to lead his team to a second-place finish behind the eventual World Champion New York Yankees.

The luck soured for Manager O'Neill in 1948 and his team was able to squeak just beyond a .500 mark with a 78-76 record and finish the year in fifth place. Although Hoot Evers (.314) and George Kell (.304) had decent years and Hal Newhouser showed he was a master on the mound with his league-leading 21 victories, there was no Hank Greenberg around to produce a victory with one swing of the bat.

Vic Wertz proved he had physical prowess with his home run production. Later he would show that he had mental and spiritual power when he overcame polio and returned to playing Major League Baseball.

When the lights were turned on June 15, 1948, the Tigers played their first night game at Briggs Stadium.

The biggest headline made by the Tigers during the '48 season appeared on June 16 when the *Detroit Free Press* described how 54,480 fans witnessed Newhouser's 4-1 victory over Philadelphia. The important story was not the score, but that the game was played under the lights—the first night game at home for the Detroit Tigers. With this addition to Briggs Stadium, all American League teams were able to play night baseball.

George Kell nosed out Boston's Ted Williams by a fraction of a point for the 1949 batting title in the American League. His .343 average prevented Williams from winning the "Triple Crown" — leading the league in home runs, RBI and batting average. Even the mighty bat of Ted Williams, however, could not overcome the crafty managing of Casey Stengel, first-year skipper for the New York Yankees. Joe DiMaggio was out for half the year due to injury and illness. In his absence, Stengel used substitution and an innovation he called "platooning," i.e., utilizing right-handed hitters against lefties and vice-versa, to win the pennant by one game over the Red Sox.

The 1949 Tigers also began the year with a new manager—Robert Abial "Red" Rolfe. The former

Yankee third baseman had to follow in the footsteps of a beloved pilot. His predecessor, Steve O'Neill, did not have a losing season during his six-year stint with Detroit. Unfortunately, neither Rolfe nor any of his players was unable to generate headlines. Manager Rolfe and his Tigers had to settle for a fourth-place finish.

Besides Kell's splendid hitting, the only other batter to crack the .300 mark was Vic Wertz (.304), who also led the Bengals that year with 20 home runs.

Newhouser (18-11) and Trucks (19-11) were consistent, but not overpowering as in previous campaigns.

Red Rolfe and his Tigers showed considerable improvement in 1950 by finishing second, just three games behind the soon-to-be World Champion New York Yankees. George Kell's 218 hits led the majors, but his .340 average fell 14 points shy of Billy Goodman of the Red Sox. While not leading the league in homers, the Tigers did show some extra-base muscle as Kell was the league leader with 56 doubles, and Hoot Evers copped the same honors with his 11 triples.

Hometown boy Art Houtteman was a so-so pitcher for five years with the Tigers. In 1949, however, his star shone brighter. He posted a superb 19-12 mark and led the American League with four shutouts. Fred Hutchinson (17-8) and Dizzy Trout (13-5) were masterful in the clutch, but Hal Newhouser dropped to 15-13 with an ERA of 4.34.

The 1950 season marked the last of Harry Heilmann in the broadcast

Walter Briggs, Jr. - better known as "Spike" - took on increased duties during the time his father owned the team.

booth. He was able to overcome bouts with arthritis, but not cancer. He died the following July. Replacing him was veteran Ty Tyson, who took the mike for two seasons before retiring a second time.

In 1951, the Tigers had their first losing season in nine years when they finished fifth with a 73-81 record. The only Tiger to hit better than .300 was reliable George Kell (.319). For the second year in a row, Kell led the league in fielding average for third basemen. Kell, sore knees and all, had to use every ounce of quickness to reach a ball hit to the left side of the infield. His teammate, Johnny Lipon, known

Eddie Gaedel, the infamous number 1/8, has his one and only major league at-bat against the Tigers. (Photo: *National Baseball Hall of Fame Library – Cooperstown, N.Y.*)

more for his hitting than his fielding, led all shortstops for the second year in a row with 33 errors.

Another native Detroit hurler, Ted Gray (7-14), and Dizzy Trout (9-14) had the "honor" of tying for the league lead in losses. Newhouser's 6-6 record showed everyone, including himself, that his best days were behind him.

No record of the 1951 season would be complete without recalling the introduction of the most famous midget since Tom Thumb. On August 19, in Sportsman's Park during a game against the Tigers, St. Louis Browns' owner Bill Veeck sent to the plate 3' 7", 65-pound, Eddie Gaedel. Standing at the

plate, wearing the number 1/8 on his back, the crouching Gaedel gave Tiger Pitcher Bob Cain a strike zone of less than two inches. Gaedel walked on four straight pitches. The next day, American League President Will Harridge negated Gaedel's contract, claiming that his appearance was "detrimental to baseball."

On January 17, 1952, a chapter of Detroit Tiger history came to a close. Walter O. Briggs, the sometimes outspoken, often benevolent, always fan-conscious owner of the Bengals, died at his winter home in Miami. The reins of the team fell into the hands of his son, Spike.

The 1952 season was less than

half over when young Spike Briggs realized that team ownership meant having to make unpleasant decisions. The Tigers had won only 23 of 72 games, were mired in last place and showed absolutely no promise of challenging the Yankees for the American League pennant. He called Manager Red Rolfe into his office for a meeting. Before the ink was dry on Rolfe's letter of resignation, Fred Hutchinson was called from the mound to take over as manager.

In an effort to turn the team around, on June 3, 1952, the Tiger front office ratified an unpopular trade. Current Tiger hero, George Kell, along with Dizzy Trout, Johnny Lipon and Hoot Evers, were traded to the Red Sox for Walt Dropo, Bill Wight, Fred Hatfield, Johnny Pesky and Don Lenhardt. Fans were furious. They believed the Tigers were self-destructing.

Hutchinson had three strikes against him from the first day on the job. First, he had to convince the players that he was no longer their teammate, but their boss. Second, he came to the job without one day's managerial experience in either the major or minor leagues. Third, he was asked to lead a squad that would eventually compile its worst record ever (50-104) and, for the first time in its history, wind up in the American League basement, 14 full games behind seventh-place St. Louis.

No pitcher ended the season with a winning percentage and Art Houtteman (8-20) led all hurlers in games lost. Once again, no regular player reached the .300 mark.

Throughout baseball, tension

Managing the Tigers for the 1949 season was former Yankee third baseman, Robert "Red" Rolfe.

mounted between players and owners. Labor unions had gained benefits for industrial workers, and major league players took note. During the Winter Meetings of 1952, the former pupil of Hank Greenberg, Ralph Kiner, representing players of the National League, and Allie Reynolds of the Yankees, representing American League players, attempted to meet with the owners. Because Kiner and Reynolds brought with them an attorney, the owners refused to speak with them officially. To generate a united voice in future deliberations, they formed the Major

Al Kaline, the son of a Baltimore broom maker, is the only Tiger to hit two home runs in one inning. He did it on April 17, 1955, in a game against the Kansas City Athletics—a team that had just relocated to the heartland from their original home in Philadelphia. Kaline accomplished this remarkable feat in the sixth inning, hitting a solo shot off Bob Spicer to open the frame and a two-run blast off Bob Trice to close out a nine-run rally that propelled the Tigers to a 16-0 victory.

In the first inning, Kaline had connected off John Gray. Those three homers gave him almost as many home runs in a single game as he hit during the entire previous season (4).

The brightest new name on the Tiger roster was a youngster fresh out of high school. His name: Albert William Kaline.

League Baseball Players Association. Both Kiner and Reynolds insisted this was a guild, not a union, per se. Ten years later, however, it would become just that.

Prior to the 1953 season, the eyes of Tiger management turned toward

Pitcher Billy Hoeft was added in an attempt to shore up a sagging mound staff.

Harvey Kuenn, a 21-year-old rookie shortstop who played in just 19 games the previous year. He batted .325, and did not commit one error. Kuenn was no flash-in-the-pan. He became one of the few bright spots in the Tiger lineup during his first full year in 1953. He led all shortstops with 308 putouts and committed only 21 miscues in the field. On top of this, he hit an impressive .308. Another bright spot was Ray Boone, a third-sacker brought in from Cleveland to replace the departed George Kell, who hit .312 in just over 100 games. It looked as though the left side of the infield was as solid as Detroit had seen in ages.

Pitching was the weak link. Once again, no hurler compiled more than a .500 average. Prince Hal Newhouser pitched in only seven games and compiled an 0-1 record. It was not a fitting last year as a Tiger for such a brilliant mound artist.

Almost unnoticed in this dismal season was the initial appearance of an 18-year-old outfielder who had just graduated from a Baltimore high school and signed with the Tigers as a "bonus baby" for $30,000. In his first game, Albert William Kaline popped to center in his only time at bat and let a ball get by him in the outfield, allowing the winning run to score. For the rest of the year, he hit only .250 in 28 times at bat, not a flashy start for the 22-year run Kaline would make to the Hall of Fame.

All in all, Fred Hutchinson and his players were able to climb two notches, finishing the 1953 season in sixth place.

Following the unglamorous '53 season, Detroit fans began referring to the Tigers as "pussycats." A city used to winners and champions grew increasingly impatient for a contender. Attendance at the ballpark for the 1953 campaign dipped to under 900,000—the lowest in 10 years. The faithful also had no spectacular player to motivate them to frequent games. No longer could they go to the stadium to see a Ty Cobb, Mickey Cochrane, Hank Greenberg or George Kell. Harvey Kuenn was the closest to becoming a local hero. However, he was still relatively new and he did not hit the long ball most often associated with players who draw fans to the games. The Yankees had third-year sensation Mickey Mantle; Ted Williams still roamed left field in Boston; Cleveland's Larry Doby paved the way for African-American players in the American League. Each of these players also could jack one out of the park. That's what people wanted to see. Detroiters had to be content with a lot of new faces, none of which were joined to bodies packed with power. In 1954, the entire Tiger squad produced only 90 homers.

The young Kaline showed potential in right field. He hit a modest .276 but showed a fantastic arm that cut down 16 runners attempting to take extra bases. Harvey Kuenn led the Bengals in batting with .306.

A fifth-place finish in 1954 proved the Tigers were improving.

Unfortunately it was not fast enough for the fans, press or management. Stanley "Bucky" Harris—a seasoned pro who had 27 years of experience as a big league manager—replaced Manager Hutchinson.

The only genuine bright spot for the Tigers was a new star on the horizon. And he wore number 6.

Coming to the Tigers in 1952 was a shortstop with a sharp batting eye, Harvey Kuenn.

On June 3, 1947, the Tigers aired their first televised game on station WWDF-TV, which was later renamed WWJ-TV and is now WDIV-TV. Ty Tyson was the announcer as 17,114 fans attended the game and saw the Yankees win, 3-0, behind Spec Shea's five-hit pitching.

Because so few people owned television sets at the time, most who saw the televised game in black and white did so by squinting at 10-inch screens in local bars and hotel lobbies. Those who stood more than 20 feet away often tried to get a better view by looking through binoculars.

One of the fears of television station owners was that the players and announcers might be tempted to "ham it up" for the camera. Following the huge success of the first World Series telecast in 1947, that fear disappeared.

Chapter 11
The Kaline Impact

"There's a hitter. In my
book, he's the greatest
right-handed hitter in the
league. There's no telling
how far the kid could go.**"**

- Ted Williams,
  commenting
  on young
  Al Kaline

ON APRIL 17, 1955, DURING THE SIXTH GAME OF THE SEASON, young Al Kaline slammed two home runs in one inning—the only Tiger ever to do so—and one more during the game for good measure. By the time the season ended, he showed every indication that he was a future superstar. At the tender age of 20 he hit .340 to become the youngest ever to win an American League batting crown. He was also number-one in total bases (321) and hits (200). Of those hits, 27 left the ballpark, tying him for fourth place in the league.

For the first time in five years, Detroit ended the season with a winning record (79-75). Although they had to settle for a fifth-place finish, the team seemed to jell. The 1955 Tigers sent 775 runners across the plate to lead all teams in that department. Harvey Kuenn hit a solid .306 and third baseman Ray Boone clubbed 20 homers and knocked in a league-leading 116 runs. Nobody could complain about the Tigers' hitting. As in recent seasons, it was pitching that kept them in check. Only southpaw Billy Hoeft (16-7), in his fourth year with Detroit, showed consistency.

Even the experience of Bucky Harris and improved pitching could not elevate the Tigers of 1956 any higher than the year before. They won, in fact, three more games. Still fifth place, though.

Kaline's hitting (.314) was steady, but it was his defensive ability in right field that drew rave notices. Sportswriters praised the ease with which he mastered the tricky right-field caroms.

Frank Lary - "The Yankee Killer."

Charlie "Paw-Paw" Maxwell. Always on Sunday.

Billy Hoeft (20-14) had another solid year, but it was Frank Lary who astonished everyone, especially the New York Yankees. Not only did Lary, in just his third year with Detroit, lead the league with 21 victories, he also seemed to have a hex on the Bronx Bombers. The Yankees, who would go on to win their second consecutive American League crown in 1956 with a power-laden line-up of Mickey Mantle, Yogi Berra, Hank Bauer and Bill "Moose" Skowron, were anemic each time they faced Frank Lary. Each time Lary pitched against the Yankees during the '56 season, the Tigers came out ahead. From then on, Frank Lary was known as "The Yankee Killer."

Another crowd favorite in 1956 was left fielder Charlie Maxwell, purchased from Baltimore late in the '55 season. Maxwell hailed from Paw-Paw, a small town west of Kalamazoo. "Paw-Paw" Maxwell hit 28 home runs to lead the club in 1956, and many of them came during Sunday home games. Fans came to Briggs Stadium on Sunday afternoons expecting the left-handed slugger to park one in the right-field upper deck. Many times, they got their wish. During

one Sunday double-header with the Yankees, Maxwell tied a major league record when he homered in four consecutive times at bat. He hit homers on five of the next eight Sundays; each blast either tied the score or won the game.

Future Hall-of-Famer Bucky Harris closed his 29-year career as a big league manager following the 1956 season.

Also ending any relationship with the Tiger organization was the estate of the late Walter O. Briggs. Legal details that allowed the club to be sold were finally spelled out.

Bidding for ownership were two teams of investors—one headed by Bill Veeck, the other by a syndicate of 11 radio/television executives led by Kenyon Brown, Fred Knorr and John Fetzer. Loyal Detroit fans, mostly conservatives, chafed at the idea of Veeck owning their club. Veeck, the "P.T. Barnum of base-ball," was fond of gimmicks in order to draw crowds. They remembered his signing of Eddie Gaedel in 1951. Brown, Knorr and Fetzer won the bid effective October 1, 1956, and hired Spike Briggs as general manager.

Perhaps it was the lack of big-market appeal or the realization that the Tigers just didn't have the tools necessary to win a pennant or a World Series. Whatever the reason, no line of proven managers stood on the corner of Michigan and Trumbull awaiting interviews for the job as Detroit skipper. The decision caused internal bickering between Fetzer and Briggs. Fetzer wanted the veteran Al "Señor" Lopez; Briggs ignored his suggestion and hired a totally unproved entity named Jack Tighe. Tighe had not one day's experience in a major league uniform as a manager or a player. It was a long shot that did not pay off.

Angered by Briggs' decision, Fetzer forced him to resign before the '57 season was three weeks old.

The 1957 Tigers won four games less than the year before, but they were able to rise one notch in the standings to fourth place, despite the fact that not one batter reached the .300 mark. Even Al Kaline (.295), while consistent, did not produce eye-popping numbers.

Right-hander Jim Bunning, a likable Kentucky native, had won a total of eight games in his first two years with Detroit. He surpassed all expectations in 1957 by leading the American League in innings pitched (267.1) and victories (20).

Paul Foytack, fourth-year pitcher with the club, had led the league the previous year in issuing walks. In 1957, he regained enough control to end the season with a 14-11 mark.

The Tigers set off an alarm with only 21 wins in 49 games to start the 1958 campaign. Management had to make a change. Because it is much easier to fire one manager than 25 players, the inexperienced Jack Tighe was dismissed. Instead of replacing him with a salty veteran, the Tigers hired Henry "Bill" Norman, a former outfielder who played a total of 37 games in two years with the White Sox. Like his predecessor, Norman had absolutely no experience as a manager.

Norman was able to generate a few more wins and end the year with a 77-77 record and a familiar fifth-place finish.

Eleven years after Jackie Robinson broke the color barrier in big-league baseball, the Tigers and Boston Red Sox were the only teams in the majors who fielded white players only. On June 6, 1958, this changed for Detroit when a native of the Dominican Republic, Osvaldo "Ozzie" Virgil, took his position at third base at Briggs Stadium. The 29,000 fans in attendance welcomed him with a standing ovation. Virgil responded with five hits in five at-bats to help Detroit whip the Washington Senators, 9-2.

Ozzie, who was acquired in a trade with the Giants, played with the Tigers until mid-season of 1961, when he was traded to Kansas City.

Both Kaline (.313) and Kuenn (.319) got back on the plus side of .300 in '58, and Gail Harris, a first baseman who, along with Virgil, came to Detroit from the Giants, led the club with 20 home runs.

At shortstop that year for his only season with Detroit was a scrappy, but aging, ex-Yankee who would later play an even more important role with the Tigers. His

The first non-white player for the Tigers was Osvaldo "Ozzie" Virgil who, in his first game in 1958, went five-for-five.

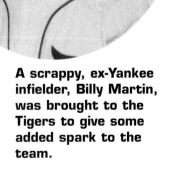

A scrappy, ex-Yankee infielder, Billy Martin, was brought to the Tigers to give some added spark to the team.

Following a 17-year career in the big leagues (10 with Detroit), pitcher Jim Bunning was elected to the U.S. House of Representatives and to the U.S. Senate.

name was Alfred Manuel "Billy" Martin. *The Saturday Evening Post* had dubbed Martin as "the most unhappy man in the major leagues." That dubious distinction became apparent when, maybe in an attempt to light a fire under his team, during spring training, he called the Tigers "spoiled babies." The normally reserved Al Kaline took issue with the remark and defended his teammates.

Frank Lary was the new American League leader in innings pitched that year (260); his 16-15 record topped the Tiger hurlers. Meanwhile, Bunning slipped to a 14-12 mark.

Following the '58 campaign, the Tiger family was shocked with the news of an auto accident that killed Mel Ott, former Giant great who, for the past three years, had shared the broadcast duties in Detroit with Van Patrick. Replacing Ott was fan-favorite George Kell. The likable third baseman, with a southern drawl that reflected his Arkansas upbringing, would become even more popular with the fans as a broadcaster.

If Bill Norman left the impression during the 1958 campaign that he could create a bona fide contender out of the players on the Tiger roster the next year, the fans, press and management would soon learn that this was all but a dream. The 1959 season began slowly for the Tigers, then ground to a screeching halt. With their club entrenched in last place with only two victories in 17 games, the Tiger brass reacted without hesitation. Out was Bill Norman; in was Jimmy Dykes—no stranger to saving teams from self-destruction. Twice before—for the White Sox and the Cincinnati Reds—Dykes had restored teams desperate for leadership. The Tigers played .540 ball the rest of the season under Dykes, climbing out of the basement to a fourth-place finish, with a 76-78 record.

Harvey Kuenn regained his batting eye and led the league with a blistering .353 average. Al Kaline was not far behind, second in the league with .327; he also chipped in 27 homers and a league-leading .530 slugging average. Charlie Maxwell led the Bengals with 31 four-baggers—12 of them on Sundays.

Jim Bunning's 201 strikeouts bettered the record of any other pitcher in 1959. Tied for the Tiger lead with 17 wins were pitchers Bunning, Lary and Don Mossi, who had come to the Tigers in a trade with Cleveland for Billy Martin.

The 1960 season was the year of unpredictable and sometimes weird changes. On the plus side, this was the first year for Ernie Harwell behind the microphone. Harwell, a future Hall-of-Fame broadcaster, would endear Tiger fans and become *the* voice of the Tigers.

Other changes were not met with as much acceptance, however. To give the team a "fresh look," Owner Fetzer and Club President

Bill DeWitt agreed to replace the Olde English "D" on the home uniforms, replacing it with "Detroit" written in script across the front of the shirt. Tiger fans resented the change and, after a one-year trial, the script was replaced with the familiar "D."

The "advance-retreat" pattern that plagued the Tigers in recent years returned. While the team was mired in sixth place on August 2, Bill DeWitt traded Manager Dykes to Cleveland for Manager Joe Gordon. It was the first mid-season managerial swap in big-league history. For one day, Coach Billy Hitchcock managed the Tigers. Detroit won the contest that evening, thus leaving Hitchcock with a most impressive percentage of victories. Gordon's 26 wins during the remaining 57 games of the season did nothing to raise the team's standing above sixth place and Gordon was not asked to return the next year.

One change that won the approval of nearly everyone was the reinstatement of Ladies' Day, following a 16-year absence. Once again, those Tiger fans of the feminine persuasion could see a game on designated days for 50 cents.

Arguably the most controversial trade in Tiger history occurred prior to the 1960 season. Harvey Kuenn, American League batting champion the previous year, was traded to Cleveland in exchange for slugging outfielder Rocco Domenico "Rocky" Colavito. The handsome New York-born Italian-American slammed 42 home runs in '59 for Cleveland to lead the league in that department. As pop-ular as Kuenn was to the fans of Detroit, Colavito was just as popular in Cleveland. Neither city endorsed the trade. In a sense, the Tigers were trading a hitter with average for a hitter with power. One of the Tiger front office staff commented to the press: "We traded hamburger for T-bone steak."

Long-time fans of Harvey Kuenn did not appreciate that characterization of the shortstop-turned-outfielder who had given them many thrills over the past eight seasons. Their anger increased as Kuenn went on to hit .308 for the Indians, while no Tiger hit .300.

The Tigers did get the home run power they sought. Colavito belted 35 round-trippers—the most since Hank Greenberg hit 44 in 1946. That onslaught brought additional fans into Briggs Stadium.

Another one of Colavito's skills that drew "ooohs" and "aaahs" from the fans was his powerful throwing arm. Once, during pre-game batting practice, Colavito threw a ball from home plate into the upper deck of the left-field stands. While his throws were not always accurate, he nabbed five runners trying to score on what would have been a sacrifice fly had the ball been handled by any other outfielder.

Making their debut for the Tigers in 1960 were two players who would figure prominently in the club's future. One was a plucky infielder from Hartford, Connecticut, named Dick McAuliffe. The other was a burly young Texan named Norman

Following a disastrous 1955 season and an almost-but-not-quite one-game miss of the Conference championship in '56, Lion's Coach Buddy Parker announced to a shocked press corps that he would resign as coach because he no longer had the confidence of his players. Replacing Parker was his assistant, George Wilson.

Wilson responded in '57 with Tobin Rote at quarterback in place of the aging Bobby Layne. The new blood shot new life into the team. They finished the season leading the division and, before 55,263 screaming fans in Briggs Stadium, clobbered the Cleveland Browns 59-14 to win the NFL Championship.

Pitcher Hank Aguirre was a fan favorite in spite of his anemic batting average. Over a 16-year career in the majors (10 with Detroit), he hit only .085. When batting in a game, if Aguirre fouled off a pitch, he sometimes received a standing ovation from the Tiger Stadium faithful.

"Stormin' Norman" Cash, who handled duties at first base. Cash, who spent two seasons with the White Sox, smacked 18 home runs in 1960 and hit .286. The following season, he would increase those figures dramatically with a "secret weapon."

Pitching tapered off in 1960. Frank Lary led all moundsmen in innings pitched (274) but could muster only a 15-15 mark. Bunning slipped to 11-14. The Tigers did, however, find a solid stopper in Hank Aguirre when they turned this left-handed starter into a reliever. It wasn't enough, though, as the Tigers finished with a 71-83 record and in sixth place.

Major League Baseball initiated drastic changes the next year. Until this time, the National and American Leagues fielded eight teams—the same number with which they started back in 1876 and 1901, respectively. Two more teams were added to the American League in 1961. At the request of owner Cal Griffith, the Washington Senators moved to Minneapolis and became the "Minnesota Twins." A new group of players formed another version of the "Washington Senators," and another 25 players formed a team in Los Angeles called the "Angels." Because of the added teams, the schedule was increased by eight to 162 games.

On Opening Day in Detroit, the name of the familiar stadium on the corner of Michigan and Trumbull was officially changed to "Tiger Stadium"—the last name that would ever be placed on the outside of its walls.

Grabbing most of the headlines in baseball during the 1961 season was the chase by Mickey Mantle and Roger Maris of Babe Ruth's all-time record of 60 home runs in a season. The "M and M Boys," as reporters dubbed them, battled until mid-September when Mantle, now hobbled with aching knees, fell behind, while Maris continued his assault and hit 61. It was a major league record that would stand until 1998, when the Cardinals' Mark McGwire won headlines by smashing 70 home runs.

Roger Maris wasn't the only one hitting homers in 1961. Detroit's Rocky Colavito clubbed 45, and Norm Cash hit 41. Under new manager Bob Scheffing, the Tigers clawed their way toward a whopping 101 victories and a second-place finish. That would have been enough to win the pennant easily during most seasons, but the Yankees were just too strong, and finished eight games ahead of Detroit.

This was the most incredible recovery in Tiger history. Scheffing, with basically the same team that won only 71 times the year before, motivated his players to new, unexpected heights.

It wasn't exactly motivation that pushed Norm Cash to hit 41 homers and increase his batting average by 75 points to a league-leading .361 and rack up 193 hits, more than any other player in the junior circuit. Instead, as Cash later admitted, he had a secret weapon. He corked his bat. To "cork" a bat, a player drills a hole approximately 15 inches deep from the end of the barrel down through the center of the bat, stuffs it with cork, then plugs the end of the bat with wood. With a lighter weight bat, Cash was able to generate more speed in his swing and more "spring" as the ball hit the bat, giving him an unfair advantage over other hitters.

If one of his bats should break and reveal what he had done, Cash would have been subject to a fine and suspension. Norm did not want to push his luck. Consequently, following the 1961 season, he never again used a corked bat.

Frank Lary (23-9) hurled an amazing 22 complete games, more than anyone else in either league. Jim Bunning (17-11) was his old self, and Don Mossi was 15-7.

On July 17, 1961, newspapers around the nation carried the announcement that Tyrus Raymond Cobb, age 79, died from internal bleeding and hard living.

The man hailed by many as the game's fiercest competitor was laid

Norm Cash in 1961 waving two of his "secret weapons."

Ty Cobb was buried in a mausoleum in a tiny cemetery in Royston, Georgia, in 1961. Contrary to myths promoted by some critics, his funeral was attended by masses of people.

to rest next to his mother and father in a mausoleum at the City Cemetery, Royston, Georgia. Some historians, even the creators of a recent movie based on his life, claim that only three people attended Ty Cobb's funeral. Charlie Cobb, grandson of The Peach, disputes that myth. "They're wrong. I was there," he says. "The funeral was packed. Little Leaguers lined the walk as his casket was carried to the mausoleum. Hundreds of townspeople crowded the cemetery. Even an ailing Mickey Cochrane attended." To this day, from his insurance office in Edgewater, Florida, Charlie Cobb reminds us that his

grandfather never received credit for the immense amount of charitable work he did.

"Even his own teammates did not know that he supported orphanages in Detroit and regularly sent money to Mickey Cochrane when he was sick, as well as to some widows of former ballplayers, because Major League Baseball had not yet had a pension system," Charlie Cobb says. The people of Royston certainly loved Ty Cobb. They built a museum in his honor which is now part of the Royston-based Ty Cobb Healthcare System. He was never too busy to autograph a baseball for a youngster and spoke freely

In appreciation for the contributions made by Ty Cobb, former club secretary Harry Sesson, general manager Jim Campbell and owner John Fetzer help unveil a memorial at the corner of Michigan and Trumbull. The inscription tells it all.

with friends and neighbors, many of whom he knew most of his life.

Shortly after he retired, Cobb gave a reporter $2,000 to give anonymously to an injured ballplayer. That act of kindness never to made it into the papers. In 1949, Ty Cobb gave $100,000 to start a hospital in Royston that bears his name.

When the final record is written, Cobb's life should be put into balance. To many reporters of his time and to many modern-day historians, Ty Cobb was a great player but perhaps the meanest, most acid-tongued man ever to step between the white lines of a baseball diamond. Those who knew him and understood him saw another side. He was a hard-fighting man who used every weapon— physical or psychological—to win a game. He was also a shy man who shunned publicity for his good deeds; perhaps he feared being misunderstood by the opposition as being soft. But the only thing soft about Ty Cobb was his heart.

Just ask the good folks of Royston, Georgia.

On November 14, 1961, John

Announcer Ray Lane (second from right) did not announce the approaching fires from outside Tiger Stadium in 1967 for fear of causing a panic.

Fetzer became sole owner of the Detroit Baseball Club following the unexpected death of his partner, Fred Knorr. Despite this tragedy, the Tigers were able to generate some degree of stability amidst unsettling changes in the Detroit area during the early '60s. The city was showing signs of racial polarization. Whites moved to Southfield, Birmingham, Royal Oak, Oak Park, Madison Heights and other suburbs. Downtown businesses also relocated to Northland Mall and to other venues more attractive to suburban shoppers. Violent crime within the city limits increased.

Many families who used to drive downtown for shopping or recreation now feared driving south of Eight Mile Road, especially after sundown.

In 1962, Norm Cash, sans corked bat, managed to hit 39 home runs, but regressed in consistency. His average dropped more than 100 points to .243, as his team ended the season in fourth place. Al Kaline (.304)—the only Tiger to hit over .300—slammed 27 homers. His figures would have been even more impressive had he not broken his collarbone while making a game-ending somersault catch of a ball hit by Yogi Berra in Yankee Stadium in May, keeping Kaline out of the lineup for nearly two months. Rocky Colavito had to pick up some of the slack. He blasted 37 round-trippers and collected a league-leading 309 total bases as the Tigers finished fourth with a record of 85-76.

Manager Scheffing summoned Hank Aguirre from the bullpen and made him a starter. The strategy paid off as the tall southpaw compiled a 16-8 record and led the league with a 2.21 ERA. Ace of the staff was Jim Bunning with a record of 19-10.

A mere 24 wins in the first 60 games of 1963 plunged the Tigers to ninth place. Recently appointed General Manager Jim Campbell, in an attempt to stop the train heading nowhere, called for Scheffing's resignation and hired Charles Dressen, a manager of proven competence. This time, experience paid off. Under Dressen's leadership, the club played better than .500 ball to end the season in a fifth-place tie with Cleveland.

Once again, Kaline's .312 average was the only one better than .300 in 1963. His home run total of 27 was one better than Norman Cash's to lead the club.

Another piece of the puzzle that would provide the basis for clubs of the future was a young, 6' 3" catcher. Bill Freehan, a Detroit native and graduate of the University of Michigan, accepted a $100,000 signing bonus from the Tigers two years earlier. To the delight of Campbell, Dressen and the rest of the Tiger brass, Freehan demonstrated amazing maturity for his 21 years in the way he handled pitchers and kept potential base-stealers honest.

Phil Regan (15-9), a fourth-year right-hander from Otsego, Michigan, and relief specialist Terry Fox (8-6) were the only two pitchers to have more wins than losses.

Two rookie pitchers in 1963 who later would become dynamic forces were southpaw Michael "Mickey" Lolich, who drew few praises with his 5-9 record, and a brash right-hander from Chicago named Dennis Dale McLain. Denny appeared in 19 games that year and produced two wins in three decisions.

Catcher Bill Freehan's bat and baseball instincts made him an ideal on-the-field leader.
[Photo: *Thomas Donaghue*]

Following the '63 season, Tiger management had to admit the addition of Rocky Colavito to the line up was not paying the dividends for which they hoped. In November, he was traded to Kansas City.

Following a 12-13 season with the Tigers, pitcher Jim Bunning was traded to the Philadelphia Phillies of the National League. Bunning would pitch eight more seasons (and a perfect game in 1964) before moving from the baseball diamond to political circles. He was elected a United States Congressman from Kentucky in 1986, then a U.S. Senator in 1998.

Attendance at Tiger Stadium dropped to 821,592 during 1963, because of the relatively poor showing of the club and because of the increasing fear of fans to attend games in downtown Detroit.

The tension-filled atmosphere of the Motor City became even more acute when, on Friday, November 22, President John F. Kennedy was cut down by an assassin's bullet in Dallas, Texas. Adding to the unrest was a decision on the part of the Detroit Lions to play a scheduled football game on Sunday at Tiger Stadium. To many Detroiters, especially the poor, this was a slap in the face to the memory of their fallen champion.

The city that *Look* magazine described earlier that year as the "city on the go" for poor people who wanted to fulfill the American dream elected Jerome Cavanaugh as mayor. Cavanaugh, who resembled President Kennedy in looks and charisma, promised to initiate a renaissance with the mission of restoring Detroit to a safe, prosperous environment.

A renaissance of another type took place in 1964 at Tiger Stadium. The Bengals ended the season in fourth place with a record of 85-77. Part of the reason for the improvement was a new fixture at third base. Don Wert, in his sophomore year, was not known for his potent bat but he was able to field his position. Outside of Baltimore's Brooks Robinson, he ranked with the best in the league at fielding the hot corner.

Another second-year player for the Tigers was left fielder William James "Gates" Brown. The left hander showed modest power with 15 home runs. It was not so much Gates' performance on the field that concerned management as was his potential for trouble off the diamond. Gates Brown had been recruited from a federal penitentiary, where he had just completed serving a sentence. Gates, however, demonstrated that people can change. He was a model citizen who dedicated himself to the Tigers and to the community.

Bill Freehan continued to

Don Wert fielded third base with the best of them.

improve not only behind the plate, but also in the batter's box. His .300 average and 18 homers proved just that.

Right hander Dave Wickersham, obtained from Kansas City in the trade for Rocky Colavito, had a fine 19-12 year. Showing improvement were Mickey Lolich (18-9), plus relievers Fred Gladding (7-4) and Larry Sherry (7-5).

Willie Horton's star burned brightly in 1965. He hit 29 home runs and knocked in 104. Teamed with stars such as Norm Cash (30 homers and 82 RBI) and pitchers Mickey Lolich (15-9), Denny McLain (16-6), Hank Aguirre (14-10) and Joe Sparma (13-8), one would think the Tigers would be serious contenders for the pennant. The best the Bengals could do with all this talent was to finish in fourth place, 13 games behind the Twins.

Highlighting the team's performance in 1965 was a relief appearance on June 15 against Boston by Denny McLain who, in one of the rare moments of his colorful career, came out of the bullpen and fanned the first seven batters he faced. Denny went on to strike out 15 batters in 6 2/3 innings, leading the Tigers to a 6-5 win. Five days later, Al Kaline notched his 1000th career RBI as the Tigers rallied form eight runs behind to defeat Kansas City, 12-8, for their eighth consecutive victory.

In November 1965, Ford Frick resigned as baseball commissioner and was replaced by William D. Eckert, a retired U.S. Air Force general. Like his predecessor, Eckert lacked the power and the boldness of a Judge Landis who might have prevented some future problems that would threaten the foundation of America's pastime, primarily the rise of the player's union and the issue of the reserve clause.

The Tigers got out of the gate quickly in 1966, winning 16 of their first 26 games. Unexpectedly, Manager Dressen walked into Jim Campbell's office and announced he would have to leave the team because of failing health. On May 16, he suffered his second heart attack in as many years.

Detroit Coach Bob Swift took over for the ailing Dressen and led the team to 24 wins in 42 games until he, too, became incapacitated with a stomach problem and was hospitalized. Coach Frank Skaff, once again, became acting manager. Barely three months later, on August 10, 67-year-old Charlie Dressen died in a Detroit hospital.

Through all this emotional upheaval, the Tigers were able to capture a third-place finish, and Denny McLain became a 20-game winner. Although no batter hit over .300, steady performances by Kaline, Cash, outfielder Jim Northrup (called the "Silver Fox" because of his prematurely graying hair), McAuliffe, Wert, Horton, Stanley and Freehan kept the Bengals in every contest.

Following the 1966 season, Kansas City Athletics owner Charles O. Finley announced he was moving the franchise to Oakland beginning with the 1968 campaign. Also in 1966, the Major League Baseball Players

The first player the Tigers selected in the inaugural amateur draft in 1965 was catcher Gene Lamont who was the 13th pick overall.

Lamont homered in his first major league at-bat on September 2, 1970, and went on to hit three more home runs and compile a .233 average during his 87-game major league career spent exclusively with the Tigers from 1970-1975.

Lamont later became the manager of the Pittsburgh Pirates.

Association (MLBPA) elected Marvin Miller, who had resigned as assistant to the president of the United Steelworkers of America, to serve as its legal director. The articulate Miller, who looked more like a Wall Street executive than a union representative, calmly voiced his positions to the press. He took up the cause of Curt Flood who, two years earlier, argued that baseball's reserve clause—which bound a player to a team even after he was eliminated from the playing roster—was unconstitutional and not in the best interest of either baseball or the player. The players, he said, were no more than "slaves" (a claim initially used in 1879 by the Cincinnati Redstockings that paved the way for Detroit to enter the National League) in a system that was immoral. As labor unrest brewed, the Tigers of 1967 played one of their finest, yet most frustrating seasons in history. During this year of turmoil, a few key plays allowed the American League pennant to slip out of their hands, just as a few key events turned the Motor City into a war zone.

The Tigers began their 1967

Big Earl Wilson was not only an outstanding pitcher but a respected hitter as well.

season on a positive note. Still mourning the death of former skipper Charlie Dressen, the players and staff rallied behind Manager Mayo Smith. The white-haired Smith, who resembled an ideal grandfather, immediately developed a group of promising ballplayers into a pennant contender.

No single player was the key to success. Al Kaline (.308), for instance, was again the only one to hit over .300 as he led his club with 25 home runs. Instead, the secret to Smith's formula for winning was balance.

Ray Oyler, a slender, 165-pounder on a good day, barely hit over .200, but gave the Tigers a solid glove at shortstop. Freehan established himself as the premier defensive catcher in all of baseball and added 20 home runs to the Detroit attack. Cash (22 home runs), McAuliffe (22 home runs) and, playing in his third full season with Detroit, outfielder Willie Horton (19 home runs) let opposing pitchers know that any of these Tigers could change the score with one swing of the bat.

The most pleasant surprise in 1967 for Mayo Smith and the Tiger faithful was pitching. For so long the weak link in the Tigers' chain, the mound staff was now second to none. Earl Wilson, picked up in a mid-season trade with the Red Sox the year before, had a banner year by tying Boston's Jim Lonborg with a league-leading 22 wins. Joe Sparma (16-9) also had his best year in his fourth season with Detroit. Rookie Mike Marshall, a native of Adrian, Michigan, was a doctoral candidate in kinesiology at Michigan State University who used a scientific approach to pitching. After spending two years with Detroit, Marshall would develop into the league's most respected reliever for several other teams.

Throughout the year, the Tigers battled the Boston Red Sox led by Triple-Crown winner Carl Yastrzemski.

During the heat of the pennant drive, however, another battle was being staged outside the park. At 6:15 p.m., on Saturday, July 23, Detroit police raided a "blind pig"—an after-hours illegal gambling house on Twelfth Street, just north of Clairmount, in the heart of the ghetto. The raid was not an unusual activity for this kind of neighborhood, but for some unknown reason, a significant number of citizens viewed the police action as a chance to strike back. The city, torn more than ever by racial strife and a 15 percent unemployment rate, was a powder keg ready to erupt. On that night, the explosion in downtown Detroit was heard around the nation. Buildings were set afire. Gangs of rioters looted stores.

Those who attended the Tigers-Yankees game on Sunday afternoon were unaware that trouble was moving closer to the stadium. Police and some lawless marauders drew battle lines just a few blocks away. When smoke rose in the sky over the left-field stands, the public address announcer was told not to cause an alarm with an announcement. "Jim Campbell and radio station WJR told us not to mention anything about the smoke," said

radio broadcaster Ray Lane. At the game's end, the public address announcer advised the fans that certain scheduled buses would not be able to meet them. Manager Smith urged his players to return home as quickly as possible.

The warning was of particular concern to Tiger slugger Willie

The Tigers often scheduled special days that brought new fans to Michigan and Trumbull.

Special events such as "Lutheran Night" or "Ladies Day" helped fill the ballpark.

Horton, who lived in the burning city. Instead of escaping to the trenches of the suburbs, he initiated a brave attempt to quell the disturbances. "I could not believe the riot," he said. "I went on my own to Livernois and the freeway in my uniform." Some fans close to being stranded due to curtailed bus service yelled encouragement to Willie Horton: "Willie! Save our city!"

But even someone as popular as Willie Horton could do nothing to stem the onrushing crowd set on destroying anything in its path. Mayor Cavanaugh, a promising Democratic politician, saw his career collapse with each building. Michigan Governor George Romney waited several hours before requesting federal troops. When he did, more than 4,700 uniformed soldiers flooded the streets. Army tanks and Jeeps crowded Woodward Avenue. Shots were fired.

Over the next seven days, 43

The future of baseball lies with the youth. Hence, Little Leaguers and members of the Dugout Club were given special consideration.

people were killed, more than 7,000 were arrested, and more than 1,700 businesses were ransacked.

The Tigers' scheduled games for July 25 and 26 against the Orioles were shifted to Baltimore.

The riots ended on July 30, but aftershocks remained. Nearly 70,000 citizens moved from the city limits of Detroit to other parts of Michigan and the nation. Tension even mounted in the stands at the stadium. Fights between fans were common. Some threw debris at ballplayers who angered them. Television commentators described Detroit as "a city of violence."

The official seal of the City of Detroit offers a motto: *Resurget Cineribus*—"It will rise from the ashes." Detroit faced the challenge of making that hope a reality.

The Tigers had the best team on paper in 1967, but Boston, led by Triple-Crown winner Carl Yastrzemski, stayed close behind. The nerve-racking strain created

"Bat Day" was always a favorite ...

Larry Doby, the first black player in the American League, played 18 games for Detroit in 1959, his last season in the majors.

by such a drive for the pennant along with the disruption outside the stadium tested the patience of the best. Even Al Kaline, the quiet, unassuming model of deportment, succumbed to the pressure. Following a game toward the end of the season when he left men on base after grounding out, he returned to the dugout, slammed his fist against the water cooler and broke his hand. That rare display of anger cost Al Kaline one full month of playing time.

The only hope for Detroit fans in 1967 was the quest for the pennant. Coming down to the last day of the season, the Tigers trailed the Red Sox by a half game. A Tiger sweep, coupled with a Red Sox loss would give Detroit the pennant; or a Tiger sweep and a Red Sox win would force a best-of-three playoff between the clubs.

The Tigers kept their hopes alive as they won the front end of the twinbill, 6-4, behind the strong pitching of Joe Sparma and the timely hitting of Willie Horton who had a homer and a double. In the nightcap, the Tigers trailed in the ninth, 8-5. With runners on first and second and one out, Dick McAuliffe, who hit into only one double play all year long, hit a weak grounder to second that resulted in a twin-killing. Meanwhile, Boston defeated Minnesota, 5-3, to win their first American League Pennant in 21 years.

The fans, with the echoes of the summer riots still ringing in their ears, stormed the field in frustration. They fought with each other. Some threatened stadium guards and police. They ripped up the pitcher's mound, tore out home plate, grabbed chunks of grass and tore seats from the bleachers. By the time order was restored, Tiger Stadium, torn to bits, resembled the feeling of the Tiger players, many of whom sat in the clubhouse silently sobbing.

Sportswriter Joe Falls described it best: "It was the lowest point in the history of baseball in Detroit."

That display of mob violence,

...as was "Family Night." Here, "Umpire" Sonny Eliot and catcher Jim Price admire a hit by one player's son.

both inside and outside their stadium, gave the Tigers even more to think about over the long, cold winter that lay ahead.

Chapter 12

The Year of the Tiger

"It was Christmas, the Fourth of
July, Halloween, V-E Day and
Mardi Gras all wrapped
into one.**"**

> - *The Detroit News* editorial
> describing the Downtown
> celebration of
> October 10, 1968

**Skipper Mayo Smith was masterful in leading the
Tigers to the '68 league championship and made some
gutsy moves in the World Series.**

DURING THE BASEBALL SEASON OF 1968, major league pitchers combined to post a 2.98 ERA. It was the lowest such mark in nearly 40 years. For the most part, batters were subdued. Only one American League hitter—Carl Yastrzemski—hit over .300, and by just a hair. His .301 average was the lowest ever for a batting champion. Among the starters, Willie Horton led the Tigers with .285.

Baseball experts offered plenty of reasons for this anemic display of offense. Some pointed to the fact that pitchers were stronger and faster. Hurlers such as Denny McLain, with his exaggerated leg kick and high overhand delivery, took full advantage of the 15-inch mound height and generous strike zone allowed by umpires.

Baseball fans throughout the nation, therefore, proclaimed the '68 season the "Year of the Pitcher." Tiger fans had a different perspective. They were convinced that, for them, this was to be the "Year of the Tiger," just as it was in China.

If a movie could be made about a baseball season the story of the 1968 Detroit Tigers would serve as the perfect model for an ideal script. There would be only one problem. Even for Hollywood, this drama would be "unbelievable."

After coming so close the year before, the Tigers and their fans approached spring training at Lakeland that February with guarded enthusiasm. They knew the team was blessed with talent. There was Kaline, Northrup, Cash, Horton, McLain and Lolich. But, with the exception of the steady Kaline, who could predict what year anyone else would have?

Pitching was the main concern. Denny McLain had the raw stuff and was coming off a fairly good season (17-16, 3.79 ERA). At the same time, questions loomed about his outside involvements. Denny's favorite hobby—flying private aircraft—raised the anxiety level for some of the more conservative Tiger management who could picture him losing an engine and crashing his plane.

Mickey Lolich (14-13) had been impressive the previous year with his league-leading six shutouts.

Mickey's favorite mode of transportation also caused concern. He was an avid motorcyclist.

Whenever Lolich reached the clubhouse on his Harley-Davidson in one piece, Manager Smith gave a quick sigh of relief.

Big (6' 3", 216-pound) Earl Wilson, acquired from Boston in a 1966 trade earlier, not only led the league with 22 victories in '67, but also wielded a mean bat. He became one of the few pitchers used as an effective pinch-hitter.

Reserve veteran infielder Dick Tracewski provided some team leadership. He later became one of the Tigers' most respected coaches.

The year did not get off to a rousing start for the Tigers. Boston beat Detroit, 7-3, on April 10 before a disappointed Opening Day crowd, despite a home run by Wilson. In the next game, pinch-hitter-supreme Gates Brown clubbed a 9th-inning home run to win 4-3. That was a taste of things to come. The Tigers went on to win the next nine games in a row. On May 10, Detroit took over sole possession of first place and refused to let go.

Throughout this marvelous season, the gods of baseball blessed the Tigers beyond measure and allowed mortals to view from the stands and via television, a modern-day miracle in progress. Victories came via the strangest routes: bloop singles that fell just inside the foul lines ... last-inning grand slam home runs ... even a triple play.

The Tigers won 40 games that year in the 7th inning or later; they won 30 games in their final at-bat.

Denny McLain was on a tear. Each time he took the mound, he acted as one accustomed to winning. On his way to compiling record statistics, Denny sometimes toyed with opposing batters. He tantalized some by telling them what kind of pitch he would throw and actually dared them to hit it. Late in September, for example, when the Yankee's Mickey Mantle made his last appearance at Tiger Stadium and the Tigers were well on their way to winning the game, McLain served up "lollipops"—i.e. soft, slow pitches that would not fool a Little Leaguer. Mantle realized what was happening. He dug into the batter's box, took a mighty swing at a belt-high pitch and sent the ball deep into the second deck of the ball park for the 535th home run of his brilliant career. As the aging slugger rounded the bases and the Tiger Stadium organist played "East Side, West Side," McLain doffed his cap to the hobbling slugger. Vince Doyle of WWJ radio commented on his broadcast the next morning that this was "a fine gesture of respect for the legendary Mantle."

That may have been one of the rare moments during which a Detroit sportscaster ever accused McLain of showing respect for anyone.

Other Tigers played better than they knew how. Gates Brown became baseball's most feared pinch-hitter as he batted .370. Jim Northrup connected for four grand-slam home runs—all of which won games.

Each contest, it seemed, produced a new hero. Al Kaline hit his 307th career home run on May 18, surpassing Hank Greenberg's club record of 306. On July 19, for example, rookie Daryl Patterson (2-3) was brought in from the bullpen to face the Baltimore Orioles who had the bases loaded and no outs. Patterson calmly struck out the side. In the dog days of July, more than 53,000 Detroit fans cheered Tom Matchick, a .203 hitter who had never hit a home run during his two-year stint in the majors, when he connected for a three-run homer with two out in the ninth to defeat the Orioles by a score of 5-4. On August 17, Bill

Freehan slammed a home run over the "Green Monster" in Boston to cap an 11th-inning victory; four days later, Jim "Big Guy" Price, a back-up catcher, hit a 10th-inning homer to beat Chicago, 3-2.

The 1968 Tigers, however, were not free of adversity. Slugger Willie Horton was knocked unconscious in a collision with Ray Oyler, the club's diminutive shortstop. Earl Wilson spent part of the year on crutches due to a jammed foot. Veteran Eddie Mathews, brought in from Houston the year before to add left-handed power, hurt his back and was limited to only 31 games during the '68 campaign. Dick McAuliffe was regarded around the league as a quiet gentleman, but he got into a knock-down-drag-out fight with the White Sox pitcher Tommy John on August 22. That scuffle cost "Mac" $250 and a four-game suspension.

The biggest blow to both the Tigers' offense and defense came on May 25th when the Athletics' Lew Krausse hit Al Kaline with a high, inside fastball and broke the Tiger right fielder's throwing arm, causing the veteran to miss more than 50 games.

Slugger Willie Horton was a constant long-ball threat and led the Tigers in '68 with a .285 average.

"I was raised at Tiger Stadium. We used to slip in at 11 and 12 years old, and when I had enough of getting caught, I started working in the clubhouse. It's the people that I remember— everybody was so close you got to know them by their faces."

- Willie Horton on Tiger Stadium

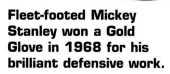

Fleet-footed Mickey Stanley won a Gold Glove in 1968 for his brilliant defensive work.

Pilot of this rambunctious cast of characters was mild-mannered Mayo Smith, who looked more like the owner of your local hardware store than a big league manager. Yet it was this sort of personality that was able to control such a boisterous gang. Later that year, Smith was to make decisions that would forever leave his imprint in Tiger history.

Jim Northrup left no doubt that he would be a factor when on June 24, he hit not one, but two grand-slam home runs against Eddie Fisher and Billy Rohr in a 14-3 romp over the Indians. Benefactor of those blasts was, of course, Denny McLain who notched his 13th win. Just five days later, Northrup blasted another grand-slam against the White Sox for a 5-2 victory. And the winning pitcher was ... who else ... McLain.

By the All-Star break, the Tigers led second-place Cleveland by 9 1/2 games.

It was just July 27 when Denny grabbed his 20th win, shutting out the Orioles on three hits. Home runs by Horton (2), Kaline, Don Wert and McAuliffe gave the Tigers all the offense they needed. After the game, McLain, no friend of local sportswriters, credited Detroit's success to the fact that the newspapers were on strike.

"The writers are not around demoralizing the players," he said.

McLain won his 25th game on August 16. It was another shutout of the Boston Red Sox, giving Denny a 16-0 road record.

Denny's 27th win was highlighted not so much by his pitching prowess as his fielding. The Orioles had come to Detroit for a crucial three-game series over the Labor Day weekend. The Tigers and Orioles had split the first two games. In the third game, with Detroit leading 4-3, Baltimore had two runners on with no outs when clean-up hitter Boog Powell stepped to the plate. Powell lined a shot up the middle. McLain snagged it for one out. He quickly threw to second before the runner got back for out number two. McAuliffe tossed it to Norm Cash at first, in time for a triple play.

Victories seemed to come naturally for McLain now. On September 6 he fanned 12 batters as he won his 26th game against the Minnesota Twins by the score of 8-3. Aiding the cause was slugger Willie Horton's five RBI via a home run (his 32nd) and a double.

It was Denny McLain the slugger four days later. He nailed a triple and two singles as he defeated the Angels 7-3 for his 29th win.

The stands of Tiger Stadium were filled to capacity on the afternoon of September 14. Each fan and reporter hoped to witness history in the making.

Dennis Dale McLain was gunning for his 30th win of the year. Among the spectators was Jay Hanna "Dizzy" Dean—the last man to accomplish such a feat 34 years earlier (although there's evidence to support the claim that Dean should have been credited with only 29).

From the start of the game, it was obvious that Denny didn't have his best stuff. Oakland's Reggie Jackson pounded him with two long blasts into the upper deck of Tiger Stadium.

With the Tigers trailing 4-3 in the bottom of the ninth, the thousands of fans in attendance and the millions viewing on national television concluded that Denny would have to wait until his next turn on the mound to grab that coveted 30th win. However, Kaline, pinch-hitting for McLain, walked. Stanley singled, sending Kaline to third. Kaline scored on a throwing error. Willie Horton followed with a sharp single to left, scoring Stanley with the winning run. Once, again, the amazing Tigers pulled another rabbit out of the baseball cap.

Denny leaped from the dugout to embrace Horton and his fellow teammates. In his excitement, McLain hit his head on the roof of the dugout and nearly knocked himself unconscious. "My body wouldn't allow that to happen," said McLain. "I would worry about the pain later. Now was the time to celebrate."

On September 17, Detroit hosted the New York Yankees. If they won the game or Baltimore lost to Boston, the Bengals would claim the American League flag.

Joe Sparma was having one of his more impressive outings, shutting out the Yankees until the top of the ninth when they scored a run to knot the game, 1-1. The standing-room-only crowd at the corner that evening was unaware, however, that the Red Sox had already defeated the Orioles, 2-0. Jim Campbell rendered a controversial decision. He opted to not show the score on the center-field scoreboard for fear that fans would run onto the field in celebration, thus forfeiting Detroit's game.

In typical Tiger fashion for that year, with two outs in the bottom of the ninth, third baseman Don Wert (a .200 hitter) stroked a single to left-center field, scoring Al Kaline with the winning run. That sent the long-denied Tiger fans into rapture.

> "When you can do it out there between the white lines you can live any way you want."
>
> - Denny McLain

During the same game, reliable Al Kaline hit a single that put the Tigers ahead to stay.

At that precise moment, the final score of the Baltimore/Boston game was flashed on the scoreboard. As Jim Campbell feared, fans flowed onto the field to congratulate their hometown heroes. Some of the more rowdy spectators elected to grab clumps of the outfield grass, bases and anything else they could carry home as a souvenir. After order was restored, the field of Tiger Stadium resembled a cow pasture.

Most of the jubilant fans elected to celebrate in a more civilized manner. Cascading Downtown streets, while hugging complete strangers, they shouted to anyone who would listen to a slogan associated with the '68 team: "Sock it to 'em, Tigers!" Radio stations throughout the night played over and over again a popular song heard many times that year: "Go Get 'em Tigers!"

The next stop was Busch

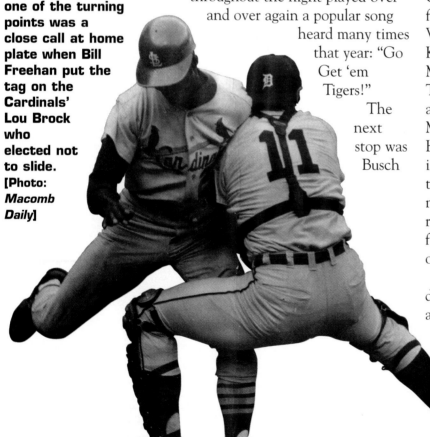

In Game Five of the 1968 World Series, one of the turning points was a close call at home plate when Bill Freehan put the tag on the Cardinals' Lou Brock who elected not to slide. [Photo: *Macomb Daily*]

Stadium, St. Louis, and the World Series.

Detroit finished the season 12 games ahead of second-place Baltimore. Although hitting a petty .235 as a team, the Tigers committed only 105 errors and led the league with 185 home runs. Willie Horton's 36 blows were second only to Frank Howard who hit 44 for the last-place Senators.

Then came the Series—that marvelous, unforgettable Series. The Tigers, said the experts, were underdogs. The first game was billed as the classic match-up between the two premier right handers of the game—Denny McLain and the St. Louis Cardinals' Bob Gibson.

Prior to the start of the Fall Classic, Manager Mayo Smith was faced with a perplexing problem. What should he do with Al Kaline? After the errant pitch of May 25 broke the arm of the Tigers' right fielder, an outfield alignment of Northrup in right, Mickey Stanley in center and Horton in left produced a chemistry unmatched by any other team. But Kaline was Detroit's role model. The one whom many regarded as the league's best right fielder had given the city 15 years of steady, brilliant play.

Kaline, sensing his manager's dilemma, volunteered to step aside and let the younger players start.

Smith had another idea. In a bold move, he brought Stanley in from center field to play shortstop in place of the steady-fielding, weak-hitting Ray Oyler. Stanley, a Gold

Glove outfielder, had appeared in only nine games at shortstop during his five years in the majors. Even the most loyal Mayo Smith supporter raised an eyebrow at this decision.

Game One at Busch Stadium in St. Louis highlighted the pitching prowess of Bob Gibson. The fire-balling right hander who held National League batters in check with 22 wins and a flimsy 1.12 ERA, mowed down the Tigers and set a World Series record of 17 strikeouts, two better than the previous mark set by Sandy Koufax. During the hot and muggy afternoon, McLain lasted five innings. The final score was St. Louis 4, Detroit 0. The only bright spot for Detroit was that Stanley handled every grounder flawlessly at short.

Willie Horton blasted a gargantuan home run in Game Two that finally got the Tigers into the scoring column. "Stormin' Norman" Cash also plunked one into the right-field seats. Al Kaline made two sensational catches to stifle Cardinal threats. The most bizarre moment came in the third inning when pitcher Mickey Lolich connected off a shocked Nelson Briles for the only home run in his major league career. At game's end, Mickey posted his first Series win easily by a score of 8-1.

Al Kaline lined two home runs and Dick McAuliffe another in Game Three at Tiger Stadium. But their efforts were not enough to overcome three-run homers by Tim McCarver and Orlando Cepeda, along with Lou Brock's three stolen bases. St. Louis had a 2-1 edge in the Series after the 7-3

humiliation of the Tigers. It looked as though the baseball experts were right.

Prior to Game Four in Detroit, singer Jose Feliciano, a blind Puerto Rican recording artist with hits that included "Light My Fire," sang an upbeat version of the national anthem while accompanying himself on the guitar. The unorthodox version caught everyone off guard. Many in the stands booed loudly. Most sat in shocked silence. More than a thousand protest calls overloaded the switchboard at Tiger Stadium. "How could anyone disgrace America with such a rendering of our anthem?" they asked. Complaints came mostly from people over 35 years old. In a year of discontent, when American flags were burned in protest to actions of our government, this rendition of the national anthem bordered on the sacrilegious. This was particularly true of Detroit fans who were used to hearing a straightforward, powerful version of the anthem sung at home games by Bob Taylor, affectionately known around town as "Fat Bob the Singing Plumber."

Before the midway point in Game Four, Commissioner William Eckert had to call the umpires to his box, cautioning them to prevent another potential problem. The Tigers were being

Denny McLain regained his form in Game Six when he led the Tigers to a 13-1 victory.

The stage was set for Game Seven. Starting pitcher was southpaw Mickey Lolich.

"All of the fat guys watch me and say to their wives, 'See, there's a fat guy doing OK. Bring me another beer.' Fat guys need idols, too."

- Mickey Lolich

handcuffed by (who else?) Bob Gibson. Behind 4-0 in the third inning, the Bengals prayed for rain. Their prayers were answered. The game was delayed 74 minutes. When play resumed, some of the Tigers attempted to stall, hoping the rains would return and wash out the game before the required five innings needed to make it an official contest. An equal number of Cardinals employed a not-so-subtle hurry-up agenda by intentionally making outs. Commissioner Eckert took decisive action. He instructed the umpires to order both managers to stop the mockery immediately.

Under the gloom of overcast skies, Gibson continued his methodical domination as he bested both McLain and the Tigers a second time. The 10-1 score told the story. Would the next day be the finale of a wonderful season for Detroit?

The crowd entering Tiger Stadium on October 7 resembled a funeral procession. Many felt as though it were just a matter of time before the burial. Mickey Lolich, fortunately, didn't agree.

With St. Louis ahead 3-2, fleet-footed Lou Brock (hitting .524 in

the Series through four games) doubled to open the fifth inning. Julian Javier followed with a sharp single to left. Brock raced around third for home. Left-fielder Willie Horton, known more for his bat than his fielding, unleashed a mighty throw on the fly to catcher Bill Freehan. Brock didn't slide, which proved to be a big mistake. Instead, he missed the plate and collided with Freehan. Freehan held onto the ball. Umpire Doug Harvey paused for a second, then yelled: "Yer out!"

Cheers from the fans showed their first burst of enthusiasm all afternoon.

With one out in the seventh and the Tigers still behind by a run, Manager Smith made another strange decision. He allowed Lolich—a .114 hitter that year—to bat for himself. Lolich made Smith a genius when he blooped a pop fly to right that fell in for a base hit. McAuliffe followed with another base hit. Stanley walked. With the bases full, Al Kaline stepped to the plate. He jumped on the third pitch—a low outside fastball—and dumped it into center field, scoring two runs. The partisan crowd erupted. The Tigers were in the lead for keeps. The roar from the stands seemed to rock the light towers.

After a 5-3 victory, Detroit fans were jubilant. Could the team become a baseball phoenix and rise from the ashes as promised by the city's motto? If so, the Tigers would have to win the last two games in St. Louis. That was a long shot at best.

Two days later, in Busch

Stadium, Tiger players reached inside themselves in search for yet another miracle.

Denny McLain finally regained his form. The Tigers, led by Northrup's grand-slam home run, pummeled the Cardinals 13-1, in Game Six.

That set the stage for a script bordering on fiction. On October 10, Game Seven featured a head-to-head confrontation between the mighty Gibson and the Tigers' Lolich, who had but two days rest. Both had won two games during the Series.

Everyone knew that you could not beat Gibson in this situation. Well … almost everyone.

The game was scoreless for six innings. The Cardinals threatened in the sixth with singles by Brock and Curt Flood, but Lolich picked both off first base.

In the top of the seventh, the Tigers had two on with two out when Jim Northrup swung at a Gibson fast ball and hit a screaming line drive to deep center. Flood hesitated for a second, then ran back. He was too late. The ball fell behind him and rolled all the way to the wall. By the time Flood retrieved the ball, Northrup was on third and the Tigers were ahead, 2-0. Eventually, Detroit scored two more runs; the only offense generated by St. Louis was a ninth-

With Game Seven scoreless in the top of the seventh, Jim Northrup slammed a long triple with two runners aboard to put the Tigers ahead.

inning homer by Mike Shannon. When catcher Bill Freehan squeezed Tim McCarver's foul pop fly behind the plate at 4:06 p.m., the game and the season ended gloriously. By a 4-1 score, the Detroit Tigers became Champions of the World.

Detroiters—more than 150,000 of them—headed for Downtown. They filled nearly every street in Cadillac Square. Traffic was at a standstill. Office workers who were just getting off the job had no possibility of returning home for hours. Many succumbed to the obvious and

At 4:06 p.m. on October 10, 1968, Tiger catcher Bill Freehan celebrates the final out of the game, lifting World Series hero Mickey Lolich into the air.

To date, a total of 11 hitters have slugged two grand-slam home runs in one ball game. "What's astounding to me," says former Tiger Jim Northrup who hit two in one game on June 24, 1968, "is two grand slams in one game is rarer than the perfect game. There have been 13 perfect games pitched. That's astounding."

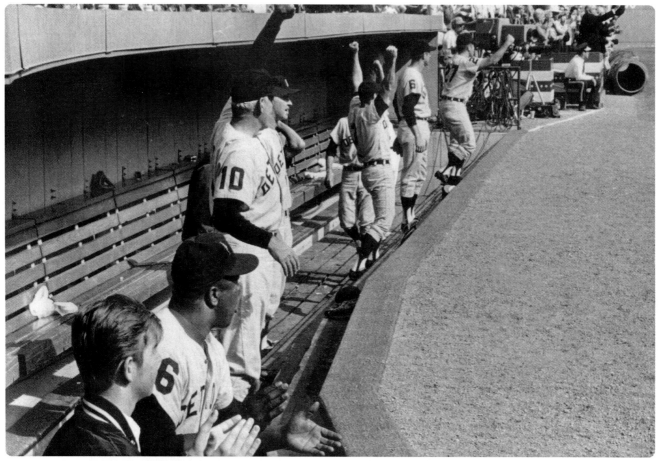

The Tiger players cheered the final out. They were now World Series Champions.

The celebration continued in the Tiger locker room as Willie Horton embraces Al Kaline.

headed for Jimmy Butsicaris' Lindell A.C., one of the popular watering holes for the Tigers and other professional athletes. But unlike the mobs that terrorized local businesses a few months earlier, this crowd was determined only to celebrate.

The party continued until sunrise. As proof that Detroiters still had some class and respect for the rights of others, police reports revealed not one person was injured that night, and no property was destroyed.

In all fairness, there was one massive disregard for the law. More than 35,000 fans invaded Detroit Metro Airport to greet the charter flight carrying their hometown heroes. In their eagerness to show their appreciation to the team, some of the more exuberant scaled the outer fences and ran onto the taxiways and runways. Air traffic controllers ordered the airport shut down, and diverted the Tigers' chartered plane to suburban Willow Run Airport. Soon after the plane landed, World Series hero Mickey Lolich was whisked by helicopter to Metro Airport where he spoke to a cheering throng of delirious fans.

Denny McLain ended the regular season with an incredible 31 wins, only 6 losses, a 1.96 ERA and 280 strikeouts. To no one's surprise, he was named the American League's Most Valuable Player and winner of the Cy Young Award. His counterpart in the National League—Bob Gibson—earned the same honors. It was the first time in history that pitchers swept the four awards.

Individual awards are noteworthy, indeed. But no die-hard Tiger fan will ever forget that 1968 team. Some claim it was the best Tiger team in history.

They may be right.

> If there was a baseball season about which a movie could be made, the story of the 1968 Detroit Tigers would serve as the perfect model for an ideal script. There would be only one problem. Even for Hollywood, this drama would be deemed as "unbelievable."
>
> - John McCollister

Detroit Tigers
1968 World Champions
Top Row - Cash, Matchick, Lolich, Sparma, Dobson, McLain, Hiller, McMahon
Third Row - Face, Wyatt, Northrup, Freehan, Brown, McAuliffe, Price, Tracewski, Patterson
Second Row - Behm *(trainer)*, Hand *(equipment manager)*, Moreno *(batting practice pitcher)*, Stanley, Oyler, Lasher, Wilson, Warden, Creedon *(traveling secretary)*
First Row - Wert, Kaline, Cuccinello *(coach)*, Moses *(coach)*, Smith *(manager)*, Naragon *(coach)*, Sain *(coach)*, Comer, Horton

Chapter 13
Aftermath

"I don't think Mayo [Smith]
had any idea of the effect of
Denny's actions on the rest
of the team.**"**

- Bill Freehan, 1969

**General Manager Jim
Campbell proudly displays
the 1968 World Series
trophy.**

SOUNDS OF POPPING CHAMPAGNE CORKS AND CHEERING CROWDS still echoed in the ears of the Detroit Tigers as they gathered in Lakeland for spring training in March 1969. The newly-crowned Champions of the World were household names. World Series hero Mickey Lolich was a coveted guest on national television shows and at high-priced banquets. Fans relished an opportunity to hear Jim Northrup talk candidly about his towering triple that sailed over the head of a stumbling Curt Flood. Denny McLain proudly displayed his Most Valuable Player and Cy Young Award trophies above the mantle in his home in suburban Detroit.

Baseball went through major readjusting in 1969. With pitchers dominating the game as they did the year before, attendance in both leagues dropped dramatically. By agreement among owners who felt the sting of lost revenue, the pitching mound was lowered to 10 inches in height. Umpires cooperated by shrinking the strike zone. The results were astounding. National League batting averages rose seven points. American League hitters more than doubled that mark with a 16-point increase. American League clubs hit 27 more home runs on the average, and the senior circuit averaged 33 more round-trippers per team.

Two new clubs—the Kansas City Royals and the Seattle Pilots—were added to the league. In addition, each league was divided into two divisions: the East and the West. Detroit joined Baltimore, Boston, Cleveland, New York and Washington to form the American League East. By vote of the baseball owners at the end of the season, the two

Celebrations included a trip to the White House. Denny McLain is congratulated by President Richard M. Nixon for his phenomenal 31 victories in 1968. Looking on is Commissioner Bowie Kuhn. McLain and Kuhn would cross paths again, soon.

division winners would face each other in a best-of-five series to decide who would represent their respective leagues in the World Series. These changes rocked the comfort zone of baseball traditionalists, who continued to feel that Major League Baseball should be kept to eight teams per league.

Another change following the '68 season was the forced resignation of the ineffective William Eckert as commissioner of baseball.

His replacement was Bowie Kuhn, a Washington attorney who would have a significant impact on the career of one Dennis Dale McLain.

The Tiger camp had its share of unsettling moments. Grand master at generating unrest was McLain who, in a newspaper interview and in one of his appearances as an entertainer (Denny was an accomplished organist) in Las Vegas, described teammate Mickey Lolich as having a "million-dollar arm

When the '69 season began, Tiger Stadium eagerly awaited the triumphal return of its heroes.

and a ten-cent brain." Also, Denny continued to agitate the media by giving a reporter from *The Detroit News* a "scoop," then, a few minutes later, cornering a reporter from the *Free Press* and whispering another story completely opposite of the one revealed earlier. Denny delighted in reading the conflicting stories in the papers the next day.

From Opening Day in 1969, the Baltimore Orioles dominated the American League and never looked back. The Tigers, on the other hand, were poor imitations of the 1968 World Champions.

By the first of May, they were playing less than .500 baseball.

Those former benevolent gods of baseball now donned devilish costumes and delighted in playing mischievous tricks on Detroit. Everything seemed to go so right for the Tigers just a short year earlier. Lazy pop fly balls dropped for singles in front of opposing outfielders; ground balls with "eyes" dribbled beyond the outstretched reach of enemy infielders; late-inning rallies made hometown fans shake their heads in amazement that they had witnessed yet another "miracle" at Tiger Stadium.

For the most part in 1969, the luck of the Tigers turned south. The breaks mysteriously vanished.

Fans and players welcomed Opening Day of 1969.

To everyone's astonishment, not one Detroit player batted over .300. While Baltimore played like Superman, winning 109 games, the Tigers (90-72) resembled Clark Kent and finished in second place, a whopping 19 games behind Manager Earl Weaver's Birds.

Occasionally, the '69 Tigers showed signs of the power and spark they exhibited throughout the previous year. On August 29, for example, Jim Northrup went 6-for-6 against the A's, including a dramatic 13th-inning, game-winning home run over the right field roof of Tiger Stadium. But such moments were few and far between.

Denny McLain, in spite of the problems he generated in the clubhouse, remained the consummate professional on the field. He picked up where he left off the year before. His league-leading 24 wins earned him a second consecutive Cy Young Award which he shared with the Orioles Mike Cuellar. Lolich (19-11) and Wilson (12-10) both contributed.

In 1970, the Seattle Pilots ended their one-year existence and became the Milwaukee Brewers. The only change for Detroit that

Commissioner Kuhn presents World Series Hero Mickey Lolich with his ring.

The first designated hitter for the Detroit Tigers was Gates "Gator" Brown on April 7, 1973, before 74,420 fans at Cleveland's Municipal Stadium. Mickey Lolich and the Tigers fell victim to Gaylord Perry and the Indians, 2-1. Gates went 0 for 4.

On April 11, Opening Day at Tiger Stadium, Gates filled the role as designated hitter, going 1 for 2 against Jim Palmer and the Baltimore Orioles. Manager Billy Martin lifted Brown for another designated hitter, Frank "Hondo" Howard, when the Orioles brought in a right-handed relief pitcher. Howard also went 1 for 2. The Tigers eventually lost a 12-inning contest 3-1, before 46,389 disappointed fans.

Gates Brown continued to demonstrate that he was the best pinch-hitter in the business.
[Photo: *Thomas Donaghue*]

And Jim Northrup remained brilliant not only at the plate but also in the field.
[Photo: *Jim McKnight*]

In 1969, Tiger fans voted for the "Greatest Tigers Ever." Appearing at a special ceremony were (L-R) Hank Greenberg, Hal Newhouser, Billy Rogell, Al Kaline, Owner John Fetzer, Denny McLain, George Kell, Charlie Gehringer.

year was a worse record as the Tigers slipped to fourth place. The glory days were history. With Willie Horton (.305) the only hitter to crack the .300 mark and Mickey Lolich leading the league, this time in losses with 19, it was no mystery as to why the once-potent Tigers ended the year with a record of 79-83.

Following the season, Mayo Smith was relieved of his duties as Tiger manager.

The biggest story of the year,

however, was McLain.

A story in *Sports Illustrated* disclosed how Denny was tied to organized crime and bookmaking. Because of baseball's strict codes against gambling and association with gamblers, Commissioner Bowie Kuhn suspended McLain until July 1, 1970. Denny returned that night to pitch against the Yankees and the largest crowd in eight years—53,863 fans—packed Tiger Stadium to welcome him home. He pitched barely over five

Larry Osterman (L) and George Kell shared announcing duties for the Tigers in 1970.

innings and was not involved with the decision. But Denny wasn't through. On August 28, General Manager Jim Campbell suspended him again, this time for throwing buckets of water over the heads of two Detroit newspaper writers. One week later, Commissioner Kuhn suspended him for carrying a pistol on a Tiger road trip.

The patience of the Tigers was exhausted. On the eve of the 1970 World Series, Jim Campbell announced that Denny had been traded to the Washington Senators along with Don Wert, Elliott Maddox and Norm MacRae for infielders Eddie Brinkman and Aurelio Rodriguez and pitchers Joe Coleman and Jim Hannan.

Denny McLain won only 15 games over the next three years with Washington, Oakland and Atlanta. He eventually lost everything—his wife, his money, even his freedom. Twice he was convicted of felonies and sentenced to serve time in a federal penitentiary.

Denny *had* everything. Denny *lost* everything.

Following a disappointing '69 season, fans renewed their hopes on Opening Day, 1970. Joining in the festivities were (L-R) Michigan Governor William G. Milliken, Detroit Mayor Roman Gribbs, Tiger Owner John Fetzer and singer Pearl Bailey.

Al Kaline had a fair year in 1970, batting .278, with 16 homers and 71 RBI. Most players would accept these statistics, but not Kaline. Shortly following the season, General Manager Jim Campbell, the lovable, balding, cigar-smoking Scotch-Irishman wanted to show his appreciation to the genial right fielder by offering him the first $100,000 contract in the club's history. Kaline refused the raise in pay. "I don't deserve such a salary," he said. "I didn't have a good enough season last year. The ball club has been fair and decent to me. Enough so that I'd prefer to have you give it to me when I rate it."

When you look up the word "class" in the dictionary, you'll see the photo of Al Kaline.

Chapter 14
Riding a
Roller Coaster

**"From one day to the next,
you never knew which
Billy Martin would
show up."**

\- Norman Cash

**In 1971, the Tigers
hired feisty Billy Martin
as their manager. He
was a stark contrast to
his predecessor, the
laid-back Mayo Smith.**

I N THE SAME YEAR THAT WALT DISNEY WORLD OPENED ITS GATES in
Orlando, Florida, the Detroit Baseball Club initiated its own version
of "Adventure Land" by hiring Alfred Manual "Billy" Martin as its
field manager. A striking contrast to the laid-back Mayo Smith, Martin
came to the Tigers in 1971 with all the patience of a gerbil. In spring
training, Martin was put to the test when John Hiller, one of his prime
relief pitchers, announced that he had suffered a life-threatening heart
attack a month before reporting to camp.

While Hiller rested at home, Martin lit a fire under the rest of the
club. Again, no Tiger hit higher than .300, but an offensive attack with
balanced power complemented a 20-win season for pitcher Joe Coleman,
plus a league-leading 25 victories and 308 strikeouts for Mickey Lolich.
The reward for such a splendid team showing was a second-place finish,
12 games behind Baltimore.

Throughout the season, Martin was criticized by many in the media
as being too hot-tempered to be effective. "Temper is something the
good Lord gave me," admitted the Tigers' skipper, "and I can't just throw
it out the window."

Helping to keep things in perspective, pitcher Mickey Lolich, not
the best physical specimen of an athlete, was also chided by the media.
The focus of their concern was his pot-bellied appearance. Although he
was a fierce competitor, he looked horribly out of shape. During one
radio interview when pressed about the issue, Lolich responded, "All of
the fat guys watch me and say to their wives, 'See, there's a fat guy doing

OK. Bring me another beer.' Fat guys need idols, too."

Perhaps the one moment best remembered at Tiger Stadium in 1971 was the All-Star Game July 13. Each of the rosters contained a powerful lineup filled with future Hall-of-Famers. Johnny Bench, Hank Aaron and Roberto Clemente hit home runs for the National League. The American League answered with circuit blows by Frank Robinson, Harmon Killebrew and a gigantic blast by Oakland's Reggie Jackson—one that would have cleared the roof in right-center field had it not struck a light tower. As they left the stadium following the game, few people talked about the 6-4 American League victory. Most just shook their heads in awe at the sight of the monstrous shot by Jackson.

The 1972 season got off to a horrible start for the Tigers and everyone else associated with baseball. Before the season, owners felt the rumblings of players. Spring training, normally a marketplace for optimistic predictions, became a feeding ground for discontent. Fans became disgruntled when players, by a vote of 663-10, chose to follow the advice of Marvin Miller, executive director of the Major League Baseball Players Association, and walk off the diamonds in protest of the current pension plan, along with baseball's sacred "reserve clause." The strike robbed those heretofore loyal fans of their annual season of hope. During spring training of 1972, the nation came to grips with the realization that baseball would never be quite the same. The game had

arrived at an intersection of a bygone era marked by men who played primarily for the love of the game, and the hard-core, perhaps caustic, belief that baseball is just another business.

Most of the nation's newspaper editorials, sports commentators and everyday fans blamed both owners and players for allegedly putting a dollar sign ahead of everything else. Commissioner Bowie Kuhn expressed what was in the hearts of most baseball diehards: "Obviously the losers in the strike action are the sports fans of America."

Negotiations ground to a halt. Egos were bruised. By the time the players union and the owners finally reached an agreement, baseball lost 13 days and a total of 86 games from its schedule.

Once the first pitch of the new season was thrown, however, the Tigers and most of their fans appeared willing to put ill will behind them. Billy Martin and his crew fought their way to an 86-70 record to win the American League East by a half game over the Red Sox.

Mirroring the '68 club, the 1972 Tigers did not have a superstar that outshone the rest. Norm Cash led the team with only 22 home runs. Mickey Lolich had 22 wins and Joe Coleman won 19. Statistics aside, Manager Martin's aggressive approach generated a win-at-all-costs spirit in his players. That attitude came back to haunt him in the American League Championship Series against the Oakland A's.

Even with their flamboyant manager, the Tigers were symbols

of conservatism next to the Oakland players. With flashy green and gold uniforms, beards and shaggy hair, they resembled refugees from the beatnik ghettos of San Francisco in the 1960s. From the opening pitch, however, they played each game with the sort of seriousness that would produce three consecutive World Championships.

Game One of the best-of-five American League Championship Series of 1972 went 11 innings. Al Kaline put the Tigers ahead by one run in the top of the 11th with a home run, but his throwing error in the bottom of the frame contributed to a two-run rally, to the delight of the hometown Oakland fans.

In Game Two, with the Tigers trailing John "Blue Moon" Odom and the A's, 5-0, Martin ordered Lerrin LaGrow to deliberately throw at the ankles of fleet-footed shortstop Bert Campaneris. LaGrow did and knocked the batter off his feet. Campaneris jumped up and threw his bat at the head of LaGrow. The Tiger right-hander dodged the whirling bat. Both benches cleared. Martin led the Tigers in the charge. LaGrow and Campaneris were ejected.

The rest of the games were tame by comparison. Joe Coleman tossed a 3-0 shutout, and Bill Freehan hit a four-bagger as Detroit won Game Three back at Tiger Stadium.

Dick McAuliffe's home run and Jim Northrup's timely hitting paced the Tigers to a 4-3 victory in Game Four.

The final game in Detroit featured a stellar pitching perfor-

mance by the Tigers' Woodie Fryman, but to no avail. He was outdueled, 2-1, by Odom.

Oakland would go on to win the 1972 World Series against Sparky Anderson's Cincinnati Reds. Meanwhile, the Detroit organization had to endure the harsh, cold winter, bemoaning a season of promise that ended with a lot of might-have-beens, coupled with the embarrassment resulting

On September 29, 1974, Tiger superstar Al Kaline waves farewell to the hometown crowd on his last day as a player.

Pitcher John Hiller surprised Manager Martin at spring training with the revelation that he had experienced a "slight problem with his heart" over the winter.

from the strategy employed by an overly aggressive manager.

John Hiller, rebounding from his heart attack, led the league by notching 38 saves while pitching in 65 games in 1973. Joe Coleman (23-15) enjoyed the best season of his 15-year career, while Mickey Lolich slipped to a 16-15 record. Willie Horton (.316) showed consistency at the plate. But the big news all year long centered on the unpredictable manager, Billy Martin.

Erratic mood swings for the Tiger skipper were normal. As Bucky Dent, Yankee shortstop who played for Martin, said, "He was fiery and could be charming." Tiger players reported that on any given day, Billy Martin could walk into the locker room and treat you as though you were his best friend. The next day, he could give every impression that you were his enemy. Norm Cash summed up the feelings of his teammates: "You never know which Billy Martin will show up."

As did the antics of Denny McLain two years earlier, Martin's temperament wore thin with Tiger management. Only 19 games remained in the 1973 season when Martin was discharged; Coach Joe Schultz guided the team the rest of the way to a third-place finish.

The '73 season marked another radical change for the Junior Circuit. To generate more offense, American League owners voted to allow a "designated hitter" to bat in place of the pitcher. As a result, American League hitters averaged .259—a 20-point jump over the previous season; home run hitting increased by nearly a third. Also, since they were not removed from games by pinch hitters, American League pitchers tossed 25 percent more complete games than their National League counterparts.

Joining the Tiger roster in 1974 was rookie Ron LeFlore. A Detroit native, LeFlore, like so many young black men struggling to survive in this era, became involved with gangs early in life and eventually was sentenced to prison.

One of the Tiger scouts heard about this speedster and, not heeding the warnings by some conservative elements of the club, visited the prison to see for himself this young talent. The audition worked, and LeFlore was signed to a Tiger contract.

Elected to guide the Tigers in '74 was Ralph "Major" Houk. The former Yankee pilot brought a different approach to the game than did the high-strung Billy Martin. Gone were the unexpected outbursts of emotion. Gone, too, was the fire that Martin was able to generate in the players. As a result, by October the Tigers fell to the bottom of the heap in the American League East. Bill Freehan (.297, 18 home runs) and Willie Horton (15 homers) were the hitting leaders. Mickey Lolich led the league, this time in losses (21). John Hiller (known now as the "Cardiac Kid") earned high marks with a 17-14 record and a 2.64 ERA.

In 1974, Al Kaline reluctantly accepted Manager Houk's order to become the Tigers' designated hitter. Veteran Detroit fans, however, were not as understanding. Many wrote letters to the editor or called radio talk shows to protest. They felt they were being robbed of an opportunity to see the game's greatest right fielder at his best.

On September 24, Albert Kaline ensured his induction into the Hall of Fame when he smacked a double off Baltimore's Dave McNally. It was the 3,000th hit of his brilliant career.

Kaline retired at the end of the season after getting seven more hits. He left the Detroit Tigers as a player with 399 home runs and a .297 career average over 22 years, all with the Tigers. His selection as a member of the All-Star team 18 times and as winner of 10 Gold Gloves demonstrates that he was one of the game's best all-around players. He was runner-up for the American League MVP award in 1955 and 1963.

It's not surprising, then, that in 1980, his first year of eligibility, he was elected to Baseball's Hall of Fame. That same year, the Tigers retired his number 6—the first time any Tiger received such an honor.

Today, Al Kaline is a popular broadcaster of Tiger games on television.

If the 1974 season was a bad dream, 1975 was a nightmare. A

57-102 record was the worst for the Tigers in 12 years. Aging hitters and pitchers seemed to go through the motions of playing ball, although youngsters such as shortstop Tom Veryzer (.252) and pitcher Vern Ruhle (11-12) playing in their first full seasons did add some zest to the lineup. Attendance at Tiger Stadium was down 200,000 from the year before and more than 700,000 off the pace of 1972. Tiger management

Billy Martin was replaced with the veteran Ralph Houk. The "Major," although much less flamboyant than Martin, was still willing to battle for his cause when he deemed it appropriate.
[Photo: *Clifton Boutelle*]

and fans grew increasingly concerned about the future of the team. They questioned the laid back, good-guy image of Manager Houk.

Owner John Fetzer also felt the sting of criticism in 1975. He took a more philosophical approach. He described the plight of a baseball owner: "The owner is a riverboat gambler because he can either make a lot of money or lose a lot of money in one year. You have to learn to live with that. You have to look at baseball as a love of accomplishment more than just a monetary reward."

By spring training of 1976, baseball nearly repeated its disaster of four years earlier. Following the '75 campaign, Peter Seitz, a professional arbitrator who knew little about baseball, ruled that two pitchers—Andy Messersmith of the Dodgers and Baltimore's Dave McNally—were "free agents" and could negotiate with any team. Owners insisted on some kind of restriction on free agents. Since none was granted, the owners refused to open training camps. On March 17, Commissioner Bowie Kuhn stepped in and ordered the camps to open. The 1976 season would be played, but with one more layer of misgiving on the part of the fans.

Resurrecting Detroit's hopes and enthusiasm in 1976 was a remarkable addition to the mound staff known affectionately as "The Bird."

Mark Steven Fidrych, a fuzzy-haired, gangly 6' 3",
175-pound right-handed pitcher from Worcester, Massachusetts, reminded people of "Big Bird" on the popular television program Sesame Street, hence his nickname. Fidrych, who raised pigs on his farm, came to Tiger Stadium with a burst of enthusiasm for the game seldom seen in any ballpark. In the midst of a sharp dip in the economy, when the American automotive industry showed signs of running second to the Japanese auto makers, this rookie sensation gave Detroit and the nation a more positive focus.

During a game Fidrych stood on the mound, held the baseball in front of him

Ron LeFlore proved that you can turn your life around. [Photo: *Clifton Boutelle*]

and … well … talked to it. People in the stands could read his lips: "Stay down, ball! Stay down!"

Whenever an infielder made a spectacular play, Fidrych stopped the game long enough to run over and congratulate him. Before tossing the first pitch of an inning, he often got down on his hands and knees, landscaping the mound. If he surrendered a base hit, he threw the ball back to the home-plate umpire and asked for a new one. "That ball had a hit on it," said The Bird, "so I want it to get back in the ball bag and goof around with the other balls in there. Maybe it'll learn some sense and come out as a pop-up next time."

In a nationally-televised Monday night game during his jaw-dropping rookie season, Fidrych pitched a magnificent 5-1 victory over the Yankees. The nearly 48,000 fans at Tiger Stadium continued to cheer and would not leave until their new hero with the Harpo Marx hairdo made a curtain call by running around the outfield walls of the stadium, waving to the crowd.

The 1976 Tigers finished one notch higher in the standings. Ron LeFlore had a solid year, hitting .316, and Daniel "Rusty" Staub, acquired from the Mets for Mickey Lolich, was the game's best designated hitter, yet the buzz around town focused on one person—

Rookie sensation Mark Fidrych captured the hearts of all America with his unique antics such as "manicuring" the pitching mound at the start of an inning.
[Photo: *John Fulton, Jr.*]

Mark Fidrych.

Fidrych won Rookie of the Year honors with his 19-9 record. He led the junior circuit with a 2.34 ERA and 24 complete games.

Detroit loved him.

"Big Bird" and "The Bird."

Two Tiger Stadium phenoms - Mark "The Bird" Fidrych and national anthem singer Bob "The Plumber" Taylor.

With a career .262 average and an even 200 home runs, he appeared in 11 All-Star games and tied the Yankees' Elston Howard with the highest lifetime fielding percentage of any catcher—.993. He became the unsung hero of the late '60s by handling and helping to develop one of the great pitching staffs in Tiger history. He went on to become baseball coach at his alma mater, The University of Michigan.

Willie Horton was traded to Texas for pitcher Steve Foucault after only one game in 1977. Detroit fans were not fond of losing Willie. They loved this man for more than on-the-field heroics. They remembered his dauntless efforts during the riots ten years earlier. He was also a champion to hundreds of kids, once patients in Michigan hospitals, who still talked about the time Willie Horton came to cheer them up. Horton retired after the 1980 season, capping an 18-year major-league career.

At a time when baseball insiders insisted the baseball was livelier than ever, Ron LeFlore hit .325; second baseman Tito Fuentes, in his only year with Detroit, averaged a nice .309, but led all second sackers with 26 errors. Rookie right hander Dave Rozema had the finest year of his career with a 15-7 record and led the league with fewest walks per nine innings (1.40). Sophomore first baseman Jason Thompson led the club with 31 homers. Designated hitter Rusty Staub slugged 22, while right fielder Ben Oglivie hit 21 blows in his last year with Detroit before

Baseball loved him.

Just as suddenly as he flew into the hearts of Americans, the high-flying bird tumbled out of the sky. The 22-year-old sensation injured his knee and hurt his arm during spring training in 1977. He would never be the same. He compiled a 10-10 record while attempting to come back in portions of the next four seasons. In 1980, Mark Fidrych retired from baseball to tend to his pigs at his farm in Worcester.

The excitement generated in 1976 by Mark Fidrych nearly smothered the news that catcher Bill Freehan retired after 15 years behind the plate for the Tigers.

being traded at the end of the season to Milwaukee.

The Tigers moved up to fourth spot in the American League East in 1977, ahead of Cleveland, Milwaukee and the newly-added Toronto Blue Jays. For the second year in a row, the American League East was dominated by the New York Yankees, who were managed by former Tiger skipper Billy Martin. Tiger General Manager Jim Campbell and manager Ralph Houk seemed unable to find the right combination for success. Although the team had no superstar and no Bird-like crowd pleaser, Detroit fans still supported their team with more than 1.3 million attending the home games.

In the fall of 1977, Tiger management sold Tiger Stadium—estimated to be worth $8 million—to the City of Detroit for one dollar. The Tigers agreed to rent the stadium for 30 years, and the City promised to pump more than $18 million into renovating the ballpark, repaid, in part, through a 50-cent surcharge on each ticket sold.

Replaced were the familiar green wooden seats that often became superb noise-makers. In their stead were bright orange and blue plastic seats. The hand-operated scoreboard above the center-field bleachers gave way to a state-of-the-art, computerized screen with flashing lights and images of the players.

Added were luxury boxes, extra press boxes and broadcast booths.

More than 1.7 million fans came to Tiger Stadium in 1978, the club's first winning season in five years. They witnessed solid

Following his retirement as a player, Al Kaline (center) joins George Kell (l) and Jim Price in the announcer's booth.

performances by Thompson and LeFlore, along with two impressive rookies: shortstop Alan Trammell who hit .268 in his first full season and second baseman Louis "Sweet Lou" Whitaker who hit .285. For the next 18 years, Trammell and Whitaker would form the most solid keystone combination in Tiger history. In '78, the fans also cheered Jim Slaton (17-11), who, in his only year with the Tigers, led the team in victories, and Jack Billingham (15-8), another veteran in his first year with Detroit. Fan support was not enough, unfortunately. Despite finishing 10 games over .500, the Tigers could do no better than end the season in fifth place.

That was enough for Ralph Houk, who was convinced there must be an easier way to make a living.

In an attempt to save the stadium, a massive renovation project took place following the 1977 season.

Renovations were curtailed in 1977 by a fire in the press box.

Keeping track of stats was long-time scorekeeper, Walter Malek.

Always ready to lead fans in singing and cheers was organist Dan Grier.

Two rookies - Alan Trammell (l) and Lou Whitaker - made their Tiger Stadium debuts in 1978. They would form one of the most respected duos in club history.

Chapter 15

Sparky and
His "Boys"

**"Kirk Gibson raised everybody
else's performance to
another level."**

- Lance Parrish

**Manager George "Sparky"
Anderson came to the Tigers in
'79 with a solid track record. His
experience proved to be
invaluable.**

THE 1979 SEASON GOT OFF TO A FAIRLY GOOD START, despite uncertainty at the helm. New Tiger manager Les Moss was allowed less than two months to deliver a winner. In fact, Moss had led his team to a 27-26 record before Jim Campbell was able to prod Sparky Anderson out of retirement. Moss was let go, and Coach Dick Tracewski served as "caretaker manager" until Anderson could arrive in Detroit from his home in Thousand Oaks, California.

"Firing Les Moss was the toughest thing I've ever had to do in baseball," admitted Campbell. "He didn't deserve it, but I couldn't pass up someone with Sparky's credentials."

Few managers commanded more respect for their intelligence, craftiness, and knowing what it takes to win than Anderson. His resumé included two World Championships, four pennant winners and five division championships in his nine years of managing at Cincinnati.

Anderson, known for his fractured syntax punctuated with double negatives and wrong verb tenses, turned few heads with a modest 56-50 record from June 14 to the end of the season for a fifth-place finish in the American League East. But the charismatic Anderson would spend 17 seasons in the Tiger dugout, leading his club to two division titles and one World Championship. Anderson proved immediately he was a man of his word in an article in *Sports Illustrated*: "It's a terrible thing to have to tell your fans who have waited like Detroit's have, that their team won't win it this year. But it's better than lying to them."

Dominating the league in their positions throughout the decade of the '80s was shortstop Alan Trammell ...

The '79 Tigers featured solid pitching performances by Jack Morris (17-7), Milt Wilcox (12-10), Jack Billingham (10-7) and Aurelio Lopez (10-5 with 21 saves). Hitting was suspect. Left fielder Steve Kemp (.318) and flashy center fielder Ron LeFlore (.300) were the only regulars to hit the coveted .300 mark. Kemp's 26 home runs and young first baseman Jason Thompson's 20 circuit blows paced the club in that department.

The Tigers began a rebuilding campaign in 1980. With a solid

manager at the rudder, management wanted to build a team that would be worthy of Sparky Anderson's leadership.

LeFlore was traded to Montreal; added to the squad was a young, brazen ex-football player from Michigan State University named Kirk Gibson, a Waterford, Michigan, native who appeared in a dozen games the previous year.

Another fifth-place finish in 1980 and no outstanding performance by any Tiger may have tempted Sparky Anderson to rejoin his predecessor in retirement. But he was determined to build a competitive team in which the Tiger fans could take pride.

One more threat to the very existence of Major League Baseball appeared at the start of the 1981 season. America's favorite pastime was interrupted when Marvin Miller and his Major League Baseball Players Association voted to strike. Initiating the eight-week strike, which began on July 12 and lasted until the owners' strike insurance ran out, allegedly was fine print in free agent contracts.

Tiger fans, normally sympathetic with the plight of unions and players, this time took the side of management. Each night they heard the evening news reports of how Ford and General Motors were laying off workers because of a crunch in the economy. Even a giant company such as Chrysler had to be saved from bankruptcy by a federal government loan guarantee. In those uncertain times, laborers worked 40 hours each week to earn around $18,000 a year. Meanwhile, these same fans read in the newspapers that major league players earned an average of $196,000 annually for playing a "kids' game." The players' demand for more money just didn't make sense.

When baseball finally resumed after 713 canceled games, Commissioner Bowie Kuhn declared that 1981 would be a "split season" in which the "first half winners" would meet in a best-of-five playoff with the "second half winners." This makeshift remedy did little more than infuriate fans in Detroit and throughout

... and second sacker Lou Whitaker.

the nation who had, until this year, regarded baseball as one of the unchangeables in an era of constant change.

The revised playoff structure had no effect on the Tigers in 1981, as they finished in fourth place in the first half and in third place in the second half of the confused season. Kirk Gibson's

"He has so much talent. He couldn't hide it even if he played under a blanket."

- Sparky Anderson describing Lou Whitaker

both hit .292 to lead the team. Jack Morris (17-16) and Dan Petry (15-9) headed the mound staff.

During the '82 campaign, the Tigers had the misfortune to play teams that were in hot winning streaks. On July 10, for example, the Rangers' Larry Parrish hit a grand-slam home run in a 6-5 win over Milt Wilcox and the Bengals. It was the third slam for Parrish (who would become the Tigers' manager in 1998) in a week, which tied a major league record shared by Lou Gehrig and Jim Northrup.

Sparky Anderson's patience reaped dividends in 1983. First baseman Enos Cabell, in his second year with Detroit, hit .311; Lou Whitaker batted .320; Alan Trammell, .319; and Herndon, .302. Jack Morris had another 20-victory season while leading the league in innings pitched (294) and strikeouts (232). Petry fell one game short of the coveted 20-win season. The balanced attack produced a 92-70 record, allowing the Tigers to finish in second place, six games behind Baltimore.

Following the 1983 season, Thomas S. Monaghan, the owner of a giant pizza chain, purchased the Tigers from John Fetzer. One of Monaghan's first challenges was to determine the fate of Tiger Stadium. Some predicted that if the Tigers were to compete economically, they had to build a modern venue. Traditionalists wanted to preserve the park they had grown to know and love. Monaghan sided with the conservative voices. "As long as I own the team, we will not build a new stadium," he said. "I like the old sta-

On August 3, 1980, the baseball world stopped to pay tribute to Al Kaline, seen here with Commissioner Bowie Kuhn, when he was inducted into the Hall of Fame.

.328 average proved he had learned to hit big league pitching, and Jack Morris, the staff ace, tied several others in the American League during this shortened season with 14 wins.

Ex-Tiger Harvey Kuenn took the managerial helm for Milwaukee in 1982 and led his club to the American League pennant. Detroit, meanwhile, settled for another fourth-place finish, 12 games behind the Brewers. Outfielder Larry Herndon, picked up from San Francisco before the season, and rookie Glenn Wilson,

dium, and we'll do all we can to keep it. We'll be fixing it up and making it look as good as possible."

Reality and pressures from influential people altered his thinking after a while. Detroit Mayor Coleman Young commented: "The damn thing is falling down." Experts advised Monaghan that renovating the stadium and adding an inflatable roof akin to the one at the Pontiac Silverdome, where the Lions now played, would cost $100 million.

The writing was on the stadium wall.

Meanwhile, in New York, a March 3 meeting of club owners produced a new commissioner. Bowie Kuhn had worn out his welcome. In his stead would be Peter Ueberroth, the man who headed the United States Olympic Committee and was responsible for orchestrating the impressive opening and closing ceremonies at the L.A. Olympics. Major League Baseball hoped he would add some ideas to stimulate more fan appeal.

By the time the 1984 Tigers had broken spring training camp and headed north, the nation finally recognized something Tiger fans had known for several years—Lou Whitaker was the finest second baseman in the American League.

The changing of the guard. In 1983, John Fetzer [L] sold the Tiger ballclub to Thomas Monaghan [R]. Jim Campbell witnesses the signing of papers.

As the Tigers continued to win, attendance at the old ballpark increased.

Alan Trammell, mainstay of the World Champion Tigers in 1984.

Whitaker that year earned his first of two Gold Glove Awards.

Manager Sparky Anderson also sang the praises of his slick-fielding second sacker: "He has so much talent. He couldn't hide it even if he played under a blanket."

Watching

Whitaker and shortstop Alan Trammell work together was like listening to Frank Sinatra and Mel Tormé sing a duet. Sparky claimed, "Detroit will never see another pair like that again."

A baseball axiom says that the strength of a club is up the middle (catcher, second base, shortstop and center field). The '84 Tigers were a textbook example of just why this theory is endorsed by veterans. Besides the marvelous duo of Whitaker and Trammell, the Tigers had a backstop who insiders compared to Bill Freehan. Lance Parrish, in his seventh season with the club, acted like a catcher, hit like a catcher, even looked like a catcher. The 6' 3", 212-pound native of Clairton, Pennsylvania, had the build of a rugged miner from back home. His face resembled chiseled rock. His hands and arms were akin to those of an old-time blacksmith.

Parrish's strength lay in his on-the-field direction. An astute manager, Anderson recognized this and turned over much of the field generalship to his catcher. Parrish's other talent was in handling pitchers. Jack Morris, Dan Petry and Milt Wilcox won 19, 18 and 17 games respectively. Although Parrish hit a modest .238 in '84, he led his club with a career-high 33 home runs.

When he was manager of the Cincinnati Reds from 1970-1978, Sparky Anderson had a stable of terrific relief pitchers. His formula for winning games was to plan for the starting pitcher to get through six or seven innings, then wave in as many relievers as it took to get the last few outs. Because he was constantly going to the mound to bring in another pitcher, Anderson earned the nickname: "Captain Hook."

That became most apparent in 1984 as relief pitcher Guillermo "Willie" Hernandez, picked up in a trade with the Phillies at the start of the season, led all clubs by appearing in nearly half the games (80). His 9-3 record plus 32 saves in 33 attempts earned him the Most Valuable Player Award and Cy Young Award honors.

The 1984 Tigers fielded no genuine superstars. Only Alan

Trammell (.314) hit over .300. Outside of Hernandez' many trips to the mound, nobody on the Tiger squad led the league in any category. The team, however, played like a unit.

Much of that type of play was a direct result of the influence of Kirk Gibson. Gibson, the big, intimidating Michigan State University gridiron standout, brought a football mentality to the Tigers. For most people, baseball is played by nine individuals who happen to be on one team. Not so with Gibson. To him, it was one team that happened to field nine players at a time.

"Kirk Gibson raised everybody else's performance to another level," claimed Lance Parrish. "He demanded that of you if you were his teammate, and I think that's what most everybody respects."

Gibson, who always looked like he had missed shaving that morning, was a no-nonsense, gruff player who, in the spirit of one Tyrus Raymond Cobb, won by intimidation. He had power and world-class speed. Manager Anderson called him "the next Mickey Mantle"—a title that

Instrumental in the success of the Tigers was former Michigan State University standout Kirk Gibson. He brought to the team a "football mentality." He did whatever it took to win - hit, field, bunt, run. His style of play reflected that of another Tiger great - Ty Cobb.
[Photo: *Clifton Boutelle*]

would actually haunt Gibson for many years. In 1984, he did, however, put together some Mantelesque numbers: 27 homers, 91 RBI, 29 stolen bases and a .282 average.

The Tigers got off to a good start in '84, winning 35 of their first 40 games. They were in first place from day one to the finish. By season's end, they chalked up 104 wins and filled Tiger Stadium with 2,704,794 fans—an all-time team record.

Characterizing the 1984 Tigers was an expression created by WDIV-TV sportscaster Al Ackerman, who coined the phrase: "Bless you, boys." It was the perfect slogan, reflecting the strong bond between Manager Anderson and his players.

Pitcher Milt Wilcox gave added pitching strength to the Tigers.
[Photo: *Clifton Boutelle*]

Jack Morris set the pace by tossing a no-hit, no-run game on April 7, beating the White Sox 4-0 at Comiskey Park. Steady performances the rest of the way on the mound, in the field and at the plate fed the confidence of players and fans. To nobody's surprise, the Tigers easily won the American League East, beating second-place Toronto by 15 games.

In the American League Championship Series (ALCS), Detroit faced Dick Howser's Kansas City Royals. Without losing a beat, the Tigers picked up where they left off in the regular season. Jack Morris pitched a five-hitter and won, 8-1. Helping to

save the game for Detroit was Gibson, who snared a vicious line-drive by future Hall-of-Famer George Brett with the bases loaded. It was a brilliant catch of a ball that had "extra bases" written all over it.

The Tigers also won Game Two of the ALCS in 11 innings when Gibson homered and reserve out-fielder Johnny Grubb slammed a two-run double to highlight a 5-3 triumph.

Wilcox and Hernandez teamed-up for a masterful three-hit shutout and won Game Three in Detroit, 1-0. For the first time in 16 years, the Detroit Tigers were Champions of the American League.

The Tigers never let up, even when the opening bell sounded for the '84 World Series against the National League Champion San Diego Padres.

At Jack Murphy Stadium for Game One, the Tigers trailed 2-1 until the top of the fifth when left-fielder Larry Herndon, who hit only seven home runs all year, blasted one into the seats to give Detroit a 3-2 edge. Pitcher Jack Morris held the Padres in check the rest of the way, aided by a brilliant relay throw to third from Gibson and Whitaker to nail Kurt Bevacqua attempting to stretch a double into a triple.

Bevacqua got revenge the next day when he hit a three-run homer in the fifth to give the Padres a lead they would never surrender. As he circled the bases, Bevacqua raised a clenched fist and blew kisses. Game Two went to San Diego, 5-3, with Dan Petry taking the loss. Bevaqua's showboating "pushed our desire to win even higher," recalled Gibson.

Game Three in Detroit was a showcase of how some of the Tigers wins that year came from the most unexpected sources. Marty Castillo, a utility player who hit a grand total of eight home runs in his entire five-year major-league career, surprised pitcher Tim Lollar and the rest of the Padres by reaching the left-field seats with a two-run blast in the second inning. The Tigers, assisted by solid pitching from Wilcox, Bill Scherrer and Hernandez, plus 11 walks given up by San Diego pitchers, sent Tiger fans home happy with a 5-2 win.

The Game Four spotlight shone brightly on shortstop Alan Trammell, who clubbed a pair of two-run homers, accounting for all the Tiger runs in a 4-2 victory. Jack Morris scattered five hits in tossing his second complete game of the Series.

The overcast sky on that afternoon of Sunday, October 14, 1984, was a stark contrast to the upbeat mood of Tiger players and fans. They sensed this would be their day. When Kirk Gibson poled an upper-deck home run to give the Tigers a 3-0 lead in the first inning, they were ready to put the champagne bottles on ice.

San Diego had other ideas. Dan Petry's tired arm yielded three Padre runs. With the score tied in the fifth, Gibson was on third with one out. Russell "Rusty" Kuntz, a reserve outfielder in his first year with Detroit, hit a pop fly behind second base. Alan Wiggins, Padres second baseman, backpedaling, caught the ball over his head while still mov-

ing backward. Gibson defied conventional baseball strategy. He tagged up and raced for home. Wiggins, caught off-guard by Gibson's daring move, was unable to launch a strong throw. Gibson slid hard across the plate without any real challenge.

Lance Parrish lined a homer into the stands in the seventh to add to the Tigers' lead. But the real drama would unfold in the bottom of the eighth.

With runners on first and third and one out, Padres pitcher Richard "Goose" Gossage, faced Kirk Gibson. Gossage, a potent strikeout artist, had faced Gibson in the past when Gossage was with the Yankees. It was a battle between two giants. They knew it. Everybody knew it. Gossage could have intentionally walked Gibson but that would not have been fitting. On an 0-1 count, Gossage threw a fast ball, chest-high. Gibson swung. In that magical fraction of a second when everyone in the stands stops breathing and all is silent, came the unique explosion of ash hitting horsehide. Suddenly, the fans roared. Gibson crushed it. A line drive into the upper deck in right field sent home three runs. Gibson raised both arms as if to embrace the fans and the game of baseball. He rounded the bases, viewing the world from the highest hill of euphoria. It seemed as though he

The glue that kept the team playing as a unit on the field was catcher Lance Parrish.
[Photo: *Clifton Boutelle*]

The celebration known only to World Champions.

Sportscaster Al Ackerman coined the phrase: "Bless you, Boys."

covered the distance between third base and home with only three giant steps, nearly knocking over his teammates with powerful high fives. It was vintage Gibson.

The Padres went quietly in the ninth. Detroit fans erupted as their Tigers capped an 8-4 victory with their fourth World Series trophy, and Sparky Anderson became the first to manage a World Series Championship team in both leagues.

As champagne was removed from the ice and corks popped in the Tiger locker room, Gibson, Hernandez, Trammell and others basked in the glory known to few athletes in this world. Sparky joined the hoopla, and, for the wonderful opportunity he had that year, he silently whispered a prayer of thanks: "Bless you, boys."

Kirk Gibson raises his hands during a victory parade along Woodward Avenue. It was the same gesture he made after he hit the clinching home run during the last game of the 1984 World Series.

Detroit Tigers
World Champions, 1984

Top Row - Parrish, Baker, Hernandez, Lowry, Grubb, Abbott, Allen, Garbey, Lemon, Whitaker, Herndon, Scherrer, DiSalvo *(trainer)*, Dr. Livingood *(physician)*
Second Row - Behm *(trainer)*, Gibson, Berenguer, Kuntz, Evans, Bergman, Castillo, Wilcox, Rozema, Petry, Morris, Schmakel *(equipment manager)*, Brown *(traveling secretary)*
First Row - Bair, Lopez, Johnson, Consolo *(coach)*, Grammas *(coach)*, Craig *(coach)*, Anderson *(manager)*, Brown *(coach)*, Tracewski *(coach)*, Trammell, Brookens

Chapter 16
Reconstruction

"I think we're on the brink
of a whole new era in
salary negotiations."

- Jim Campbell

**While roaming the
outfield at Tiger Stadium,
Kirk Gibson eyed other
pastures. In 1988 an
arbitrator ruled he could
move on.**
[Photo: *Doc Holcomb***]**

SPARKY ANDERSON ONCE SAID OF KIRK GIBSON: "He was my toughest project." The Tiger right fielder embodied an abundance of talent. In 1985, Gibson smacked 29 homers and swiped 30 bases. At the same time, Gibson's unyielding demand for an all-out effort on the part of each player irritated many of his teammates who were struggling to regain their performance of a year before. The fact that Detroit ended the season in third place, despite Darrell Evans' league-leading 40 home runs, did little to ease the tension.

Baseball got one more black eye in 1985 when, on August 6, the Players Union voted to strike–again. Donald Fehr, a younger, brash, less charismatic figure than his predecessor, Marvin Miller, was now executive director of the union. He and Lee MacPhail, representative of the team owners, frequently locked horns over financial issues. Fan resentment in Detroit was loud and clear. Talks resumed instantly, but that satisfied no one.

The strike was settled in just two days. Baseball continued with virtually no changes in the contract agreement between owners and the Players Union. The fans, however, lost another ounce of trust.

A new plague descended on baseball during the '80s. Reports of players using illegal drugs filled sports pages. On February 28, 1986, Commissioner Ueberroth set a zero-tolerance policy for drug abuse by major league players. A total of 22 players were implicated in one case alone.

In Detroit, it was money, not drugs, that got headlines. Following some heated negotiations, Kirk Gibson became the Tigers' first million-dollar-a-year player when he signed a $4 million, three-year contract. His increased salary along with the superb pitching of Jack Morris (21-8, and six shutouts) made little difference as the Tigers finished the '86 season in third place again.

Following his fine season, Jack Morris sought the big paycheck. An arbitrator awarded Morris $1.87 million for the 1987 season. Catcher Lance Parrish, hampered by a bad back, turned down a $1.2 million offer by the Tigers and signed with the Phillies. Replacing Parrish as starting catcher was left-hand-hitting Matt Nokes, who pounded out a career-high 32 home runs. In spite of the bickering over contracts, the Tigers returned to glory in 1987. An 11-19 start did not hold much promise, but Sparky and his boys picked up momentum. Veteran pitcher Doyle

Tiger mound ace, Jack Morris, signed a huge contract with the Tigers and remained through the 1990 season.
[Photo: *Clifton Boutelle*]

Alexander, acquired in a late July trade with Atlanta, won nine straight games in the last two months of the season. Alan Trammell hit .343 with 28 homers and 105 RBI. Forty-year-old Darrell Evans clubbed 34 round trippers.

Going into the final weekend of the campaign, Detroit trailed Toronto by only one game. Like two Old West gunslingers meeting in the middle of the street for a shoot-out, the three-game set in Detroit against the Blue Jays would settle it all. The Tigers took the first game, 4-3, to tie Toronto at the top of the A.L. East. It took 12 innings for the Bengals to win the second contest, 3-2. Now with a one-game lead, Detroit sent Frank Tanana (15-10) to finish the 'Jays. He pitched brilliantly. Reserve outfielder Larry Herndon clubbed a solo shot into the stands. That's all Tanana needed as he blanked the Jays, 1-0. Tigers are division champs - again.

Detroit lost the ALCS to the eventual World Champion Minnesota Twins, four games to one. The Tigers' sole victory was a 7-6 win in Detroit, featuring outfielder Pat Sheridan's two-run homer. A disappointing and abrupt end to an exciting season.

On Opening Day 1988, a strange, sad, yet ever so sweet event took place at Michigan and Trumbull. Hundreds of Detroit fans "hugged" their stadium. Just before the start of the game, the people surrounded the stadium hand-in-hand. At a pre-arranged signal, they took one step forward toward the wall and as one, embraced the

(L-R) Jim Campbell and Thomas Monaghan introduce former University of Michigan head football coach, Bo Schembechler, as the club's new president.

cinder blocks, wood and steel that served as boundaries of a most beloved piece of real estate. In the same way one attempts to comfort a dying grandparent, some fans even kissed its walls as if to say, "Don't worry. I'll be here with you no matter what happens."

The stadium, cherished as it was, showed signs of wear. So did the 1988 Tigers. Prior to the season, another arbitrator ruled that Tiger management had restricted the movement of free agents, including Kirk Gibson. As a result, Gibson was released from his contract. The Tiger star agreed to a $4.5 million deal with the Los Angeles Dodgers. This set the stage for Gibson to become the

number-one hero in the '88 World Series when, in his only Series at-bat, he hit a last-inning home run to win Game One.

Detroit could have used some of that home run power as they ended the 1988 campaign in second place, only one game behind the Red Sox. Trammell, with a .311 average, was the only player to bat over .300. Evans home run production dropped to a four-year low of 22.

The bottom really fell out in 1989. The Tigers went from pennant contenders to basement dwellers. A miserable 59-103 record caused Sparky Anderson to lose more sleep than any other time in his managerial career.

Doyle Alexander, the pitcher who helped the Tigers to the '87 playoffs, now led the league in losses with 18. Manager Anderson put the season in perspective: "The great thing about baseball is when you're done, you'll only tell your grandchildren the good things. If they ask me about 1989, I'll tell 'em I had amnesia."

Toronto's new Sky Dome showed what baseball had become in 1989. You could get a hotel room, for example, and watch the game from an open window just behind the outfield seats. Upon seeing it for the first time, Twins coach Wayne Terwilliger remarked, "There's so much inside here. It's like a shopping center."

Tiger President Jim Campbell pitched his tent in a more conservative camp. He took a private vow to keep Tiger Stadium from falling into the trap of all such attempts to "modernize" baseball.

The '89 season was the first guided by a rare baseball commissioner. Following the resignation of Peter Ueberroth, the owners elected Dr. A. Bartlett Giamatti, National League president, a former Yale professor of Renaissance literature, philosopher, poet and a die-hard baseball fan. He became an instant hit with fans and media with his insights and genuine love of the game. That popularity would be challenged the next year when baseball shot itself in the foot again.

Whenever it seemed players and owners were winning back loyal fans who had supported the national pastime, one of the two camps elected to fan the flames of controversy. After failing to sign a new collective bargaining agreement, the owners locked players out of spring training camps. Both sides remained at an impasse until the disputes were resolved in mid-March. Baseball had only two-and-a-half weeks to get ready for a delayed Opening Day.

Several players were earning more than $3 million a year. Jose Canseco, for example, signed a pact with the Oakland A's for $23.5 million over five years. "I think we are on the brink of a whole new era of salary negotiations," predicted Jim Campbell.

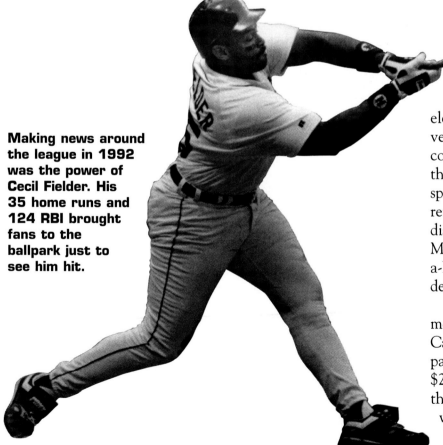

Making news around the league in 1992 was the power of Cecil Fielder. His 35 home runs and 124 RBI brought fans to the ballpark just to see him hit.

Commenting on the strike, Commissioner Giamatti said of both players and owners, "The people of America care about baseball, not about your squalid little squabbles. Reassume your dignity and remember that you are the temporary custodians of an enduring public trust."

Commissioner Giamatti took more hard-line stances and seemed to be able to nip problems in the bud. Whether or not Dr. Giamatti would have been able to prevent further strikes is hypothetical. On September 2, 1989, he died of a massive heart attack, nine days after he suspended Cincinnati's Pete Rose for gambling. Replacing Bart Giamatti as commissioner was his deputy, Francis "Fay" Vincent, who was unaware of the magnitude of the problems that lay ahead.

The 1990 Tigers attempted to restore some of the trust of the fans by playing hard and climbing to a third-place finish.

Much of the revival of enthusiasm for winning came from the potent bat of Cecil Fielder, a four-year veteran who had played the previous season in Japan. Fielder was a free-swinging first baseman and designated hitter who hit towering home runs—51 of them in 1990—to lead the league. Fielder, in fact, drew crowds to the ballpark an hour or so before the game just so they could watch him take batting practice. It was not unlike Pittsburgh fans who came to the park early to see Ralph Kiner in the batting cage or today's St. Louis fans who arrive early to see Mark McGwire give a show of power.

Fielder's home runs were not his only credentials. His 132 RBI, .592 slugging average and 339 total bases all topped the junior circuit.

In addition to his talent for hitting the long ball and moving runners around the bases, Fielder was a congenial representative of the Tigers. He was willing to sign autographs for kids and in the tradition of Willie Horton, visited children in area hospitals. For all his athletic ability and his acts of kindness, Fielder was the talk of the town long after the 1990 season ended.

Prior to the spring training strike of 1990, Owner Thomas Monaghan promoted Jim Campbell to chairman and CEO; replacing him as president was former University of Michigan Football coach, Glenn Edward "Bo" Schembechler.

In less than one year, Schembechler probably wished he had never left the relative calm of a Michigan-Ohio State football game. Late in 1990, the decision was made to replace announcer Ernie Harwell with a "younger voice" in the booth. Fans were outraged. Protest calls and letters cascaded on the Tiger front office. Schembechler, true to his football mentality, stood firmly behind the "team" of management.

On Opening Day 1991, for one of the rare times in its history, the lid-lifter at Tiger Stadium was not sold out. Many of the spectators carried fans with Ernie Harwell's image and held them in front of their faces.

Ernie Harwell wasn't just a broadcaster. He was the Tigers'

> "The great thing about baseball is when you're done, you'll only tell your grandchildren the good things. If they ask me about 1989, I'll tell 'em I had amnesia."
>
> - Sparky Anderson

"voice." The beloved announcer who thrilled America when he called Bobby Thomson's "shot heard 'round the world" in the third game of the Giants-Dodgers playoff series in 1951, became a loyal cheerleader of his Tigers. No matter if their team won or lost, Detroit fans knew they were together with Harwell. For reasons such as those, Ernie Harwell was presented the Ford Frick Award and elected to the Broadcasters' Wing in baseball's Hall of Fame in 1981.

Harwell, a born-again Christian, was one of the founders of the "Baseball Chapel." At the same time, he never used the WJR microphone to preach to his audience. He didn't have to. Those who have heard Ernie Harwell or who have seen him in person know exactly for what he stands. The 1991

Travis Fryman was another consistent home run threat.

Tigers (84-78) finished in a second-place tie with the Red Sox. Cecil Fielder led the league for a second year in a row with 44 circuit blows and 133 RBI,

becoming the first American League player to lead in that department in consecutive years since Jimmy Foxx with the Philadelphia Athletics in the 1932-33 seasons and was the first Tiger to do so since Bobby Veach in 1917-18. Pitcher Bill Gullickson, picked up as a free agent from Houston at the start of the season, tied for the top in the junior circuit with 20 victories.

Catcher Mickey Tettleton, received in a trade with Baltimore in early 1991, added power to a lineup saturated with home-run hitters. In '91, the Tigers slammed 209 homers. Besides Fielder, who led the pack with 44, Tettleton hit 31; Rob Deer, a veteran outfielder in his first year with Detroit, hit 25; Whitaker had 23, Travis Fryman, a second-year infielder, clubbed 21; and Tony Phillips, who could play infield or outfield, hit 19.

One of the fan favorites in 1991 was slugger Rob Deer. When this native of Orange, California, now in his eighth major league season, stepped to the plate, he had just one intention—to swing as hard as he could. "If I swing and hit it," he said, "it has a good chance of getting out of here." Deer was successful 25 times as he propelled balls deep into the outfield seats. Unfortunately, he had 150 more strikeouts. His .179 average showed that he approached each swing with an "all or nothing" attitude. In the end, the fans loved him simply because he was an uncomplicated slugger, not a cunning batsman.

Deer increased his home run

On August 26, 1992, at a press conference at Tiger Stadium, Michael Ilitch, founder and owner of Little Caesars Pizza, assumed his new role as owner of the Detroit Tigers.

output to 32 and his average to .247 in 1992. Cecil Fielder again led the league with 124 RBI, becoming the only player besides Babe Ruth (1919-21) to lead in that department three years in a row. Left fielder Tony Phillips, in his third year with the club, was the league leader in runs scored (114). These impressive statistics were not enough to elevate the Tigers, however, as the club finished in sixth place.

On August 26, 1992, Thomas S. Monaghan sold the Detroit Baseball Club to the owner of Little Caesars Pizza, Michael Ilitch. One of Monaghan's last official duties before cleaning out his office desk was to fire Bo Schembechler and to give walking papers to Jim Campbell, ending Campbell's 43-year association with the Tigers.

Chapter 17

From Darkness to Light

"Major League Baseball:
No Balls and
A Strike!"

- The Sporting News

Before he played in the Detroit Tiger organization, young Mike Ilitch played infield for the U.S. Marines.

FORMER U.S. MARINE MICHAEL ILITCH HAD HIS SIGHTS SET on a major league career. He was a pretty fair infielder for the Class B Tampa Bay Smokers until a bad knee forced him out of the game. Mike Ilitch, the energetic, imaginative new Tiger owner, had a unique credential. He knew baseball from the perspectives of both the fan and the player. He also knew how to attract modern-day crowds to the ballpark.

He launched an $8 million face-lift for Tiger Stadium. He turned the players' parking lot adjacent to the stadium into "Tiger Plaza"—a food court for the fans. There, before and after the games, fans could relax, eat, have a beer, wine or soft drink, and listen to a three-piece Dixieland band. Even waiters were available to serve you.

Aware that some people were concerned about walking to Tiger Stadium after dark, Ilitch added more day games and began the evening contests a half-hour earlier.

Other attractions to the ballpark included fireworks, ball days, bat days and helmet days. On Fan Appreciation Day, the players even took off their shirts and gave them to lucky fans.

In 1993—Ilitch's first full season as owner—1,971,421 fans passed through the turnstiles. It was the sixth-best attendance year in the club's history. The only possible explanation for the increased support had to be the promotions. The huge number of fans was not generated by the club's play in '93. Finishing in a third-place tie with Baltimore, 10 games behind the American League East Division Champion Toronto Blue Jays, was not enough to generate the sort of pennant fever that would

Opening Day 1995.

place on the all-time list for managerial wins with 2,126.

Detroit ended the 1994 season with a 53-62 record. There's an easy explanation for why the team record reflected less than 75 percent of the scheduled games. Baseball's darkest days fell in the last quarter of the season. On August 12, 1994, the Players Union voted to stop play for the eighth time since 1972.

Prior to the strike, both the American and National Leagues voted to divide into three divisions—the East, Central and West. Detroit was to be in the East along with New York, Baltimore, Boston, and Toronto.

Had the Detroit Tigers won the East Division, they would have had no chance to play in the World Series in 1994. History's most tradition-rich sports event was canceled due to the strike.

Baseball was in a funk.

The most pointed slogan of the year was published in *The Sporting News*—"Major League Baseball: No Balls and a Strike." The situation failed to improve over the winter months. By spring training in 1995, players and owners were still miles apart in negotiations. Even the most optimistic fans knew the impasse would not be resolved before Opening Day.

Major league clubs voted to open their spring-training camps with so-called "replacement players." With few exceptions, the caliber of talent

stir up fan excitement.

The fans appreciated seeing, again, one of their favorites—the hero of the '84 World Series, Kirk Gibson, in the role of designated hitter and part-time outfielder. Gibson would not disappoint the fans, smacking 13 out of the park that year.

Mike Moore, picked up in the free agency draft, topped the pitching staff with 13 victories but allowed more than five runs per game. Reliever Mike Henneman (5-3) recorded 24 saves that year, thus becoming the Tigers' all-time saves leader.

The 1994 season contained a few highlights and one gigantic thunderbolt that nearly ruined baseball. On the plus side for the Tigers, Kirk Gibson looked like his old self when he batted .276 and hit 23 home runs. Also, on June 27, Sparky Anderson, in a 3-1 victory over the Florida Marlins, passed Joe McCarthy into fourth

shown by these minor leaguers and sandlot players in no way came close to that of established major leaguers.

The strike finally was settled, not at the bargaining table but in a courtroom less than a week before the scheduled start of the season. On March 31, a U.S. District Court forbade owners from implementing new financial working conditions. Both owners and players were ordered to revert to the rules of the previous season.

Eighteen games were trimmed from the 1995 schedule, and teams were given time to prepare for the season. This time, baseball fans were slow to forgive.

During the dark days of the strike, much of the national media focused on Tiger manager Sparky Anderson. Unlike his contemporaries, Sparky refused to participate in spring training or any part of the season as long as the regular players were on strike. "I'm not looking forward to no replacement thing. That's not for me," he said.

Attendance on Opening Day, May 2, 1995, was 39,398. While the visiting Cleveland Indians unloaded on Tiger pitching with an outburst of hits and runs, the more disgruntled fans threw onto the field magnetized schedules given them earlier as free tokens of appreciation. Batteries, cans, cups, bottles even a restaurant napkin dispenser followed. Cleveland center fielder Kenny Lofton ran for cover. Umpires stopped the game and pointed to spectators they saw throw objects. One fan interrupted the game by running from the outfield stands and sliding across

home plate to the cheers of some onlookers.

Following an 11-1 shellacking by the Tribe, Detroit was now the subject of more bad press. Police reports showed 34 arrests that day in the stadium. Reactions varied. A reporter for the *Free Press* wrote: "The fans … were acting out [their] collective contempt for the national pastime." Kirk Gibson had another view: "That's pure ignorance. I think the protest is an excuse."

The 1995 season was the first to use a "wild card" scheme for the playoff games. Under the new format, the three division winners and the second-place team with the best winning percentage would compete to represent their respective leagues in the World Series.

This year marked Sparky Anderson's final campaign. He had grown weary, especially in leading a team that finished 60-84, 26 games behind the East Division leading Red Sox.

After three sub-par seasons, Mike Moore was released. Kirk Gibson left, finding it difficult to play with a team that had lost its

The Tiger logo shows itself prominently throughout Tiger Stadium. Here it marks a row of seats.

One of the first decisions of Michael Ilitch was extremely popular - to bring back to the microphone Hall of Fame announcer, Ernie Harwell.

fire. About the only one with any credentials worth noting was center fielder Chad Curtis, acquired from California in a trade for Tony Phillips in April, who hit .268 and slammed 21 homers.

Two other additions to the Tigers in '95 proved to be positive moves. One was the hiring of John McHale, Jr., as president and CEO. The son of a major league player (John, Sr., played for the Tigers for five seasons and was named general manager in 1957), McHale had grown up with the Tigers. As a lawyer with more than ten years of private practice and a labor arbitrator for the American Arbitration Association, McHale came equipped with the sort of training that would serve the Tigers well in contract negotiations.

John McHale, distinguished by his ever-present bow tie, threw himself into shaping the Tiger organization and into the work for the community. He serves on the board of directors of CATCH (Caring Athletes Team for Children's & Henry Ford Hospitals) and has served for the past few years as the Southeast Michigan WalkAmerica Chairman for the March of Dimes.

The second welcomed newcomer was Randy Smith in the role of general manager. Smith, the son of long-time baseball executive Tal Smith, prepared for his new responsibilities by serving as assistant general manager of the Colorado Rockies, and at age 29, became the youngest general manager ever in Major League Baseball with the San Diego Padres.

The Tigers tried to instill more new blood into the organization by hiring David Gus "Buddy" Bell as manager in 1996. Bell, son of former major leaguer Gus Bell, was an 18-year veteran third baseman with the Indians, Astros, Reds and Rangers.

The new blood didn't generate many wins at first. The club, in fact, got off to a miserable start. By June 1, the team was entrenched in last place, 18 games out of first. "This is a much bigger job than we had in San Diego," confessed Randy Smith.

The Tigers were running on

empty. On the night of the trading deadline, they sent popular slugger Cecil Fielder to the Yankees, thus giving him the opportunity to play for a pennant contender.

Along with Fielder, a total of 52 other players wore Tiger uniforms sometime during the '96 campaign. They combined to post a 53-109 record—the second-worst in Tiger history.

Following the disaster of '96, the Tigers introduced more fresh faces into their lineup. Only seven Tigers from the roster the year before were present for the 1997 Opening Day game. Following a month of "here we go again" moans from fans and writers, the Tigers began to jell. In fact, the Tigers improved to a 79-83 record, in third place, 19 games out of first.

With Detroit's minor league affiliates posting a .531 winning percentage, the Tigers were named "Organization of the Year" by *Baseball America* magazine. With improved major league standing and the solid potential of its minor league prospects, the Tigers gave the appearance of a team on the move in 1997.

Center fielder Brian Hunter, who came to the Tigers in a trade with Houston prior to the season, led the league with 74 stolen bases. He was the first Bengal to lead the league in that department since Ty Cobb in 1917. From the hitters' box, Tony Clark, Travis Fryman and Bobby Higginson each knocked in over 100 runs.

One Tiger mainstay was missing in 1997. In January, George Kell announced his retirement from broadcasting games. Since 1959, Detroit fans had been accustomed to hearing his familiar: "Hello, everybody. I'm George Kell" that opened each broadcast. His easy-going southern drawl and folksy manner, coupled with keen insights into the game, made him a treasured addition to both radio and television.

Fifteen years earlier, Kell had left the booth to spend more time with his family in Swifton, Arkansas, after his initial five-year contract to broadcast all games had expired. Following a one-year sabbatical, Kell was persuaded by owner John Fetzer to return on a reduced schedule.

George Kell's biggest thrill came in 1983 when the Veterans Committee voted him into Baseball's Hall of Fame.

The Tigers entered the 1998 season as part of the newly-shaped Central Division (along with the White Sox, Indians, Royals and Twins). In spite of what might be deemed weaker competition, the Tigers ended the year far out of the running—in last place, 24 games behind Cleveland. In fact, the 1998 Tigers were often the subject

Another noteworthy decision by Owner Ilitch was to hire John McHale, Jr., as club president. Here, during a television interview, the new president shares the spotlight with his father, John McHale, Sr., (R) former general manager for the Tigers.

At the groundbreaking ceremony for Comerica Park on October 29, 1997, Owner Ilitch gives a "thumbs up" for the future of the club.

of a Jay Leno monologue as he began *The Tonight Show*. On Opening Day, for example, Leno announced: "The Detroit Tigers, today, have been mathematically eliminated from the American League pennant."

With Tony Clark (.291) the only regular to hit near .300, and Brian Moehler (14-13) as the ace of the mound staff, the Tigers appeared to make Leno a modern-day prophet.

As expected, taking the brunt of criticism was manager Buddy Bell, who was replaced by bench coach Larry Parrish on September 1. Parrish, called "LP" by his friends, was a 15-year veteran player and two-time All-Star selection. He was a popular choice with both fans and players. In the season's final month of play, the Tigers went 13-12. "We think he has excellent qualifications that will enable him to lead the club into the coming years of Tiger baseball," said General Manager Randy Smith. The Tigers finished last in the Central, 24 games back of Cleveland.

Not all was dismal, though, for the Tigers in '98. Tony Clark (34 homers), Damion Easley (27 home runs) and Bobby Higginson (25 homers) showed that the Tigers still had muscle at the plate. Rookie Matt Anderson (5-1) was impressive, especially when he threw a fastball clocked at 103 mph.

The 1998 season ended on another positive note. In November, the Tigers announced that popular broadcaster Ernie Harwell, dismissed by the Tigers eight years before, would return as the team's play-by-play announcer for the 1999 and 2000 seasons. Ex-catcher Jim Price would join him in the radio booth, while Al Kaline—"Mr. Tiger"—would continue as a television analyst.

The fans missed listening to Harwell's famous expressions such as: "He stood there like the house by the side of the road," his pointed description of a batter who had just been called out on strikes. Another quality the fans appreciated was Harwell's apt descriptions of the game itself. Some of the more philosophical listeners recalled Ernie Harwell's observation in *The Game for All America*: "Baseball? It's just a game—as simple as a ball and a bat. Yet as complex as the American spirit it symbolizes. It's a sport, business—sometimes even a religion." One of his quotes also appeared in *The Sporting News*: "Baseball is ballet without music. Drama without words. A carnival without Kewpie dolls."

How appropriate that, in the same year, this Hall-of-Fame announcer, who has also earned laurels as a songwriter for top-name recording artists, was selected for induction into the

An aerial view of The Grand Old Lady circa 1993.

Radio Hall of Fame. Quite a fitting tribute to mark the 50th anniversary of his first major league broadcast.

Ernie Harwell sat in his rightful place in the announcer's booth on April 12, 1999, as 47,449 fans filled the aging Tiger Stadium for its last Opening Day. A 12-inning, 1-0 loss to Minnesota put no joy in the hearts of the Tiger faithful. Yet even if the final score had been in favor of the Bengals, those in attendance would have left the stadium with a touch of sadness. The reality sank in. This scarred, weather-beaten old park had just begun its last season for Major League Baseball.

People crowding the exits paused to share with complete strangers some priceless memories—the gargantuan home runs of Greenberg, Horton and Fielder … the slick fielding of Gehringer, Kell and Whitaker … the masterful pitching of Bridges, Newhouser and Lolich … the timely hitting of Cobb, Heilmann and Kaline.

They also talked about the characters of the game—Schaefer, Cash and Fidrych—and the managerial genius of Jennings, Cochrane and Anderson.

"There's no other stadium like it," remembered 1984 World Series hero Alan Trammell. "It'll probably hit me hard on Opening Day next year. But it's time to move on."

Chapter 18

A Pictorial Salute to Opening Day 1999

On April 12, 1999, The Detroit Tigers faced the Minnesota Twins for the last Opening Day at historic Tiger Stadium.

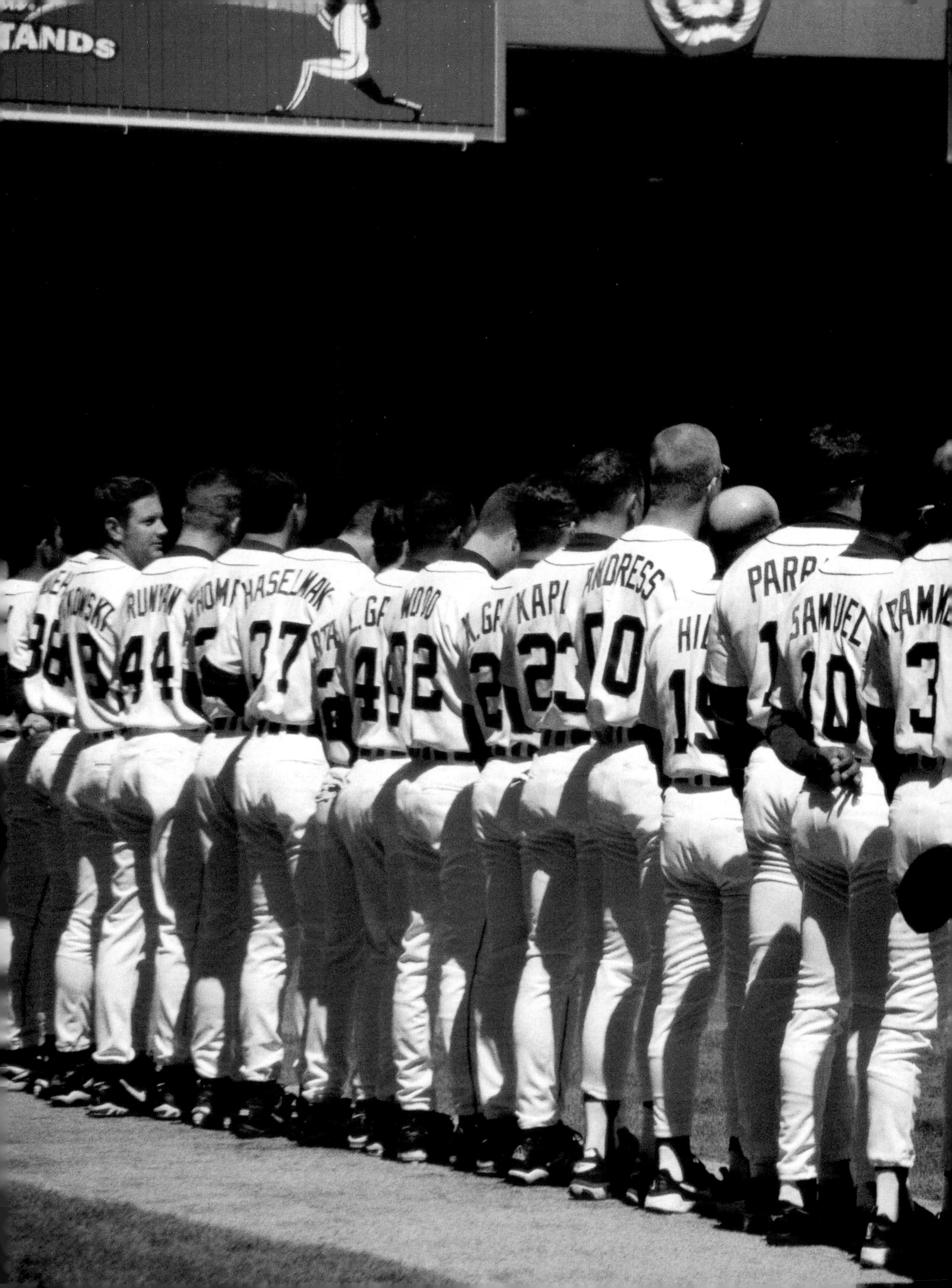
RUNYAN
44
37
ANDRESS
SAMUEL
10

Former Tiger star Kirk Gibson, now an analyst for Tigers telecasts.

Chapter 19

A New Stadium;
A New Era

**"I want to bring baseball
back to the fans."**

- Michael Ilitch

**Tony Clark belts
another one.**

WHAT MAKES MICHAEL ILITCH RUN? Why would one man who seems to have everything that life has to offer, subject himself to the challenges of owning and operating a baseball club? Ilitch has one answer—the fans.

"Many owners want to bring the fans back to baseball; I want to bring baseball back to the fans," he says. "Nothing would make me happier than to realize that baseball has, once again, become part of the fabric of Detroit."

The man who once focused his hopes on a major league career until an injured knee ended his dream, knows firsthand the joy that baseball can bring to a fan and to a family. "When we started a tradition of allowing children to run the bases following some of the Tiger games, we could see the fire and excitement in the eyes of the kids and of their families. That's what it's all about. Baseball is a family game that reflects solid family values.

"We now have a young team of dedicated, aggressive players who want so much to win for the fans. We pledge to give each man, woman and child who attends the ballpark a 100-percent effort to do our best and to make them proud to be Tiger fans."

While some of the traditionalists and more conservative elements bemoan the fact that Tiger Stadium could no longer be a viable venue for big league baseball, Ilitch and his staff began work on providing a new stadium for the people of Detroit. So, on October 29, 1997, more than 60 city and county officials broke ground for Comerica Park that

would be part of a new, exciting sports/entertainment complex on 80 acres of ground across from the Fox Theatre.

Beginning on Opening Day, 2000, it's a new era. The 40,000-capacity stadium allows intimacy between players and fans. The open-air design with real grass is a throwback to the kind of baseball atmosphere that has been a part of America. It also brings the city into the park. With no upper level seats in the outfield, the park enables fans to view the magnificent skyline of Downtown Detroit.

Combined with the old-time baseball atmosphere are modern conveniences. Clean rest rooms, state-of-the-art lighting, efficient concession areas and a main scoreboard larger than any other facility in existence.

Other parts of the Foxtown Sports/Entertainment Complex will be a new stadium for the Detroit Lions, theaters, restaurants and amusement centers. "It will be a destination for those who want to enjoy family entertainment in a convenient, safe atmosphere," according to owner Michael Ilitch.

Ensuring the safety of all visitors, Owner Ilitch has added a comprehensive security system that will make Foxtown one of the safest environments in the nation for families who want to celebrate life to the fullest.

Turning Comerica Park from a dream into reality was a cooperative venture. Owner Ilitch, himself, invested $175 million into the stadium. Comerica Bank, from which the new ballpark got its name, was a guiding force and

instrumental in forming a working agreement with the Detroit Tiger Baseball Club.

Sumitomo Bank led a syndication of banks (including Societe General, First Chicago NBD, Provident Bank of Maryland, First of America Bank, Standard Federal Bank and Michigan National Bank) for $145 million in financing. Public financing participants included the Michigan Strategic Fund, City of Detroit Downtown Development Authority and Wayne County.

The design team for the new ballpark included the Detroit-based Smith, Hinchman and Grylls, along with HOK Sport and the Rockwellgroup. Hunt-Turner-White served as general contractors.

"None of this, however, would be possible without the support of the greatest baseball fans in the world," admits Ilitch. "I promise Tiger fans everywhere I shall do whatever I can in order to provide for them the best I can give and the best baseball can give. I am proud to be a part of Detroit Tigers baseball. Now, let's go win a World Championship!"

Comerica Park, in various phases of construction.

- Epilogue -

"For all the years I was blessed to be there, I never saw nothing like how those Tiger fans were. Those people were the real deal."

- George Lee "Sparky" Anderson, Tiger manager, 1979 - 1995

DATELINE: APRIL 28, 1896. The paint had not yet dried on the outside walls of a new ball field in an area of Detroit, Michigan, known as "Corktown," named by immigrants from Ireland's County Cork. The hastily built stadium was constructed on a vacant lot bordered by National Avenue, Michigan Avenue, Trumbull Avenue and Cherry Street—the site of an old hay market. The unnamed stadium, designed to seat 5,000 spectators, opened its gates to the eager mass of people who had been waiting outside for over an hour. The new field cost owner George Vanderbeck $10,000 to construct. An overflow throng of 8,000 cheering fans, some of whom had to sit on the outfield grass, assured the owner his investment was wise. His enthusiasm grew as the game progressed. The hometown baseball team known as the "Detroits" dominated the visiting Columbus Senators by a score of 17-2.

Highlighting the runaway contest were the actions of one of the onlookers seated in the outfield. Perhaps in his enthusiasm to help the home team, an over-zealous fan rushed out on the playing field and collided with an unsuspecting visiting middle fielder (the designation in that day), rendering the hapless player unconscious. It was the start of a 104-year history of a baseball team and its magnificent ballpark that would brim with passionate expressions of enthusiasm for the sport by players and fans alike.

This opening game marked the beginning of both a new era and a fresh attitude for the residents of this callow metropolis of fewer than 300,000 residents. Prior to the acceptance of their baseball team into the major leagues, Detroiters seldom wasted time on celebrations. Anything resembling a party atmosphere was shunned in this city that took pride in the fact that most families endorsed a Puritan work ethic. The prevailing religion was a daily devotion to hard physical labor.

This is the sort of attitude that has made Detroit one of those rare, made-in-the-USA communities. It's a tough town in which only the equally tough are expected to survive.

Even the weather offers unique challenges to this rugged city of muscles and calluses. The familiar gray skies of winter can bring bone-chilling storms carried on waves of sub-zero winds that numb the body. During the summer months, those normally overcast skies give way to a scorching August sun. The air, saturated with humidity, creates a hot-house effect. Office workers rushing to grab a quick sandwich during the noon hour feel their shoes sink slightly into the softened asphalt of Lafayette or Congress streets.

Detroit is blessed with neither the lure of the year-round sunny beaches of Florida nor the glamour and glitz of Hollywood or Las Vegas. Instead, its chief claim to fame has been the automotive industry. Its pioneers are the likes of Henry Ford, Walter Chrysler and Henry Kaiser. From these giants came a legacy that the respected laborer earned a day's pay for an honest day's work.

At the same time, Detroit is not, by nature, a unified city. Instead, it's a combination of smaller cities, towns and villages clustered around the Detroit River and Lake St. Clair. Each community reflects part of the recipe for the melting pot that has been the backbone of America. The humble Polish settlement in Hamtramck and the African-American concentration along Jefferson Avenue house many descendants of the laborers responsible for transforming this nation from a horse-and-buggy mode of transportation to one in which an automobile became not merely a means of getting places, but also a symbol of status. Then there is Greektown with the world's most scrumptious lamb chops. And, of course, owning a home amid the society-page elite of Grosse Pointe shows everyone, including yourself, that you've "arrived."

One of the most loyal groups of fans to follow the Detroit Tigers is the Mayo Smith Society. Founded in 1983 by Dale Petroskey, Denny Petroskey and Bill Mackay, the club has grown to be the largest Tiger fan club today. Since 1985, the organization has published a newsletter called *Tiger Stripes* that offers statistical insights into the Tigers. The Mayo Smith Society also sponsors an annual spring training trip to Lakeland, Florida, and holds an annual meeting each summer in Detroit to raise money for charitable causes.

On July 19, 1999, Society founder Dale Petroskey was installed as president of Baseball's Hall of Fame in Cooperstown, New York.

Just as its citizens have always demanded a work-by-the-sweat-of-your-brow approach to life, so they embraced a baseball team composed of hard-nosed, in-your-face, dirty-shirt players who gave a hundred percent on the hallowed diamond, known as Tiger Stadium.

Baseball on this corner of Michigan and Trumbull dates back to 1896 when Detroit was part of the Western League. Through the years the name has changed—Bennett Park (1896-1911), Navin Field (1912-1937), Briggs Stadium (1938-1960) and Tiger Stadium (1961-1999). To the genuine fan, however, it mattered little what name appeared on the outer wall of the place. This was their home for precious memories.

Tiger Stadium offered a majestic setting for a baseball game. Unlike many multi-purpose stadiums that seem to be cut from a common mold with all the creative imagination of a cookie-cutter, Tiger Stadium radiated an intangible quality called "character." As soon as you crossed its turnstiles and entered the stands, you knew you were at a place unlike any other. The glow of the freshly mowed green outfield grass and the neatly manicured infield would be the pride of a skilled landscape architect. Lingering odors of cigars smoked the day before blended with the mouth-watering aroma of sausages grilled at the concession stands, of hot-roasted peanuts and cotton candy. Players taking batting practice on the diamond wore the same basic uniforms made famous by icons of the game: Cobb, Gehringer, Greenberg, Kell and Kaline.

Then there were those unforgettable moments filled with awe and majesty often used by veteran fans to mark time: Hank Greenberg's last-inning home run to win the 1945 pennant … Al Kaline's single in Game Five of the '68 Series that turned the game around … Denny McLain's 30th victory that same year…. For those of us who were there, those moments remain as clear in our minds as if they happened yesterday.

Sometimes the stadium itself contributed to a game's outcome. Two-tiered stands wrapped the park from the left-field foul pole, around home plate and down the right-field line. When filled with spectators, they created a baffle for ear-shattering cheers and gave the hometown heroes an extra shot of adrenaline.

In right field, the floor of the second deck actually hung ten feet over the front edge of the first deck. Many a visiting outfielder gaped in amazement as he stood on the warning track ready to catch a deep fly ball, only to watch it disappear above for a home run.

The right-field wall created a weird angle that often caused a batted ball to bounce off in an unexpected direction, turning a routine single into a double or a triple. A flagpole was located in center field in the field of play.

In spite of these distinctive features, Tiger Stadium remained sensitive to the solemn traditions of baseball. It eschewed splashy gimmicks designed to orchestrate fan reaction. No messin' around here. None was needed. Those who attended games at Tiger Stadium didn't have to be told when to cheer or applaud. They were far too sophisticated for that.

This is not to imply that Tiger Stadium was always the perfect spot to see a game. For some fans, the view was partially obstructed by two-foot-wide steel beams that supported the upper deck or roof, much like the design of Ebbets Field, Fenway Park and Forbes Field.

Few complained, however. This was all part of the game of baseball and they were proud to be in this place that overflowed with history.

Even the paint reflected Detroit's no-nonsense approach to the game. The grass was green; walls were green; seats were painted green; even the roof was green.

In spite of attempts to add spice through fancy make-up, Tiger Stadium remained for the baseball fan what Gettysburg is to an American History buff. This was the site where monumental things happened. Just being there awakened passions for the excitement of a bygone era.

On an off day, when nobody else was in the park, if you listened closely, you could hear the unmistakable sound of ash hitting horsehide. Echoing around the stands was the minced oath of an opposing second baseman who was just cut by the cleats of a hard-sliding Ty Cobb. Perhaps you could even imagine the play called with the calm, Arkansas drawl of George Kell or the perfectly timed quips of Ernie Harwell.

Tiger Stadium, for Detroit, was more than a setting for some of the best games ever played in Major League Baseball. It offered us a sense of stability when we needed it the most. During the woeful days of the Great Depression, for example, factory workers were laid off in record numbers. They were unable to afford the cost of a trolley ride, let alone a ticket to the game. They could, at least, listen to WWJ radio and announcer Ty Tyson describe the magic of Charlie Gehringer, who made fielding a tricky ground ball look like a graceful ballet.

During the riots of 1967, parts of downtown Detroit were set afire and turned into war zones. Replacing cars and buses that normally transported factory workers on Woodward Avenue were different modes of transportation—military Jeeps and tanks—carrying soldiers wielding loaded weapons. The scene gave every appearance of a police state. It was an ugly, divisive time for the city. One year later, within the span of a few short months, Martin Luther King, Jr., was shot on a motel balcony in Memphis and Senator Robert F. Kennedy lay dying on the kitchen floor at a Los Angeles hotel. Detroiters, along with millions of other Americans, shook their heads in disbelief. They asked the pointed question posed in a popular song: "What's It All About, Alfie?"

Young people did more than ask questions. They openly defied a government they thought was conducting an illegal war on a remote piece of real estate known as Vietnam. On top of this, they

"My first impression was when we came into the old train station. I was sitting by Johnny Pesky, and he said that we'd be passing by the stadium on our way in. It looked almost like a battleship from the outside.

"The next day, I walked from the hotel to the ballpark. I was only 18 at the time, and I had a hard time getting through the security gate into the park. When I first looked in, all I saw was green— green seats, green field. What a sight!"

- Al Kaline's first impression of Tiger Stadium

dared challenge standards of speech, dress and decorum long accepted by their parents and grandparents. They openly followed gurus who told them that it was their obligation to protest and uproot anything deemed to be "establishment." Meanwhile, their parents pasted bumper stickers on their cars that promoted a more conservative opinion: "America! Love it or leave it."

The nation was being ripped asunder by a new kind of civil war.

Amid all this confusion about what constituted a proper sense of ideals and values was the stability of baseball and Tiger Stadium. The bases remained 90 feet apart; the pitching mound was 60 feet, six inches from home plate; foul lines were still 325 feet to right field and 340 to left. It was one of the few places you could go and be assured it would look the same as the last time you were there.

When it appeared Detroit lay on the brink of self-destruction, the 1968 Tigers captured the hearts of the Motor City and the rest of the nation by overcoming incredible odds as they defeated Bob Gibson and his mighty St. Louis Cardinals in the World Series. For one priceless moment, the City of Detroit was united.

During the '70s, interest rates soared through the roof. Car owners waited in line for hours to purchase gasoline that had risen to more than two dollars a gallon. Executives at the local automotive plants awoke to reality and were obliged to confess that Japan was now manufacturing better cars than they could. Into this boiling cauldron of spiraling inflation and uncertainties came 21-year-old Mark Fidrych—a rookie sensation known affectionately as "The Bird." The lanky right-handed pitcher fascinated local fans when he actually talked to the baseball or paused to congratulate a teammate who had just completed a spectacular play.

These were just a few of the moments of glory that emanated from Tiger Stadium and gave us a diversion from the problems of the work-a-day world and a society in the agonizing process of re-identifying itself. For this reason, alone, Detroit fans considered Tiger Stadium more than just a ballpark. It was a shrine.

Alas, sentiment eventually gave way to the realities of the day. Tiger Stadium had grown too old. Costs for repairs and reconstruction became prohibitive. The only sensible solution was to construct a new ballpark. As of Opening Day, 2000, the Tigers' new home is Comerica Park, located east of Woodward Avenue across from the Fox Theatre.

If, during the 21st century, Comerica Park brings as much joy and cherished memories as did Tiger Stadium over the previous 104 years, today's Tiger fans are, indeed, most fortunate. There's a heap of thrills in store for all of us.

104 Years at Michigan and Trumbull

April 28, 1896 — Detroit defeats the Columbus Senators by the score of 17-2. Nearly 8,000 fans cram into **Bennett Park** to watch this Western League game to open the season.

April 25, 1901 — Detroit makes its American League debut by defeating Milwaukee 14-13. Some of the overflow crowd of over 10,000 has to stand behind ropes in the outfield.

October 8 - 12, 1907 — The Tigers play in their first World Series and lose the World Championship to the Chicago Cubs.

October 10 - 14, 1908 — Detroit repeats as American League Champions, but again loses the World Series to Chicago four games to one.

October 8 - 16, 1909 — The 1909 World Series is hyped as a duel between Ty Cobb of the American League Champion Tigers and Honus Wagner of the National League Champion Pittsburgh Pirates. Wagner and the Pirates come out on top four games to three.

April 20, 1912 — In the first game ever played at **Navin Field,** an overflow crowd of 24,384 fans cheer Ty Cobb as he steals second and home in Detroit's 6-5 win in eleven innings against Cleveland.

Opening Day ceremonies for the contest include dignitaries and a marching band parading across the stadium grounds to a huge flagpole in center field for the raising of the American flag.

This event marks the beginning of the transformation of The Corner into the familiar sight that is to be the home of the Tigers through the 1999 season.

April 26, 1923 — Opening Day at the stadium is delayed for one week in order to complete the expansion of Navin Field. The stands from first-to-third-base are double-decked and a press box is added to the roof. Seating capacity increases to 30,000.

October 7, 1935 — For the first time in its history, the Detroit Tigers win the World Series when Goose Goslin singles home Mickey Cochrane with two out in the bottom of the ninth to defeat the Cubs in Game Six of the Series 4-3.

April 17, 1936 — The Detroit Tigers family mourns the death of owner Frank Navin as more than 32,000 fans brave the snow to see the newly expanded facility capable of seating 36,000.

April 22, 1938 — Another overflow crowd of 54,500 crams inside a newly enlarged ballpark now named **Briggs Stadium.** Large dougle-decked stands in left and center field make this the first double-decked enclosed stadium in the major leagues.

October 18, 1938 — The Detroit Lions football team begins play at Briggs Stadium. The Lions win 7-5 against Sammy Baugh and his Washington Redskins.

September 20, 1939 — Heavyweight Champion and Detroit native Joe Louis knocks out challenger Bob Pastor in the eleventh round before 33,000 people at Briggs Stadium.

October 2 - 8, 1940 — Detroit loses the World Series to Cincinnati four games to three in a heart-breaking 2-1 loss in the final game in spite of a splendid pitching performance by Bobo Newsom.

July 8, 1941 — More than 54,700 fans cheer Boston's Ted Williams when he slams a towering home run into the upper deck of Briggs Stadium in the bottom half of the ninth. The game-winning blast gives the American League a 7-5 victory over the National League in the ninth All-Star Game.

October 3 - 10, 1945 — The Tigers are baseball's World Champions for the second time in history. Slugger Hank Greenberg, recently released from military service, and pitcher Hal Newhouser lead Detroit to victory over Chicago in the seven-game Series.

June 16, 1948 — Night baseball begins in Detroit – the last American League city to play its home games under the lights.

July 10, 1951 — Hometown heroes Vic Wertz and George Kell hit home runs in the All-Star Game. They aren't enough, however, to overcome the depth of the National Leaguers who win the contest by a score of 8-3.

April 11, 1961 — Tiger Stadium is the new name for the ballpark and Bob Scheffing is the team's new manager. Unfortunately, the Tigers lose the home opener to Cleveland.

October 2 - 10, 1968 — Following a 23-year drought, the Tigers tame the St. Louis Cardinals in a come-from-behind World Series victory. Led by 31-game winner Denny McLain and Series hero Mickey Lolich, the Bengals win four games to three.

July 13, 1971 — Six home runs dominated the All-Star Game at Tiger Stadium, but none is more memorable than the shot by Oakland's Reggie Jackson that hits the light tower above the right field roof. The American league won the game 6-4.

October 7 - 12, 1972 — Detroit wins the Eastern Division Championship but loses the ALCS to Oakland three games to two.

November 28, 1974 — The Detroit Lions end nearly four decades of play at Tiger Stadium before a Thanksgiving Day crowd of 53,314. Coach Joe Schmidt and his Lions lose to the Denver Broncos, 31-27.

October 5, 1984 — Detroit's Milt Wilcox shuts out Kansas City 1-0 as the Tigers win the ALCS three games to none.

October 14, 1984 — Kirk Gibson's dramatic home run at Tiger Stadium caps an 8-4 victory over San Diego in Game Five of the World Series, and the Tigers become World Champions.

September 25, 1993 — British rock star Rod Stewart performs a concert to a sell-out crowd on a rainy night at Tiger Stadium.

July 13, 1994 — The Eagles, featuring Royal Oak native Glenn Frey, entertain 36,500 fans at the ballpark.

July 17, 1999 — In their only North American appearance of 1999, the Three Tenors – Jose Carreras, Placido Domingo and Luciano Pavarotti – thrill 31,441 with their world-class artistry.

September 27, 1999 — Tigers and their fans bid farewell to The Grand Old Lady at Michigan and Trumbull in a game against the Kansas City Royals.

The New Comerica Park

October 29, 1997 — Owner Mike Ilitch is among the 60 dignitaries who share groundbreaking duties before thousands of Tiger fans at the site of the new ballpark across from the Fox Theatre on Woodward Ave.

December, 1998 — An agreement is reached with Comerica Bank in naming the new home of the Tigers.

April, 2000 — It's Opening Day at Comerica Park.

Features

Seating Capacity — Slightly more than 40,000 will enjoy the games at Comerica Park. The new ball field features approximately 30,000 chair seats, 3,000 club seats, 2,000 suite seats and 5,000 bleacher seats.

View — Fans appreciate the unobstructed view of Detroit's magnificent skyline beyond the outfield walls.

Hall of Fame Museum Walk — The entire family can relive the rich history of Tigers baseball. Paintings, artifacts, statues, interactive exhibits, even a carousel and Ferris Wheel, envelop the entire circumference of the main concourse area. It's a baseball buff's dream.

Scoreboard — As wide as the face of the Fox Theatre Office Building across the street, this 202-foot-wide scoreboard is the nation's largest and will keep fans abreast of action on the field and around the major leagues.

Concessions — What's a ball game without a hot dog? At Comerica Park, however, you won't have inning-long waits in line. An increased number of concession stands allows fans to get back to their seats in record time. In addition, open-air courts off the first- and third-base sides allow fans to enjoy a picnic atmosphere.

www.detroittigers.com
- Website for the Detroit Tigers

- Appendix -

NO-HITTERS (9 or more innings) in TIGER HISTORY:

George Mullin, July 4, 1912 (7-0 vs. St. Louis)
Virgil Trucks, May 15, 1952 (1-0 vs. Washington)
Virgil Trucks, August 25, 1952 (1-0 vs. New York)
Jim Bunning, July 20, 1958 (3-0 vs. Boston)
Jack Morris, April 7, 1984 (4-0 vs. Chicago)

GOLD GLOVE AWARDS:

Frank Boling, 2B, 1958
Al Kaline, OF, 1957, 1958, 1959, 1961, 1962, 1963, 1964, 1965, 1966, 1967
Frank Lary, P, 1961
Bill Freehan, C, 1965, 1966, 1967, 1968, 1969
Mickey Stanley, OF, 1968, 1969, 1970, 1973
Ed Brinkman, SS, 1972
Aurelio Rodriguez, 3B, 1976
Alan Trammell, SS, 1980, 1981, 1983, 1984
Lance Parrish, C, 1983, 1984, 1985
Lou Whitaker, 2B, 1984, 1985
Gary Pettis, OF, 1988, 1989

TRIPLE CROWN WINNERS:

1909 - Ty Cobb

RETIRED NUMBERS:

No. 2 — Charlie Gehringer, 2B
No. 5 — Hank Greenberg, 1B
No. 6 — Al Kaline, OF
No. 16 — Hal Newhouser, P
(Note: Since numbers were not issued to players prior to 1931, Ty Cobb wore no number to retire.)

MOST VALUABLE PLAYER AWARDS:

Mickey Cochrane, C, 1934
Hank Greenberg, 1B, 1935; OF, 1940
Charlie Gehringer, 2B, 1937
Hal Newhouser, P, 1944, 1945
Denny McLain, P, 1968
Willie Hernandez, P, 1984

MANAGER OF THE YEAR AWARDS:

Sparky Anderson, 1984, 1987

CY YOUNG AWARDS:

Denny McLain, 1968, 1969
Willie Hernandez, 1984

TIGERS in the HALL OF FAME (with the year selected):

Ty Cobb, 1936
Dan Brouthers, 1945
Hugh Jennings, 1945
Mickey Cochrane, 1947
Charlie Gehringer, 1949
Harry Heilmann, 1952
Ed Barrow (executive), 1953
Al Simmons, 1953
Hank Greenberg, 1956
Sam Crawford, 1957
Heinie Manush, 1964
Goose Goslin, 1968
Waite Hoyt, 1969
Billy Evans (executive) (umpire), 1973
Sam Thompson, 1974
Earl Averill, 1975
Bucky Harris (manager), 1975
Eddie Mathews, 1978
Al Kaline, 1980
George Kell, 1983
Rick Ferrell, 1984
Hal Newhouser, 1992
Jim Bunning, 1996
Ned Hanlon (manager), 1996
Larry Doby, 1998

ROOKIES OF THE YEAR:

Harvey Kuenn, SS, 1953
Mark Fidrych, P, 1976
Lou Whitaker, 2B, 1978

DIVISION CHAMPIONS:

1972 - Lost to Oakland
1984 - Defeated Kansas City
1987 - Lost to Minnesota

NATIONAL LEAGUE CHAMPION:

1887 — Defeated the St. Louis Browns of the American Association in a 15-game exhibition following the season.

AMERICAN LEAGUE CHAMPIONS:

1907 — Lost to Cubs
1908 — Lost to Cubs
1909 — Lost to Pirates
1934 — Lost to Cardinals
1935 — Defeated Cubs
1940 — Lost to Reds
1945 — Defeated Cubs
1968 — Defeated Cardinals
1984 — Defeated Padres

WORLD SERIES CHAMPIONS:

1935 — Chicago, 6 games
1945 — Chicago, 7 games
1968 — St. Louis, 7 games
1984 — San Diego, 5 games

- Index -

Farewell to Tiger Stadium

September 27, 1999

Photos courtesy Mark A. Hicks, Action Image

The excitement of the last pitch at Tiger Stadium.

The excitement of a new era for the Tigers and their fans.

Standing Room Only

The Grand Old Lady has endured,
and earned her repose ...

The roars rejoicing the seasons past are
but faded, distant echoes ...

But we will have her with us,
always in our reveries ...

Sellout after sellout, Standing
Room Only for memories.